ENDOR

ΙΠ Ε

ΛΤΗΕΙSTΙC
THEIST

"Jeff Turner has written a manifesto for the millennial generation. Utilizing cutting edge theological thinkers such as Shults and Zizek, Turner masterfully demonstrates why faith in a deus ex machina is a hopeless enterprise. I found myself asking 'Really?' or 'You think so?' as I avidly read *The Atheistic Theist*. I gladly commend this book to American Evangelicals and others who are on the edge and just need light to see the way. This book is that intelligently argued. Highly recommended!"

-MICHAEL HARDIN

Executive Director of *Preaching Peace*,
and Author of *The Jesus Driven Life*

"We often receive our beliefs while growing up, as beautifully wrapped gifts from our family and community. For many these gifts remain wrapped as unexamined assumptions until much later in life. If you are at a place where you are ready to honestly look at the implications of your beliefs, Jeff Turner's book is an invaluable help in this process. Ironically, it is what we believe about God that can keep us from experiencing God, and so losing our beliefs about God becomes an essential part of the process of encountering the God who is larger than our convictions."

- ANDRE RABE

Director of *Mimesis Academy*,
and Author of *Desire Found Me*

"Insightful, timely, and provocative. *The Atheistic Theist* is a must-read for both skeptics and honest people of faith."

- JOSHUA TONGOL

Author of *So You Thought You Knew*

"Jeff Turner's *The Atheistic Theist* is a book that you could not only put into the hands of any theist interested in walking the path of Jesus, but also into the hands of any atheist who has walked away. As adherents of the Christian faith are leaving the institutional church in droves—and who's to blame them?—the Church will need books like this in order to rediscover the real Jesus, and in order to heal and move forward through and past the 21st century. A timely book, and highly recommended."

- MATTHEW J. DISTEFANO

Regular Contributor for the *Unfundamentalist Christians* blog on Patheos, and author of *All Set Free* and *From the Blood of Abel*

"On the charge of 'atheistic theism,' Jeff Turner is guilty as charged, and he's in very good company as I read the early church fathers and mothers! In this work, he banishes some of Christianity's cherished gods and a few of her sacred cows.

Ironically, in the aftermath, my instincts tell me we've drawn much nearer to the Real Deal."

-BRADLEY JERSAK [PHD]

Author of *A More Christlike God*

THE

why there is no god

ATHEISTIC

and you should follow him

THEIST

JEFF TURNER

CONTENTS

LOSING GOD IS FINDING GOD

It was at the feet of Jesus that I discovered atheism, and at the feet of atheists that I rediscovered Jesus.

I'll never forget walking out of our local Barnes and Noble with an uncomfortably heavy bag of books in my hand. The reason it was so heavy was that, while shopping, I had sandwiched one particular book between several others in order to avoid being seen carrying it around the store, and when I got up to the register I just ended up buying them all in order to avoiding looking awkward.

As I walked to my car, I felt like every eye in the county was fixed on and peering into my bag, examining its contents and zeroing in on the one book I had purchased so sheepishly, but was nevertheless very eager to read. The book in question was *The God Delusion*, by the rather infamous Richard Dawkins. Why was I so uncomfortable purchasing it, you might ask? Well, because I was a devout Christian, for starters, not to mention a pastor, and it just wasn't the sort of thing I wanted a church member to spot me toting around.

Now, in reality, there could have been a dozen or more reasons I had been perusing the rather small *atheist* section at our local bookstore, and settled on one of the most reviled (by Christians anyways) books written from an atheistic perspective in the last hundred years. Maybe it was just for research. You know, I was getting ready to do a sermon series on atheism and belief, or something like that, and just wanted to see what arguments were out there. Or maybe I'd gotten lost in the terribly Godless *New Age* section, and so, with a spirit that was vexed to its limits, reached in desperation for anything with the word *God* in the title. Or maybe I bought it as part of an Elijah-like showdown with an atheist friend who promised he'd read *The Purpose-Driven Life* if only I'd read a little Dawkins. And maybe, just maybe, that friend would get gloriously "born again," and grow up to be the next Billy Graham.

I mean, aside from the Billy Graham bit, all of those scenarios would have sounded plausible, and the likeliest of scenarios, had I run into any church going folk, would have been that no one would have even noticed the books I was carrying. So why was I so nervous then? In all honesty, it was because my faith was in crisis and threatening to fall to pieces, and I was in a desperate search for answers to questions I'd only, at that point, recently begun allowing myself to ask. Hence my paranoia.

My Christian experience up until just several years prior, had been quite different from what I was experiencing, and this whole "questioning" and "deconstructing" thing was not what I was used to. I was raised in a Christian home by literally two of the greatest humans a child could ever hope to call parents, who also happened to be two of the greatest Christians one could ever hope to know. For some unfortunate reason, though, somewhere in my childhood I picked up the idea that God was an angry, disapproving being, who was displeased with me far more often than he was pleased. That did not dissuade me from trying to please him, though. No, no, it only fueled my desire to please him, and ignited an unholy fire of discontentment in me that nothing but the pleasure of my God-concept would be able to satisfy.

Due to the wholly unpleasable nature of that same God-concept, though, my spiritual life became one of great toil, pressure, and legalism. I literally cannot calculate the hours I spent in anguished prayer, tearful repentance, attempted fasting, and intense worship, all in order to earn the favor and approval of the one I called God. Had I a dollar for each of those hours, though, I would have probably retired at 17, and presently be cruising the Caribbean on my private yacht, sipping some umbrella drink. Maybe that's a bit of an exaggeration, but you get the point.

To make a long and painful story pleasantly shorter, let's just say that I wasn't being paid a dollar per legalistic action, and instead ended up burning myself out and then some. By the tail end of my early twenties, I was thoroughly exhausted, and at the end of my rope as far as my Christianity was concerned. As I've already stated, I eventually became a pastor, but did so way sooner than I should have, and after just a few short years, because of my intensity, felt like I'd been doing it for a lifetime.

To top it off, pastoring exposed me to human suffering on a level that I was woefully unprepared to deal with. I was Charismatic in my beliefs, meaning that I believed in spiritual gifts like healing and so on, and so watching church members die slowly and painfully of diseases that God certainly ought to have been able to heal through someone as devoted as me, was bewildering, to say the least.

In the midst of this, I was also radically rediscovering my faith. I began to take the person of Jesus more seriously than I ever had before, and in so doing became convinced that I'd formerly had God figured completely wrong. My "god" had been one of anger, wrath, violence, and hellfire, but the God I was beginning to see in Jesus was one of love, forgiveness, mercy, and inclusion. This caused me a lot of emotional stress, since I had been tasked with helping to lead a congregation, and all the while was having to completely reconfigure my understanding of the very One toward whom I was supposed to be leading them. For the most part, I had to keep this deconstruction and rethinking of my faith under wraps, talking only with a select few about any of it, and even then in a very guarded manner.

In this place of questioning, rethinking, and deconstruction, I began to search for teachers, thinkers, scholars, and theologians who could point me toward a better way of approaching the subject of God, and a more intellectually honest and spiritually enriching approach to scripture and spirituality. Along the way I discovered many voices that were of great encouragement to me, and who helped me salvage and then transform my faith into something that actually worked in the real world. But along that same way I found myself sitting among and learning from individuals who pastors simply ought not to be learning from: *Atheists.*

By the time I walked out of Barnes and Noble with my own personal copy of *The God Delusion* in hand, I was already extremely familiar with the works and words of individuals like Richard Dawkins, Sam Harris, the late Christopher Hitchens, Daniel Dennet, Dan Barker, Laurence Kraus, and more. In the early phases of my own deconstructive journey, I began to find that I resonated with the words of many of these radical atheists, some even identifying as *anti*-theists, more so than I did with my fellow Christians.

At first this really troubled me. I mean, I didn't hate God. I didn't even hate the concept of God. Sure, I was tired, burnt out, frustrated with the lack of results, and worn as thin as the book of Philemon from my constant strivings after God, but I didn't hate him. Sadly, atheism is often mistaken by people as a hatred for God, or a manifestation of anger toward religious institutions or people, and I too had absorbed this misconception along the way. I was none of these things, though, and yet I was more and more finding Christian teaching to be the opposite of refreshing, and the lectures and talks given by many atheist philosophers and teachers to be a breath of fresh air.

This experience in itself helped break down many of the misconceptions I'd built up concerning atheism. Atheists weren't necessarily hateful toward God or Christianity. They just simply didn't believe. Some just come to a point where they can't, despite wanting to, continue believing, and this was something I was beginning to experience for myself. I was ceasing to believe in God as I'd always imagined God, despite trying with all of my might to continue. So many people are quick to accuse the one losing their faith of *choosing* to lose it, or of changing their beliefs in order to justify an immoral lifestyle, but for me, it was exactly the opposite. I felt as though my morals and ethics were coming more and more in line with what I saw in the Jesus of the Gospels, and in increasing disharmony with the image of God I had held in mind from my youth. Life was happening all around me, forcing me to grow, and I simply could no longer consider sacred things that, more and more, I was finding repugnant.

Ideas like original sin, a violent atonement, and an eternal hell just stopped making any sense to me whatsoever. I didn't set out to "disprove" these ideas, nor was I on the warpath, trying to tear down traditional beliefs and construct some newfangled version of Christianity that stood in opposition to them. I was simply living, breathing, experiencing life, and attempting to take seriously the God I had decided to follow in my teens. I couldn't help asking the questions I was asking, or thinking the thoughts I was thinking. I didn't necessarily want to, but I just couldn't help it. Life forced me into a corner where I could either be dishonest, and push it all down, or ask, wonder, and pull at threads until my faith unraveled like a poorly-knit sweater. Having never been one to opt for dishonesty, I did some serious thread-pulling, and soon found myself with nary a shred of faith left.

That might sound a bit traumatic, especially for a pastor helping to lead a faith community, and that's because it was traumatic, especially for a pastor helping to lead a faith community. And although I'm glad I endured the initial trauma and discomfort that comes with deconstruction, I won't sugarcoat it-it was painful, mostly because of how painfully lonely it was. There wasn't a soul I felt comfortable bearing my own soul to in those days, simply because I didn't know anyone who would understand. And that's how I discovered the likes of Dawkins, Hitchens, and the rest. These allowed me to ask questions I would have never asked on my own, mostly by asking them for me. I began to find comfort in listening to their lectures, and reading their works, simply because everything I had wanted to say, think, and ask, they said, thought, and asked freely, without any fear of divine retribution.

It was refreshing, liberating, and reminded me that I was not alone in my doubts and my questioning.

Tim Whitmarsh, in his book, *Battling the Gods: Atheism in the Ancient World,* documents the phenomenon of atheism in the cultures of ancient Greece and Rome. In discussing the public performances of plays based on the works of atheists like Diagoras of Melos in the theaters of the ancient, and intensely *theistic* city of Athens, which were considered sacred, even religious spaces, Whitmarsh asks:

> Is it possible to imagine a monotheist equivalent? Is there any synagogue, mosque, or church where the ideas of Richard Dawkins, Christopher Hitchens, and Sam Harris are expounded seriously and constructively? If such places exist at all, they are extremely rare. But then Greek religious culture had no sacred text, no orthodoxy, no clear sense of what was ruled in and out of the sacred sphere, and as a result it was not blasphemous to subject the nature of the gods to radical questioning.

Such a space would have been a dream come true in those early days of my own deconstruction, but as Whitmarsh suggests, it is extremely rare, if not impossible, to find a Christian community willing to entertain such thoughts. Our problem, as he also suggests, is the vise-grip like manner in which we hold onto ideas of orthodoxy, and devote ourselves to sacred texts. It isn't that we, as Christians, should not consider our text sacred, but that we ought to be humble enough to recognize that it is often just our *interpretation* of this text that we consider sacred and orthodox, and that maybe we've missed what it is that truly makes it sacred. But what I had, and what I was surrounded by, was an inflexible orthodoxy that told me what and what not to think. I could not, in any public sense, ask my questions and bear my soul, and so my un-bearable soul itself became the "Athenian theater" where such ideas could be shared, and given due consideration. And it was a host of atheistic biologists, neuroscientists, astrophysicists, activists, and everything in between, along with a few theologians, philosophers, and I'd like to think Jesus himself, who became my deconstructive companions. What I could not think upon, and what I could not discuss in church or a home fellowship group, I could freely think upon and consider in their company.

This was an enriching, spiritual experience that, at first, far from damaging my faith, greatly enriched it. As I said in my opening line, it was actually Jesus who drove me to explore atheism. It was seriously considering his love, his ethics, and merciful nature that made me to question and reconsider the nature of my god-concept to start with, but that radical questioning eventually led me to a place I never expected to end up in, but was nonetheless critical to my spiritual development.

The more time I spent with my deconstructive companions, the more I began to see, not only an honest portrayal of my god-concept, but an honest portrayal of myself as well. I began to see how I looked to those who did not share my worldview or background, which is something I'd never taken even a moment to consider. Seeing myself, the backwardness of some of my beliefs, and even the danger inherent in so many of them, shook me to my core.

I'll never forget, for instance, hearing it suggested by Christopher Hitchens that teaching a young child about a very real hell, where God eternally punishes his enemies, was tantamount to child abuse. My oldest daughter was just beginning to ask me questions about heaven, hell, and the afterlife, and on a few occasions I had, through gritted teeth, grudgingly told her that, yes, according to how I understood scripture, God would send unbelievers to hell forever. I always felt sick when forced into that position, but thought it would be ultimately more damaging to *not* teach her about hell, since ignorance concerning its existence could apparently land you there. Or so goes the story, anyways.

Hearing it suggested that what I thought was a loving act from a Christian father was abusive at first made me extremely angry, until the truth of the statement dawned on me. I don't have an abusive cell in my body, and most certainly not where my children are concerned, and so I know that I never intentionally harmed them. Yet hearing the critique of one from the "outside" allowed me to see how monstrous and terrifying what I saw as normal parenting looked like to those who live on the other side of my very small circle. I didn't feel shamed or ridiculed, but more just had this realization that I had been living in a hermetically sealed environment, and was only considerate of the opinions and views of those similarly sealed. When I allowed my god-concept to be critiqued by these "outsiders," I saw, not just how horrifying my god-concept was, but how horrifying of a person it was turning me into.

Honestly, I think this was the worst part of my deconstruction experience. I mean, it's one thing to realize you were wrong about an idea, but it's another to realize how damaging that idea had been to you, and consequently to those you love. Realizing that the terrible image of the vindictive, violent "god" was often just a projection of an unrealized part of myself that, once externalized, became justification for acts that I would have never engaged in on my own, was beyond disturbing. In my small little circle of people who thought and acted just like me, I would have never noticed such things, or if I had, would have thought them perfectly normal. Once I allowed others with drastically different views and opinions in, though, I caught a glimpse of a Jeff Turner I'd never glimpsed before, and I was frightened by what I saw.

I was a man who loved my wife, but, because of my god-concept, had become neglectful, controlling, and distant. Worse yet, some of these tendencies that I may have naturally outgrown on my own, were justified and vindicated by my beliefs, and were allowed to flourish unchecked.

I was a father who loved his children dearly, but, because of what I believed was truth, was forced into a position where I had to teach them things that I knew full well could lead to maladjustment, fear, and anxiety.

In my pastoral role, I was a man who loved those I was tasked with pastoring, but, because of my beliefs, was forced to agonizingly preach a God of wrath, hellfire, hate, and holy terror. More disturbingly, though, is the fact that on more occasions than I'd like to admit, I know very well that the traits I presented as divine were merely my own, and were used by me to keep people believing and living a certain way.

At this point in my journey, when I started to realize how damaged I had been by my theology, and how *damaging* I was becoming as a consequence, things really started coming unraveled.

I had already concluded that my god-beliefs were royally screwed up, but was now beginning to see how royally screwed up I was because of them. Not only had I suffered, struggled, and toiled beneath the weight of a certain god-concept, but I had absolutely nothing to show for it, morally speaking. I wasn't better because of it, but worse, and I had left a lot of hurt people in my wake.

Now, when you're just deconstructing beliefs, it can actually be kind of exciting, fun even. When you're forced to come to terms with the damage done to yourself and to others by those beliefs, though, it gets real heavy, real fast. It was at this point in my journey that atheism became more to me than just an edgy conversation partner, but started to seem like an appealing and viable option worth exploring.

In this season of my life, I lost God, and I don't mean that I couldn't find God in an experiential sense, or that my prayer life became dry and "drudgerous." I mean that the very concept of God became lost to me. The God I had known died to me. I no longer saw any value, relevance, or reality in any of it, and, in fact, actually came to see precisely the opposite. Things I had thought to be true of the divine were things I had outgrown, and could no longer live out or justify. I could not rightly employ the methods in my parenting that my God, who was quickly becoming *god*, with a lowercase "g," was said to employ in his without landing myself in jail. Nor could I be the sort of husband to my bride he supposedly was to his without losing my marriage over it. I had, in many ways, become better than my "god," or at the very least better than my beliefs about him, and continuing to worship him at that point seemed like a step backwards, not forwards.

I did not want to lose "god," but my faith was slipping through my fingers, and there seemed to be nothing I could do to stop it. The more I lived, learned, and experienced, the less any of it made sense, until it finally made no sense, and I just couldn't hold onto it any longer. I passed through what I can only call, to use St. John of the Cross's words, a *dark night of the soul*, and eventually made a conscious decision to just let it all go.

Now, I know this all sounds rather gloomy, and maybe not like the sort of thing you're interested in reading about, but the truth is that every Jesus-follower must travel down this path at some point in their journey. Of course, your journey and mine aren't always going to match up exactly, but the basic crisis I'm describing is something that every honest soul must pass through.

Some try to avoid it completely, and when they feel the icy fingers of doubt, or hear the incessant tinnitus of cognitive dissonance, just insist that it isn't happening to them, and that all is fine and dandy. Many will continue in this state for years, and even transition into the next life insisting they never doubted or had such a crisis, but the insistence is itself a tell, revealing the crisis they're undergoing to be a most hellish and unspeakable one. It is, ironically enough, the unspeaking that makes such crises all the more hellish, though, and this I know from personal experience.

Others have embraced the notion that such experiences are unavoidable, but have tried to domesticate them by making doubt or the passage through the "dark night" a part of the Christian experience, just like prayer or communion. Many of my progressive friends take such an approach, and while I see the validity in what they're trying to do, you simply can't ritualize an experience like this.

Jesus, when questioned about why his disciples did not fast, which was essentially a ritualization of the experience of mourning, responded that:

> 34 ..."You cannot make wedding guests fast while the bridegroom is with them, can you? 35 The days will come when the bridegroom will be taken away from them, and then they will fast in those days."
>
> -Luke 5:34-35, NRSV

In other words, he was saying that one cannot ritualize the experience of loss, but that when he is literally taken from them through death, they will have an experience that transcends mere ritual. They will feel something so deeply that they won't be able to eat, but it will not be fasting as religion understands and defines it. It will be real, painful, and penetrative. And that's precisely what it was.

The disciples had to experience the death of their god-concept, were they to ever truly discover God, and my own experience was no different. The "bridegroom," as it were, was quite literally taken from me, and I was plunged into a season in which I could not tell up from down. It was not a cutesy, ritualized loss, or even just an exercise in which I explored the theological and philosophical concept of the "death of God." It was a season in which I could do little more than sing with the Lutheran hymn writer, Johannes Rist: "O great woe, God himself lies dead..."

And yet somehow, in this darkness, in this place of the utter loss of God, I found God again. I can't fully explain why or how, but in watching my God die, and in becoming an atheist, I discovered God, as if for the first time. Perhaps this is what Jesus had in mind when, just after speaking of his disciple's imminent loss of him, he spoke this parable:

36 He also told them a parable: "No one tears a piece from a new garment and sews it on an old garment; otherwise the new will be torn, and the piece from the new will not match the old. 37 And no one puts new wine into old wineskins; otherwise the new wine will burst the skins and will be spilled, and the skins will be destroyed. 38 But new wine must be put into fresh wineskins.

-Luke 5:36-38, NRSV

Jesus seems to suggest here that we must rediscover God, who is spoken of here metaphorically as a garment and wine. One cannot simply take new concepts, represented by a patch from a new garment, or a new wineskin, and add it to their old conceptions. No, there needs to be an overhaul of the entire system. The rediscovery of God necessitates the loss of all former conceptions of God. Old garments must be lost, and old wineskins tossed if we are to ever discover god afresh. And since this is said directly after Jesus' statement about his disciples own loss of him, maybe he is suggesting that all would-be followers of his must have the "Bridegroom taken from them." And maybe it is here, in this place of loss, this place where we realize that everything we once held sacred must go, that we actually discover the sacred. Perhaps Jesus is telling us here that it is only in losing God that we find God, and that it is only in becoming atheists that we can truly become theists.

Simone Weil has written that: "There are two atheisms of which one is a purification of the notion of God" and Paul Tillich, whose words I'm admittedly taking a bit out of their context here, has written similarly, "It is safe to say that a man who has never tried to flee God has never experienced the God Who is." There is no ritual, no religious, philosophical, or intellectual exercise that can do this for you. You *must* have the "Bridegroom taken" from you. Whether it's through a conscious leaving behind of God, a fleeing, as Tillich says, or a slow, un-helpable process in which you find yourself unable to believe, you and I must, at some point, feel the utter and complete loss of "god" we once knew in order to discover the God who is. We must experience the legitimate and worshipful experience of atheism in order to experience a theism that can stand up in the world as it stands at present. It is this loss, this fleeing, this atheism that is, to quote Weil, "a purification of the notion of God."

I was smack dab in the middle of this loss when I walked out of Barnes and Noble with my heavier-than-normal bag of books in tow that day. There was not a soul in the world that I thought would understand what I was going through, or who would allow me to express this experience without warning me of deception or apostasy. So I took refuge in my own soul with the words of a man who had no orthodoxy restraining him from asking the hard questions, and poking holes in the holy. And it was ultimately the words of such unflinchingly anti-religious individuals like

Dawkins, that led me back to the feet of a God who looked like Jesus. When the "god" of my youth and of my imagination had been thoroughly crucified and deconstructed, something arose from the grave that was unencumbered by all of the darkness, dogmas, and doctrines that drove me to question him in the first place. Like the men on the road the Emmaus, who mourned their God, and then found him in an unexpected form, I too found the Father who looks like the Son on the other side of having thoroughly mourned his inexistence and irrelevance.

Maybe you're walking out of a bookstore hiding this book between a few more acceptable titles, or maybe not, but the fact that you're reading it tells me that you know a thing or two about the journey I've described above. You've either been through it, are on the other side of it, and maybe gearing up for round two, or are standing at the edge of the woods, wondering if it's safe to go in. Wherever you're at, one thing is for sure, though, and that's that if you've determined to follow this Jesus, this God who "refuses to be God," you're going to come to know this well-worn path very, very intimately.

I wrote this book for those like you and like me. I wrote it for those sheepish book-buyers who have no safe place in which they can share their doubts and questions or bear their souls. I wrote it for those in the midst of their own deconstruction, trying desperately to figure out if there is anything of their faith worth saving or holding on to. I wrote it for the one who maybe isn't even looking for answers, but maybe just for someone to stand with them while they question and let them know that it's ok. And I also wrote it for those who are too afraid to ask, and need someone to do it for them.

I still have far more questions than I have answers, and am admittedly lacking in certainty more than I'm in possession of it. I don't know how many more times I'll go through a similar experience before all is said and done, and all I have to share with you is my journey thus far. And so what follows is precisely that: my own theological and philosophical journey over the last decade plus. We will cover a lot of ground, some of it a bit abstract, some of it more practical and theological, and some of it existential and personal. It is the story of how my "god" died, and how my God was reborn. It is the tale of my own journey away from a "god" whom I could no longer worship, toward one whom I can't help but worship.

I hope, dear reader, as I bring the "book" of my own life and beliefs out of hiding, out from among the more palatable and acceptable titles that I'm sometimes tempted to hide it between, that you're somehow able to find yourself in its pages. I hope that my story and my journey somehow, someway, helps you on your own, and gives you a safe space to ask your questions, and speak your truth. And ultimately, I hope that me, bringing my own "book" out of hiding, somehow gives you the courage to do the same.

1 | JESUS IS AN ATHEIST

"Yes, we are atheists -- if you mean that we do not pray to or believe in all of the gods that we are expected to worship."
-Octavius, second century CE

"...it is thanks to God that I am an atheist...I have become an atheist thanks to Jesus' existence."
-Gianni Vattimo

I tried to be an atheist, but I wasn't a good enough Christian to pull it off.

Now, what in the name of all Gods, existent and non-existent, could I possibly mean by that? What I certainly *do not* mean is that I didn't have enough faith to be an atheist what with all of this evidence demanding a verdict (if you grew up in the church, congratulations on getting those references), or some other passive aggressive Christian insinuation that atheism is, itself, some sort of religion. What *is* concealed in my statement are my beliefs about what a true atheism looks like, something the Slovenian Philosopher, Slavoj Zizek, suggests is not to be found in what we often think of when we speak of atheism, but in Christianity. Zizek even goes as far as to call Christianity the "so-called religion of atheism," saying of it elsewhere, "Christianity is much more atheist than the usual atheism..."[1] Now, it's obvious he has in mind a brand of Christianity, or at least an approach to it, that is very different from what

---

[1] Fiennes, Sophie, James Wilson, Martin Rosenbaum, Katie Holly, and Slavoj Žižek. 2014. The Pervert's Guide to Ideology.

we see today, and while I don't claim to have a complete grasp on what he means, I do believe there is truth in his words. Christianity, when lived in the manner that following Jesus and taking seriously the implications of the Gospel story will eventually lead us to, will appear to the religious as atheism. Beyond just appearing as such, though, I would agree that it actually *is* atheism, at least in my experience.

So, rather than just explaining right up front what I mean by, "I tried to be an atheist, but I wasn't a good enough Christian to pull it off," I'll just assure you that we'll get there, but it will take an entire book to do so. Even then I'm not sure I'll do the subject justice, but I can assure you I'll try my best.

EARLY CHRISTIAN ATHEISM

To get us started on this journey, let's back up 2000 years or so, and briefly talk about the early church. According to the book of Acts, those who followed "the way," that is, early followers of Jesus, eventually came to be called *Christians,* first at Antioch. There was something so genuine, so Christ-like, about their Christ-following that it seemed logical to refer to them by his name. But this same Christ-likeness eventually led to them becoming the bearers of another title-a title that many 21st century heirs of the Christian title would have no desire to be associated with. This title, borne with a degree of pride by some early Christians, is now understood as representing the very antithesis of Christianity.

So, what is this title I'm referring to? What is this designation that was synonymous with Christianity in its earliest days? You may have already guessed it based on the title of the book you're reading, but here it is:

Atheists.

That's right, you read correctly. Along with being called Christians, early Jesus-followers were also called atheists. But why, exactly? Justin Martyr, writing nearly two millennia ago, laid out the accusation of atheism brought against himself and his fellow Christians, in a work known as the *First Apology*. He writes:

> For not only among the Greeks did reason (Logos) prevail to condemn these things [idols] through Socrates, but also among the Barbarians were they condemned by Reason (or the Word, the Logos) Himself, who took shape, and became man, and was called Jesus Christ; and in obedience to Him, we not only deny that they who did such things as these are gods, but assert that they are wicked and impious demons, whose actions will not

bear comparison with those even of men desirous of virtue.[2]

And here he addresses the charge directly:

> Hence are we called atheists. And we confess that we are atheists, so far as gods of this sort are concerned, but not with respect to the most true God, the Father of righteousness and temperance and the other virtues, who is free from all impurity. But both Him, and the Son…and the prophetic Spirit, we worship and adore, knowing them in reason and truth, and declaring without grudging to everyone who wishes to learn, as we have been taught.[3]

The charge is not only an historically documented reality, but something that was happily embraced within a certain context: "And we confess that we *are* atheists," Justin Martyr wrote, "so far as gods of this sort are concerned." In the face of the lustful, violent, licentious idols of their contemporaries, early Christians gladly bore the title, as it uncoupled them from what was popularly worshipped in the day, as well as from the values these deities represented.

Another early Christian document called *Octavius*, in which two fictional characters, Octavius, a Christian, and Caecilius, a non-Christian, engage in a dialogue concerning the way the church was viewed by outsiders, again reveals the charge of atheism early Christians came up against:

> CAECILIUS: What concerns me is what you really are. This is the reason that you are hated across all the lands of this vast empire. Let's get to the real problem. You are atheists.

> OCTAVIUS: Yes, we are atheists -- if you mean that we do not pray to or believe in all of the gods that we are expected to worship. But these are not gods. We worship the one true God, the Lord over all.[4]

In yet another early document called *The Martyrdom of Polycarp*, a crowd is said to have yelled "away with the atheists!" in calling for the arrest and killing of the bishop of Smyrna, Polycarp:

---

[2] A. Cleveland Coxe, Ante-Nicene Fathers: Volume 1: The Apostolic Fathers, Justin Martyr, Irenaeus [1885]

[3] Ibid.

[4] https://archive.org/stream/octaviusofminuci00minuiala/octaviusofminuci00minuiala_djvu.txt

> So after this all the crowd, wondering at the nobility of
> the God-loving and God-fearing people of the Christians,
> cried out: "Away with the Atheists; let Polycarp be
> searched for.[5]

Once Polycarp is found and arrested, he is called upon to avoid
execution by swearing his allegiance to Caesar, and rejecting Christianity
by proclaiming, "away with the atheists," just as it was said of him by the
unbelieving crowd. We read:

> Therefore when he was brought forward the Pro-Consul
> asked him if he were Polycarp, and when he admitted it
> he tried to persuade him to deny, saying: "Respect your
> age," and so forth, as they are accustomed to say:
> "Swear by the genius of Caesar, repent, say: `Away with
> the Atheists'"; but Polycarp, with a stern countenance
> looked on all the crowd of lawless heathen in the arena,
> and waving his hand at them, he groaned and looked up
> to heaven and said: "Away with the Atheists."[6]

Here, atheism is clearly connected to the church's rejection of the gods
of Rome, and when called to denounce Christianity as atheism, or a
rejection of that which is divine, Polycarp essentially turns the tables on
his captors, proclaiming them and the angry crow calling for his murder
to be the true God-deniers. While Polycarp himself is not portrayed as
embracing the label, it was his devotion to Christ, and his rejection of the
gods of the empire, that welcomed it.

You see, for the earliest followers of Jesus, being a Christian was not a
matter of leaving behind a Godless life for a God-filled one, but of leaving
behind a god-filled life for a god-less one (note carefully the
capitalizations). In a world filled with deities of all shapes and sizes,
choosing "the way" of Jesus was not simply about embracing a new
belief system, but negating one, if not hundreds, of others. Hence the
charge of atheism constantly popping up in these early documents. As
the fictional Octavius states, "we are atheists...we do not pray to or
believe in all of the gods that we are expected to worship." The early
church's atheism was not a tongue in cheek statement, or an ironic title
embraced in the name of being edgy or progressive, but an accusation
that actually made sense in the context of the world in which they lived.

In his book *Theology of Culture*, Paul Tillich writes:

---

[5] Polycarp, Saint Bishop of Smyrna; Paul Hartog, Polycarp's Epistle to the
Philippians and the Martyrdom of Polycarp : introduction, text, and
commentary (Oxford : Oxford University Press, 2013.)
[6] Ibid.

> It is not by chance that not only Socrates, but also the Jews and the early Christians were persecuted as atheists. For those who adhered to the powers, they were atheists.[7]

In other words, in the days when gods were more than just fodder for comic book characters and Hollywood movies, but were backed by the power of the state, and the state by the supposed power of the gods, leaving them behind in favor of others was not seen as a simple conversion from one brand of theism to another, but *atheism*. The political power structure told you what was, and was not divine, and so the worship of any gods but those sanctioned by the state would have been considered atheistic. The early church's break with what the establishment called divinity was a true, literal atheism, then, and so the accusation was justified.

More importantly than all of that, though, is the fact that, for early Christians, Christianity was not merely a belief system, but a path, or a way of living. In fact, for the Christian, the living has always been more important than the believing. In early Christian communities, for example, becoming a Christian was not merely a matter of hearing a message and responding to an altar call, but a process of discipleship, in which one carefully considered whether or not they were willing to embrace this *way* before joining themselves to the church. And so, in a culture like that of Rome, Christianity stood out as atheistic, perhaps more for its practices than its beliefs. Yes, their refusal to worship Rome's gods was at the center of the accusation, but it was the *way* of Christianity that barred them from doing so, for these deities represented values that ran contrary to the ethics laid out in the Gospel. To the world, then, this *way* looked atheistic, because it was a way bereft of the values of the gods of culture. Most brands of theism, regardless of the gods at the helm, have certain things in common, because the gods birthed by the human brain all tend to look just like us. In Christianity, however, God becomes something completely different from everything and anything we've envisioned, and so the lives of his followers become as different from the culture as God is from the gods of that culture.

To outside observers, the Christian appeared to be living a godless life. These early churches were radical communities of love that operated without a sacred temple, a sacrificial system, and were, at least in theory, not attached to a political agenda or ideology. Their God was non-violent, non-retributive, non-sacrificial, and non-sectarian. They were strange and peculiar individuals, whose God and lifestyles did not, in any way, resemble those of the theists of their day.

---

[7] Paul Tillich, Robert C Kimball, *Theology of Culture* (London ; New York : Oxford University Press, 1964, ©1959.)

So, again, for the early Christian, choosing to follow Jesus was not a matter of leaving behind a Godless life for a God-filled life, but of leaving behind a god-filled life for a god-less life. Throwing aside the gods one was "expected to worship" by "those who adhered to the powers," as Tillich says, meant rejecting an entire way of living in the world that was considered normal, and was acceptable in the eyes of the majority. Following *the way* of Jesus did not simply alter the space the Christian occupied on Sunday morning, but everything from the majors to the minutia of their daily lives. They became radically detached from societal norms, expectations, and demands, choosing instead something so different that, to the outside observer, it could only be described as atheism. To those entrenched in theism, then, the Christian, lacking in the values considered godly, was a godless individual.

For an example of what I mean, let's look at the story of Jesus' meeting with the two men on the road to Emmaus for a brief moment. In Luke 24, Jesus, in an unrecognizable form, encounters two individuals, one of whom was named Cleopas, walking along the road from Jerusalem to Emmaus. The two are discussing the recent events of Jesus' crucifixion, and their obvious disillusionment, as they had hoped he would be the militaristic, political ruler who would free them from Roman oppression. What Jesus communicates to them, though, is that, while they were expecting a Messiah who would make their enemies to suffer and die, what they got was a Messiah who would sooner suffer and die at the hands of their enemies before stooping to become just like them:

> 25 Then he said to them, "Oh, how foolish you are, and how slow of heart to believe all that the prophets have declared! 26 Was it not necessary that the Messiah should suffer these things and then enter into his glory?" 27 Then beginning with Moses and all the prophets, he interpreted to them the things about himself in all the scriptures.
> -Luke 24:25-27, NRSV

In essence, Jesus is telling them that his Kingdom bears no resemblance to the kingdom they were hoping he would help them defeat. His was not a Kingdom that was Rome's equal in value, but something that utterly contradicted it. It was not violence, retribution, power, or subjugating others that his Kingdom was founded on, but rather giving oneself for the benefit of others, and being willing to suffer rather than bring harm or suffering upon another.

This is further demonstrated when Jesus, who throughout the conversation, keeps the disciples from recognizing him, is suddenly recognized by them in the sharing of a meal. It is not until these disciples have taken this stranger in for the night, and provide for his needs, that they realize it is Jesus, who then immediately disappears before their eyes. The point could not be more clear: Jesus' Kingdom is not about waging war, or amassing power in the name of God, but rather about realizing that giving oneself for another is how one serves God. In fact, it is God whom we serve when we serve and meet the needs of strangers.

This story was likely intended to be read as a critique of an older story about Rome's legendary founder and demigod, Romulus, whose tale of being murdered by corrupt, government officials, and subsequent resurrection and ascension into heaven was retold and reenacted annually. After the disappearance of his body, Romulus is said to have appeared, in a glorious, resurrected form, to a man named Proculus, who was travelling on the road from Alba Longa to Rome. Interestingly, the name *Proculus,* just as the name *Cleopas* from the Luke story, means to tell or to proclaim. Obviously, in both stories, those to whom the resurrected figure appears are being shown something that they are then to tell, or proclaim as being central to the veneration of said figure. In Luke, Jesus shows that it is non-violence, love of enemies, and caring for the needs of strangers that lie at the core of his Kingdom, but Romulus tells Proculus to proclaim something quite different.

In Titus Livius's *Early History of Rome,* we read these supposed words from Proculus on his encounter with the resurrected Romulus:

> "Romulus", he declared, "the father of our city descended from heaven at dawn this morning and appeared to me. In awe and reverence I stood before him, praying for permission to look upon his face without sin. Go, he said, and tell the Romans that by heaven's will my Rome shall be capital of the world. Let them learn to be soldiers. Let them know, and teach their children, that no power on earth can stand against Roman arms. Having spoken these words, he was taken up again into the sky."[8]

The Roman poet, Ovid, claims Proculus was told by Romulus:

> "Bid the pious throng bring incense, and propitiate the new Quirinius and bid them cultivate the arts their fathers cultivated, the art of war."[9]

---

[8] Livy, *The early history of Rome. Books I-V of The history of Rome from its foundation.* (Harmondsworth, Eng. Penguin, 1971)

[9] Ovid; Rolfe Humphries, *Metamorphoses.* (Bloomington : Indiana University Press, 1955.)

In both stories, men with names meaning "to proclaim" are met by their resurrected lord. Jesus appears humbly, and as a stranger, while Romulus appears in such splendor that Proculus must pray "for permission to look upon his face without sin." Then, in Ovid's account, Romulus calls himself "the new Quirinius," who, according to the Greek historian, Plutarch, was a deity associated with Mars, the god of war. Jesus, on the other hand, clearly communicates that his Kingdom is one in which we must be willing to suffer for the benefit of our enemies, as opposed to Romulus' kingdom, which had the art of war, and the subjugation of enemies at its center. Romulus ascends into heaven, disappearing before Proculus' eyes, after having commissioned him to call the Romans to take up arms, and teach their children war, whereas Jesus disappears before the eyes of his disciples, only once they've discerned the divine presence in one whom they'd formerly thought only a stranger.

It's also interesting to note that, in the Romulus story, Proculus was journeying *from* Alba Longa *to* Rome, whereas Cleopas and his companion were travelling *from* Jerusalem *to* Emmaus. The suggestion here is that the "way" of Romulus is one that has Rome, or Empire, at its center-that "all roads lead to Rome" and whatnot, whereas Jesus leads us from power and nationalism, to simple service and love for one another.

What we see here, in comparing and contrasting these two stories alone, is how huge the chasm was between the values of Rome, and the Kingdom of God proclaimed by Jesus. To follow the "way" of Jesus was to walk in the exact opposite direction of that laid out by Romulus, and to follow the "way" of Romulus was to walk in the exact opposite direction of that laid out by Jesus. No wonder, then, to the prominent theists of the day, Christians appeared as atheists! Their "way" was so contrary to everything thought to be divine, that it could only be dismissed as godlessness.

Following Jesus, from day one, has meant breaking away, not just from the gods popularly worshipped in the culture, but from culture, as it looks when informed by a belief in gods. Christianity has always been, first and foremost, a "way" of living, and a path to be trodden, and not simply a belief system. When one actually follows this path, they become completely and totally divorced from the values of the gods of culture, and the culture of the gods. To be a Christian, in that sense, is to embrace a lifestyle that so contradicts all popular theisms, that it is relatively indistinguishable from atheism. That was the case then, and it will continue to be the case whenever and wherever someone embraces the "way."

Paradoxically, though, it was precisely the early Christian's theism that informed their atheistic lifestyle. They lived as they did *because* of their devotion to the divine, but it was an understanding so contradictory to what humans had come to imagine the divine to be, that it seemed utterly un-divine. They were atheists in this world, precisely because of their theism, and it is in that sense that I refer to them as *atheistic theists*. Now, I know that seems oxymoronic, but think of it this way: many, in the name of devotion to their country, become absolutely opposed to that same country's present state and leadership. Their actions and words may come off as disloyal, or unpatriotic to their fellow countrymen, but in truth it is their loyalty and patriotism that moves them to speak and behave as they do. They are loyal, not to what their country has become, but to some version of it which they think ideal. They are *unpatriotic patriots,* who are first and foremost loyal to their country, but in a way that no longer looks like loyalty to the popular culture.

In the same way, the early church saw something in Jesus that came to define God for them, and it was this *something* that they gave themselves to unreservedly. They were theists, in a very strict sense, but their theism was so different from that of their culture, that they appeared atheistic. Hence my use of the term *atheistic theists*.

Thomas Altizer put it this way:

> The "atheism" of the radical Christian is in large measure a prophetic reaction to a distant and non-redemptive God who...stands wholly apart from...the Incarnate Word. It is precisely because the radical Christian seeks a total union with the Word made flesh that he must refuse the God who alone is God and give himself to a quest for the God who *is* Jesus.[10]

Altizer here refers to certain portrayals of the Christian God, borrowed and derived from pagan thought. But the principle applies to the early church's atheism as well. It was their loyalty to the God they encountered in Jesus that moved them to refuse the "gods" of culture, in favor of something radically different.

Now, as time passed, these same deities toward whom the early church was deliberately atheistic, became incorporated into the Christian experience. When the Roman Emperor, Constantine, converted to Christianity, the gods and values of Rome became Christianized, and the very values that the *way* of Jesus once diametrically opposed, became woven into the fabric of Christianity. The cross, the ultimate sign of forgiveness, and non-retaliation, became a sign in which Constantine claimed he was told to conquer, and the rest is bloody history. Constantinian Christianity became, and remains, the dominant form of

---

[10] Thomas J J Altizer, *The Gospel of Christian Atheism* (Philadelphia, Westminster Press, 1966)

Christianity, meaning that this once atheistic religion has been swallowed up by the very theism it opposed.

Down through the ages, all who dared break with the idolatry concealed within popular Christianity, found themselves persecuted, marginalized, burned at the stake, stoned, and worse, because, to the powers that be, they were as good as unbelievers. Yet, paradoxically, it was their belief in a God who was like Jesus, and, therefore, altogether different from empire, that animated their actions, and amplified their preaching, and proclamations. They were believers, but seen as unbelievers; Orthodox, but treated as heretics; Theists, but living like atheists.

This, I propose, is the true legacy of Christianity. It calls us, in every generation, to break from the idolatrous system that has swallowed Christianity, and masquerades as it. It may look different, and take on various forms in each successive generation, but it is the same false system at work. Those who choose the *way*, who choose to follow Jesus, and follow the implications of the Jesus story to their logical end, will always be seen as atheistic by the powers that be. We may no longer be dealing with Rome, or with Constantine here, but simply with church boards, doctrinal statements, or even fundamentalist family members, but it is the same process unfolding that has been unfolding from the beginning. Those who choose to follow the radical implications of the Gospel will forever find themselves unable to follow the gods of culture, or the culture of the gods, but when those "gods," as well as their culture, become Christianized, the Christian will also forever appear un-Christian.

In an un-Christian Christendom, then, the Christ-follower becomes the Christ-rejecter, and the theist becomes the atheist. Their lifestyles witness to an utter lack of the presence of the "god" of culture, and so, to the culture, they are as good as godless. It is God, however, who motivates this ungodliness, and a deep theism that calls for this atheism. As Gianni Vattimo has written, "it is thanks to God that I am an atheist...I have become an atheist thanks to Jesus' existence."[11] It is not a disloyalty to the Gospel, nor to the person of Jesus, that motivates this rejection of what is popularly considered true of God, but loyalty and devotion.

I don't write this as one who has merely peered into the rearview mirror of Church history, and observed this phenomenon unfolding from the safety of a library or office, but rather have lived it. For years I was considered the Christian of Christians. I was *the* guy, if you know what I mean. I was the guy who prayed 8-12 hours a day, and attempted fasting every other day of his life. If anyone was *in*, and if anyone was truly

---

[11] Richard Rorty; Gianni Vattimo; Santiago Zabala, *The Future of Religion* (New York : Columbia University Press, ©2005)

"following hard after God," it was me. And yet, along the way, something happened-I encountered Jesus. And in that encounter, I saw the backwardness of the values I once thought so Christian.

I encountered a God in Jesus who, far from being the exclusive, us-four-and-no-more being whose inner circle I took great pride in being a part of, had actually declared the borders of inclusion to be expanding exponentially, in all directions, and who, ironically, referred to those who thought themselves insiders as outsiders. I encountered a God who, far from being the nit-picky, bean-counting, sin-obsessed rule master who haunted my youth, was more concerned with the poor and needy than he was the global church's internet browser history. I encountered a God who, instead of standing behind, encouraging, and egging on the angry, line-drawing, sin-exposing, people-shaming preachers, like the one I had become, was actually standing with the people I was condemning, while at the same time loving me despite my blindness.

I encountered a God who was not in possession of quantities of wrath large enough to permanently extend even one person's stay in a cosmic, Christ-less concentration camp, let alone most of humanity. I encountered a God who pointed to the beauty, innocence, and simplicity of children as something we should emulate, instead of the "god" who damned us all as sinners before we'd even spoken our first words. I encountered a God who would sooner asphyxiate upon a Roman torture device, and use his final breaths to extend forgiveness to those who would deprive him of his own, than use his divinity to exact vengeance, or seek retribution.

In short, I encountered a God who looked nothing like the one I'd grown up imagining and worshipping. I encountered a God who looked like, wait for it...Jesus! Everything I thought I knew, everything I thought was so solid, etched in stone, and sure, became unsettled. The firm foundation upon which I thought my feet were planted seemed at once to be ground to powder, and all I could do was watch as it was carried away by the gentle breeze of love that this God was. In the wake of all of this, I soon found myself, not only bereft of certain values and doctrines, but, at least in the eyes of religious culture, bereft of God altogether. I could no longer pray as I once did, preach as I once did, or even understand the whole schema of sin and salvation as I once did. It was all gone, and what I was left with in no way looked like theism to my religiously trained eyes or mind. To top it all off, I was a pastor while all this was happening, which made the process that much more interesting.

I had become an atheist.

In fact, one sincere Christian even told me that my beliefs and way of practicing Christianity was, in their opinion, "indistinguishable from atheism." At first that hurt, and I of course thought that I must have been doing something wrong. I tried to return to my old ways more times than I can count, but those ways no longer worked. As hard as I tried, and as much passion as I put into my trying, I just could not return. And so, Jeff Turner, the pastor, the Christian par excellence, had, just like that, become a heretic, an unorthodox false teacher-an atheist. I was more devoted to the person of Jesus, and to God as I had come to understand God, than I had ever been before, and yet I'd never looked more godless to so many as I did then, and presently do.

As Altizer said, it was precisely because I sought and experienced the reality of Jesus, that I was forced to "refuse the God who alone is God and give [myself] to a quest for the God who is Jesus."

This process was strenuous. Relationships suffered as I struggled to find what, to me, is a more authentic Christianity, and many chose to politely (and some not so politely) parts ways with me. I lost many a speaking engagement, and, sadly, quite a few friends as well, simply because the God I was coming to know looked drastically different from the one I'd known before. To those looking in, this was far more than a shift in my understanding, or a growth in my knowledge of God, but was an abandoning of God altogether. And for a season, actually, while seeking a more Jesus-like way of living, I in fact was led to explore *literal* atheism, and, as you can imagine, being a pastor, that made for an interesting experience. But I had to come to the end of all of my god-concepts and beliefs, until there were none left whatsoever, so that I could come to grips with this wholly unhuman, yet wholly human God, revealed in Jesus. My palate needed to be cleansed, and the lenses through which I'd conceptualized the divine needed to fall from my eyes like scales, so that I could discover the beautiful, merciful God revealed in the Nazarene.

I had to become an atheist to find God, and then, in finding God, my atheism became solidified.

Maybe you're there too. Or, at least, maybe you feel yourself heading that way. Maybe you feel everything that you once thought orthodox, Christian, or theistic, slipping away from you, and you don't know what to do about it. Maybe you, like me, have encountered the Father of Jesus, whose nature simply disallows religion from functioning, and no longer find the path you once walked a path you can continue down any longer. Maybe you've never felt more in love with the person of God, or intent on following Jesus, and yet, ironically, never more ostracized, vilified, or atheistic in the eyes of religion than right now.

May I suggest to you that you're not in the danger zone? May I suggest that you're actually walking the path? That maybe you've stumbled upon "the way," and that you're simply tapping into the rich heritage of atheism, inherent within Christianity?

May I suggest that you've nothing to fear? That you've not gone astray, and that you're not storing up wrath for yourself? May I suggest that you're just fine?

Whether or not I receive your permission to suggest this list of "may I's," I'm going to go ahead and do it anyways. The godless path, my friend, is the Godly path. The atheistic path, is the Jesus path. Following him was always going to lead you here, so now that you're here, don't lose heart, and jump back onto the broad path. Be still. Be at peace, and know that you're OK.

You've simply stumbled onto the path of the atheistic theist, upon which I am your fellow sojourner.

Let us journey together.

2 | WHERE DO "GODS" COME FROM?

"The gods are born, and we have borne them."
-Leron Shults

"God created man in his own image and man, being a gentleman, returned the favor."
-Mark Twain

Now that we've started down the path of atheistic theism together, we need to talk about "gods." If we are to rid ourselves of them, we need to understand a little about what they are, where they come from, and why we worship them, or at the very least, reach for some understanding in this area. Remember, the "way" of Christ is not simply a way into Godliness, but into godlessness, and in order to become godless we must come to terms with their fictitious nature, by understanding them for what they really are.

So, for starters, what are gods? Well, there's no easy answer to this question, and I haven't the finger strength to type out all the possible ones, but let me try my best to explain by telling you about the bathroom door in the house I grew up in. As far as bathroom doors go, this one was unique, and its uniqueness lay in the fact that on it was painted a most bizarre mural. There was an erupting, Vesuvius-like volcano in the background, and what appeared to be hundreds, maybe thousands, of cartoon characters, fleeing the pyroclastic flow. What was even stranger about this mural, though, was the fact that new characters seemed to appear each time I took a bath.

Now, in case you're worrying about the sanity of my parents, or their odd decorating choices, allow me to alleviate your worries. The bathroom door contained no such mural. Instead of an intelligently thought out piece of art, what I was actually seeing was accidental water damage done to the door by my bath time antics. My young mind, however, saw intelligently drawn figures and shapes, where there were actually just random blobs.

While there may not have been any bathroom doors or bubble baths involved, you have most certainly experienced this mistaking of accidents for intelligence. You've, no doubt, seen shapes and figures in clouds, eyes and faces in woodgrain, or maybe even the elusive image of Christ on your pop tart. We all do this, but why? Well, over the years, our brains have developed in such a way that they over detect intention, or agency, where there is only randomness. The likely reason being that, when we were hunter gatherers, seeking to survive in primitive conditions, we were more likely to survive if we assumed a rustle in the bushes, for example, was a predator, rather than just a breeze. If you assumed it was a breeze, when it was actually a tiger, well, you wouldn't live to make the same mistake twice. If you assumed it was a lion, however, even if it was just a breeze, you were more likely to live, and to pass on your genes. And that's exactly what happened. We are the ancestors of those who assumed intelligence and intention where there sometimes was none, and have inherited this trait, and continue to do the same over detection, even today.

Dr. Andy Thomson, in a talk called *Why We Believe in Gods,* remarks, "All of us will mistake a shadow for a burglar. We will never mistake a burglar for a shadow,"[12] and it makes sense as to why we do this. It's much safer to assume a shadow is a burglar than it is to assume it's

---

[12] Dr. Thomson's full lecture can be viewed here:
https://www.youtube.com/watch?v=1iMmvu9eMrg

simply a shadow, because if you assume incorrectly, it could end up costing you your life. If you're wrong, however, and it is just a shadow, it's no skin off your back. This cognition, referred to as *agency detection*, is something we developed to keep us alive, and to keep us safe, and the fact that we are here today proves that over detecting agency works.

In the same talk, Thomson refers to religion as, "an extraordinary use of everyday cognitions," and, "a by-product of cognitive mechanisms designed for other purposes." In other words, the mechanisms we developed to help us avoid harm on the African Savannah, have been repurposed, and are now used by us to detect things other than what they were originally developed to detect.

So, imagine you're an early human, watching lightning light up the sky. What are you going to assume it is? Well, when we strike certain rocks together a certain way, sometimes they spark! So, perhaps there is an intelligent being, just like us, up there doing something similar. We detected agency where there was actually just charged particles, and assumed a mind like ours, only greater, was at work. We repeated this same mistake over and again, assuming things like the churning of the seas, human reproductive cycles, and the apparent movement of the sun across the sky, to all be the work of unseen beings. All of these things are now naturally explainable, but at the time, we lacked the knowledge necessary to understand them, and so ascribed them to the actions of intelligent beings that we came to call "gods." What we did with breezes and lions, we did with the natural world as a whole, and that's because we are hardwired to see intention and intelligence where there may just be random happenstance.

Now, I know, I know-this is a very oversimplified explanation of this phenomenon, but it still represents something close to what likely occurred. I don't mean to, in any way, suggest that our ancestors were unsophisticated dolts, who created elaborate mythologies and pantheons while being dumber than the rocks they used to carve their idols. No, these were intelligent individuals who simply worked with what they had.

In the golden era of Saturday Night Live, the late, great Phil Hartman played a character called Cirroc (pronounced Keyrock), in a sketch called *Unfrozen Caveman Lawyer*. As his name would suggest, Cirroc is a thawed out caveman, making his way in the modern world by practicing law. In each of the sketches, Keyrock, while dressed impeccably, but still sporting the thick brow ridge and other features of our Paleolithic ancestors, addresses the court in the most humorously ironic of ways. He still speaks of the modern world in the way you'd imagine one named Keyrock might, but in a smooth, lawyer-esque voice, mentioning in the same breath things like his struggle to find an interior decorator, and his desire to hunt Wooly Mammoth. In one of my favorite sketches, Hartman's Cirroc says:

> Ladies and gentlemen of the City Council, I'm just a caveman...Your world frightens me. When I see your tall building and flashing neon signs, sometimes I just want to get away as fast as I can, to my place in Martha's Vineyard...And when I see a solar eclipse...I think, "Oh, no, is the moon eating the sun?, because I'm a caveman...but there is one thing I do know. The new resort housing development proposed by my partners and myself will include more than adequate greenbelts for recreation and aesthetic enhancement.

Let's not forget that while our ancestors were capable of making mistakes about cosmology, they could also understand complex subjects, like law, for example.

All kidding aside, though, the truth is that, in a world that we knew almost nothing about, there was little more we could do than dream up myths and stories to explain the workings of nature. I'm often criticized for portraying our ancestors, and the emergence of "gods," in this ultra-simplistic fashion, but there can be little doubt that this is something close to what happened, though no one can pin it down precisely, since none of us were there. I'm not suggesting that primitive people were stupid, only that they could not help but perceive the world as they did, as their knowledge was limited, and so they worked with what they had.

"Gods," in a very real sense, were our sophisticated first attempts at answering scientific questions and decoding the natural world, but the advent of modern science has been the death of them. Now, beings like Thor, in whose name blood was once shed, are simply characters in movies and comic books, and King Neptune, who was once adored and feared, just makes occasional appearances on Spongebob Squarepants. Meteorology became the death of sky gods. Oceanology the death of water gods. Biology the death of creator gods. And on and on it went.

Some gods, though, aren't nearly as easy to get rid of.

These are the gods I want to talk about.

Once we have these gods on our hands, or in our minds, we are free to imbue them with any qualities we like. We are free to use them to justify certain behaviors, and validate our desires and pursuits. We already used the gods to answer our scientific questions, but there is a deeper need that we all feel; a deeper answer we seek. We want relief from suffering, a solution to the pain of existence, and crave meaning in the midst of what seems like meaninglessness. The "gods" had these things and more, and became expressions of our ideal selves, or sort of ultimate, super versions of us. Once we had established that there was a place populated by beings who had what we craved, and who were what we wanted to be, we could concoct ways of tapping into it, and taking it for ourselves, either in this life or the next. That is one of the many functions of religion.

Now, surely this isn't the only reason we created "gods," but just think about it for a moment. Have you ever been perusing a book on mythology, and come across a deity who does the cosmic equivalent of flipping burgers? How about one who struggles with self-confidence, or is trapped in a loveless marriage? Have you ever read about a god who is basically the guy or gal no one wants to be, but, hey, they're a god, so you've still got to worship them? Probably not. Quite to the contrary, "gods" typically always look like everything we wish we were, but aren't. They are beautiful, handsome, and of body types that we still idealize. They don't struggle to pay their bills, feed their children, or hold down jobs. They are victorious warriors, powerful, fertile and prosperous. Simply put, they're better than us.

The modern equivalent of this might be seen in our speculations about aliens. Notice how they are rarely, if ever, depicted as primitives, who've yet to invent the wheel or discover fire, and would probably share many of Cirroc's fear about the modern world. No, they've discovered interstellar travel, and, in addition to packing laser guns, have also attained planet-wide peace, rendering them just for show. The way we imagine aliens reflects upon us and our desires as a species. We don't want to return to primitive times, but to make quantum leaps forward. And so, when we imagine intelligent life elsewhere, we do it in a way that reflects our desires for advancement.

Another example of this can be observed in new age beliefs about reincarnation and past lives. When is the last time someone ever discovered that they were a sailor, who died at sea of scurvy and dysentery in a past life? Or an impoverished farmer, who died quite unceremoniously of an abscess? No, everyone was always an Egyptian Pharaoh, or the Queen of Sheba, but never a humble bean farmer. Why? Because the human heart has more than scientific questions for which it seeks solutions; like the crippling feeling of unworthiness, a fear of death, and a desire to escape from the pain of living. And so "gods" are not so much made in our image, but in the image of that which we desire to become. They are not simply answers to why the sky is blue, what lightning is, or why the seas churn, but represent the possibility of us rising above life and the world as it is.

You can imagine why such beliefs would arise from our ancient ancestors, who often lived only to the ripe old age of twenty, and regularly died of things that we can now easily treat with expired medicines kept in our bathroom cupboards. Life wasn't exactly easy, and escape routes were very much things we would have been looking for. So, once we have these "gods," who represent our ideal selves, we need to find ways to show our devotion to them through acts like ritual sacrifice, or even through waging wars against rival factions, and perhaps could get them to send a little bit of what was theirs, our way. Today we have different methods for actualizing our goals and becoming our ideal selves, but in a land and era that lacked opportunity, science, medicine, and just about everything else we now take for granted, "gods" were the answer.

"Gods" such as these, who meet emotional needs, as opposed to simply filling gaps in our knowledge, cannot simply be killed off by modern science or rationalism. They will persist, in one form or another, so long as we live lives of discontentment and dissatisfaction. They might not look like multi-headed monsters with rippling muscles, but we still obsessively pursue things that speak to that deeply felt need. Even Friedrich Nietzsche, an avowed atheist, wrote of the ideal human, which he called the *Ubermensch*[13], meaning the overman, or the superman, in the same work in which we wrote of the death of God. As a man who valued reason, and the values of the enlightenment above all else, his "superman" looked less god-like, and more like a freethinking, compassionate intellectual, but the point is that even he had god-like ambitions. Regardless of how dead he thought God to be, the desire to escape humanity as it was, and attain to something higher, was still very much alive. Now, don't misunderstand me. There's nothing wrong with having ambitions, aiming higher, or trying to extricate yourself from a state that you know is below you. Without such ambitions, I shudder to think where we'd be as a species. My point is simply that we've always imagined higher, bigger, and better versions of ourselves, and the "gods" were simply, among other things, our ancestor's version of these ambitions.

We live now in an increasingly irreligious time, and many, like Nietzsche, have discarded all notions of god or gods, and truly believe themselves to be free of their influence. Many Christians who have seen this trend think the answer is to rally to God's defense, and assure those proclaiming his demise that, "God's Not Dead," but we all know how well that typically works. The issue is not that we've edged God out, or that we've truly believed and embraced the concept of the death of God, but that "gods" are still very much alive and at work in our midst. They've taken on different forms, to be sure, but they are as present as ever. And the work of the Christian is still to call a "godly" world to godlessness, not a Godless world to Godliness.

In an era where we know that lightning isn't the work of Thor, nor the churning seas the wrath of Poseidon, *still,* no one is "coming to Jesus" in a godless state. Choosing to follow him is *still* a choice to become

---

[13] From *Thus Spake Zarathustra* (New York : Algora Pub., ©2003)

godless. From the gods who have lost their names over time, and been reduced to drives, desires, or mere ideals, to those who now masquerade under the name of the One Jesus called Father, or even under the name Jesus itself, the Gospel calls us to atheism. These old god concepts have not vanished, but simply gone undercover, living among us disguised as things we often don't think of in divine terms. And yet they are very much the same things more primitive folk might have been tempted to ascribe intelligence to and worship.

My point is that Christianity is not about adding another "god," in this case, *God*, to our lives, or somehow proving God to still be relevant, but systematically subtracting all gods, both the easily detected, and the well-hidden, from our lives. While it declares to us the truth of who God is, the Gospel also exposes and identifies the objects that we worship, even when we don't know we are worshipping them. This does not occur all in a single setting, but unfolds gradually as we follow "the way," and sometimes without us even knowing it's happened. But make no mistake, it will happen.

GOING ONE GOD FURTHER

One of the most outspoken atheists of our generation, Richard Dawkins, has famously said:

> We are all atheists about most of the gods that humanity has ever believed in. Some of us just go one god further. [14]

This statement is meant to suggest that the only thing separating the atheist from modern theists is a belief in a single deity. It is meant to show that we are all just one god away from atheism, and while I actually agree wholeheartedly, I must do so in a rather halfhearted manner. The half of my heart that agrees is the part that understands that the Gospel does, in fact, call us to continually go "one god further." In Acts 14, for example, we have the apostle Paul and Barnabas being mistaken for the gods, Zeus and Hermes, respectively, after the performance of a miracle, which provokes them to proclaim:

> 15 "Friends, why are you doing this? We are mortals just like you, and we bring you good news, that you should turn from these worthless things to the living God, who made the heaven and the earth and the sea and all that is in them. 16 In past generations he allowed all the

---

[14] Richard Dawkins, *The God Delusion* (Boston : Houghton Mifflin Company, 2006.)

nations to follow their own ways; 17 yet he has not left himself without a witness in doing good—giving you rains from heaven and fruitful seasons, and filling you with food and your hearts with joy."

-Acts 14:15-17, NRSV

Notice the content of their Gospel message: God once allowed people to worship idols, while still speaking and being present by doing good to them – that is, by providing them with rain, crops, etc. However, now, through the Gospel, God calls for a subtraction from our belief systems. God no longer wants to be present among humanity in a hidden way, but to be known by us. So we are now called away from those gods whom we once mistook the true God's blessings as coming from. We are called to go "one God further," as it were, that we might discover the One who had "not left himself without a witness in doing good," but had yet to reveal himself in Jesus. He was always present, in a sense, but now calls us to find him by losing all others; to add through subtraction. We are called to become theists by becoming atheists, and atheists by becoming theists.

In this sense, I agree with Dawkins' statement. We are called to continually go "one god further," and it is the Gospel itself that issues the call. The half of me that disagrees, however, is the half that realizes how notoriously difficult it is to *actually* go "one god further." While we may outgrow superstitious beliefs in beings living in castles in the clouds, the same drives and passions which we once mistook for the divine, still live in us, and continue to shape our lives. We may strip them of sentience and ontology, but desires that once moved us to carve idols out of wood and stone still drive us to climb corporate ladders, amass power, and overindulge in pleasure. So, while I see in Dawkins' statement something profoundly Christian, that is, something that is in alignment with Christianity's atheistic heritage of addition through subtraction, I also see in it something very problematic. And that is because I do not believe a true atheism can be found, or experienced, simply through living in opposition to what is the most popularly held to god-beliefs of the day. For every god we discard, a new one seems to arise to take its place, and while we might think of ourselves as becoming less godly, and more god-less, we are often just recycling our deities, and giving them different names and functions. Our "going one god further" brand of atheism could continue indefinitely, unless something is done to stem the tide, and keep the gods from being reborn in new forms.

Consider the fact that, throughout the Book of Acts and the epistles, turning from idols was a central theme of the Gospel, and yet, the author of 1 John, writing to a community of Christian believers, closes his letter with these words:

21 Little children, keep yourselves from idols.

-1 John 5:21, NRSV

Now, I don't think we are meant to understand that the recipients of this letter were still being tempted to worship carved idols, or the gods of the Greeks and Romans. No, these were individuals who were seemingly rooted and grounded in Christianity, but who were still being warned against idolatry. What idols, precisely, were they being warned against? Throughout the epistle, the issue of our love for one another is emphasized again and again, against the backdrop of warnings against getting tied up in systems of belief that divide and lead to hatred. It would seem that it is not things readily noticeable as idols that they are being warned against, but rather false images of the Jesus in whose name they forsook idolatry in the first place.

I bring this up only to show that, even a community who had long ago turned from their former "gods," were still capable of worshipping them, just in different forms. In this instance, that form was a distorted understanding of Jesus, the very reason they left idolatry behind. Idols, or "gods," though we forsake them, often persist, and reappear in ways that are harder to recognize.

N.T. Wright, in his book *Surprised by Scripture*, speaking of what he calls Idolatry 2.0, writes:

> One of the things we learn early in science is that nature abhors a vacuum...Well, something similar is true in philosophies and worldviews. They abhor a vacuum. You can push God, or the gods, upstairs out of sight...But history shows again and again that other gods quietly sneak in to take their place.

> These other gods are not strangers. The ancient world knew them well. Just to name the three most obvious: there are Mars, the god of war, Mammon, the god of money, and Aphrodite, the goddess of erotic love. One of the fascinating things about modern Western ideas has been the work of the "masters of suspicion," Nietzsche, Marx, and Freud, claiming to reveal the motives that lie hidden beneath the outwardly smooth and comprehensible surface of the modern world. It is all about power, declared Nietzsche. Everything comes down to money, said Marx. It's all about sex, said Freud. In each case these were seen as forces or drives that were there whether we liked it or not; we might imagine

we are free to choose, but in fact we are the blind
servants of these impulses.[15]

In other words, as much as we'd like to imagine ourselves as an
enlightened and godless society, as people who have gone "one god
further," until there are none left to speak of, the truth is that our gods
have simply changed forms. We are still driven by the same forces we've
always been driven by, and the things we sought salvation in and from in
ancient times, are still the things we seek salvation in and from today.

Wright continues:

> In each of these three cases-Aphrodite, Mammon, and
> Mars-these ancient and well-known gods have not gone
> away, have not been banished upstairs, but are present
> and powerful-all the more so for being unrecognized.[16]

Now, I am certainly not insinuating, nor do I think is Wright, that these
idols were divine in nature, even if only in the form of "demons," but only
that all our "gods" ever were in the first place were expressions of our
desires. Though our drives and ambitions seem wholly secular on the
surface, they are often very much the same drives our ancestors mistook
for the divine, and worshipped and sacrificed to. What Wright is pointing
out is that these "masters of suspicion", these proclaimers of god's death,
were not nearly suspicious enough. For even in their philosophies are the
vestigial idols of our less enlightened ancestors. Religion, like nature,
abhors a vacuum, and the vacancies left by our god-beliefs will always
find themselves filled by something else, whether it calls itself a "god" or
not. While the enlightenment claims all notions of "god" as its victim, we
all know better, for the very claim is a semi-divine one, and represents
the god-like ambitions we all carry around within us. God's don't leave,
and they certainly don't die. They're just transformed into harder to detect
forms that are all the more difficult to rid ourselves of because of the level
of difficulty involved in detecting them.

UNCLE SIMON AND THE [NOT SO] DEATH OF GOD

I'm reminded of an episode of the Twilight Zone, in which a young
woman named Barbara works tirelessly to serve the needs of her elderly

---

[15] N.T. Wright, *Surprised by Scripture: Engaging Contemporary Issues* (New
York : HarperOne, 2014)
[16] N.T. Wright, Surprised by Scripture: Engaging Contemporary Issues (New
York : HarperOne, 2014)

and ailing Uncle Simon, an inventor by trade, and curmudgeonly old jerk by choice. He is a mean, belittling, verbally abusive, bitter old man, who is constantly demanding that Barbara bring him hot chocolate, in a certain mug, prepared a specific way. Barbara, though obviously exhausted and worn as thin as a communion wafer, continues caring for her uncle, but only because she hopes to inherit his estate upon his death. Her drab appearance, short temper, and colorless wardrobe (I'm guessing here, as it's all in black and white), tell the story of a woman who has endured 25 years' worth of hell, in order to attain heaven in the form of an inheritance.

During one particularly heated exchange, which occurs at the top of a flight of stairs (always a bad place to get into a heated exchange), Uncle Simon raises his cane to strike Barbara, but she deflects the blow, causing him to lose his balance and tumble down the stairs to his death. In the scenes that follow, Barbara, who is finally feeling a bit of freedom, and eagerly awaiting word of her inheritance, learns that there are some stipulations: 1.) She must never leave the house, and 2.) She must agree to look after Uncle Simon's latest invention.

Quite unenthusiastically, Barbara accepts the terms, only to find out that Uncle Simon's latest invention is a robot programmed to behave exactly as he did in life. At first it speaks in a monotonic, robotic voice, and is more machine than man, but as the days pass, it evolves to the point that the robotic voice is replaced by the human Uncle Simon's, and it proves to be just as brash, abusive and demeaning to the poor girl as its creator. Uncle Simon 2.0 is the original's equal, both in curmudgeonliness and jerkiness, and even comes equipped with Uncle Simon's liking for hot chocolate. Barbara is again pushed to a breaking point when Uncle Simon 2.0 refers to her as, and I quote, "a peanut-headed sample of nature's carelessness," and she pushes him down the stairs, apparently to his death.

After this, you'd expect for Barbara to finally be free of her Uncle's tyranny, but you'd be expecting too much, for in the very next scene, the robot comes hobbling into the living room, and, speaking in a voice just as human, and just as angry as Uncle Simon's, demands hot chocolate, in a certain mug, prepared a specific way. All to which Barbara replies, in a very robotic voice, "Yes, Uncle."

Oh, and as for Uncle Simon 2.0's nasty tumble down the stairs? He's made a remarkable recovery, and now sports a leg brace and leans on a cane!

No matter how hard poor Barbara tries, she just can't get rid of Uncle Simon, and no matter how hard humanity tries, we just can't get rid of our gods.

You may simply let them succumb to their old age and irrelevancy, as Barbara did at first, but then you end up with "god" 2.0. You may eventually become so fed up that you go the whole murder route, and intentionally "push it down the stairs," but then it simply buys a cane, and commences walking with a limp intended to remind you that it will always be back, finding newer and more creative ways to oppress you.

Religion abhors a vacuum, thus, gods never die. So long as there is a void, be it illusory or real, gods will persist, and neither old age nor homicide, natural causes nor a good old fashioned pushing down the stairs, are enough to take them down. Hence my reservations about Dawkins's statement that we are all just one god-belief away from atheism. Vacancies will always produce deities of some kind. Tossing Yahweh or Jesus into the same mass grave with Thor or Ba'al, does not make one's atheism any more authentic or complete than anyone else's, so long as there is a void, or vacancy to be filled. You may have simply discarded an image that I've yet to discard, but neither of us should be so foolish as to believe that the discarding of an image means that we've fully done away with "Uncle Simon." Both the educated, progressive Christian, who finds their former, overly superstitious understanding of the divine succumbing to the results of rational thought, and the guns-blazing, anti-god crusader will find new ways of worshipping the old "gods."

God-concepts, or "gods," are not divine beings, but persistent, perennial and oftentimes pernicious, ideas, representing solutions to the problem of pain and existence. So, whether we call them "gods," or simply good ideas, we are still talking about the same things. They live in our heads, not the heavens, thus, the "god" does not die when we push its most recent image down the stairs. It simply finds a new image, a new form, and continues to live, making the whole idea of the "death of god" somewhat irrelevant. As long as there is a void, there will be a god-concept to fill it. The god whose demise Friedrich Nietzsche pronounces in *Thus Spake Zarathustra*, has simply changed forms, and his bold proclamation of "God is dead," should probably be read as more of a coy, "the image that was once acceptable to worship has become unacceptable, and so we're presently shopping for a new one."

Here, I can't help but be reminded of the words of the Jewish Philosopher, Martin Buber, who wrote:

> Men of all eras have heard the tidings of the death of gods. But it was reserved for our era to have a philosopher (Nietzsche) feel called upon to announce that God himself had died. Whether or not we know it, what we really mean when we say that a god is dead is that the images of God vanish, and that therefore an image which up to now was regarded and worshipped as

God, can no longer be so regarded and so worshipped. For what we call gods are nothing but images of God and must suffer the fate of such images.[17]

In other words, "gods" don't die. We can deal only with the images we ascribe to the ideas we mistake for "gods," or even the true God, but it is *only* the images we can kill, not the "gods," or God, himself. So push all of the images down the stairs you want! Slay them, mount their heads on your mantle, and boast of your freedom from them. Claim your place among the godless and revel in your liberation. But you'd better enjoy that moment while it lasts, because you'll be serving some limping specter "hot chocolate" quicker than you can say, "Yes, Uncle."

Buber continues:

> But Nietzsche manifestly wished to say something different, and that something different is terribly wrong in a way characteristic of our time. For it means confusing an image, confusing one of the many images of God that are born and perish, with the real God whose reality men could never shake with any one of these images, no matter what forms they might honestly invent for the objects of their particular adoration. Time after time, the images must be broken, the iconoclasts (smashers of images) must have their way. For the iconoclast is the soul of man which rebels against having an image that can no longer be believed in, elevated above the heads of man as a thing that demands to be worshipped. In their longing for a god, men try again and again to set up a greater, a more genuine and more just image, which is intended to be more glorious than the last and only proves the more unsatisfactory. The commandment, "Thou shalt not make unto thee an image," means at the same time, "Thou canst not make an image." This does not, of course, refer merely to sculptured or painted images, but to our fantasy, to all the power of our imagination as well. But man is forced time and again to make images, and forced to destroy them when he realizes that he has not succeeded.[18]

---

[17] Martin Buber, *Israel and the World: Essays in a Time of Crisis* (New York : Schocken Books, ©1948.)

[18] Martin Buber, Israel and the World: Essays in a Time of Crisis (New York : Schocken Books, ©1948.)

What Buber is saying is that Nietzsche's proclamation of "God is dead" was misguided, in that it mistook an image of God that was once tenable, but no longer so, for God himself. What Nietzsche was rejecting, according to Buber, was not God, but one of the many images constructed over the years with which we have sought to define him. He goes on to claim that the world will always need its iconoclastic, idol-smashers, who deface and efface the wrongheaded images that get superimposed over the real deal. Each time we build a new image, we are eventually forced to destroy it, when we realize how miserably we have failed to give proper representation to the divine.

While I love the imagery, as well as the sentiment, I can agree, again, only in a halfhearted manner. I think that the same meritorious misguidedness in Dawkins' statement of, "We are all atheists...Some of us just go one god further," is present in Buber's as well. I say this, not because I believe Buber is wrong to claim that our idols need smashing, but because a simple smashing of idols will never do the trick. Again, I love the beautiful thoughts expressed by Buber, but his underlying thought seems to be that our seeking to give expression to the divine in the constructing of images is admirable, as the thing we are seeking to express is the real God, it's just that we're incapable of getting the image right. He seems to suggest that that which we seek to express is something worth expressing, and that it's simply our misinterpreting of it that is the problem. He continues:

> The images topple, but the voice is never silenced...the voice speaks in the guise of everything that happens; in the guise of all world events; it speaks to the men of all generations, makes demands upon them, and summons them to accept responsibility...it is of utmost important not to lose one's openness. But to be open means not to shut out the voice-call it what you will. It does not matter what you call it. All that matters is that you hear it. [19]

There is a voice, Buber claims, that lies at the heart of all of our idolatry, and if we could simply smash enough images, and find that ever speaking voice, we'd find God. This is where I disagree, for the thought here is that at the heart of idolatry is a misunderstanding or perversion of the true God; that there was once a pristine, virgin revelation, that became distorted over time, hence the presence of "gods." I think, though, that all "gods" are of human origin, a result of misidentification, and the pursuit of an escape route. The voice at the bottom of the idol pile is not God's, but ours. It is the source of our angst, depression, fear, dissatisfaction, and discontentment with the world. It is the voice of our

---

[19] Martin Buber, Israel and the World: Essays in a Time of Crisis (New York: Schocken Books, ©1948.)

own existential dread, fear of death, and horror at the thought of life being meaningless. "Gods" are what assure us that there's more to existence than the ball of dirt on which we live, and give us hope that, if we discover the right path of salvation, or the right savior figure, we can be rescued from it all. In a modern context, it may just look like self-help philosophies, or attempts at escaping both the horror and humdrum of existence, and while these make no spiritual claims, they still represent desires for god-like attributes like transcendence and ascension.

UNBELIEF AS BELIEF

Even the pursuit of a wholly secular society can be the pursuit of a *holy*, or "god-like" thing, since the identifiably secular can really only exist in opposition to the identifiably sacred. The use of the term *secular* suggests that a thing exists in the same universe as the sacred, it just strives to be its opposite or is a reaction against it. The wholly secular, therefore, still derives its being from the so-called holy and sacred, and so cannot be truly godless as it needs a god-concept in order to function.

Now, that's not in any way to speak down to my atheist friends or to say that beneath the surface they are somehow actually theists, or at the very least religious. No, I believe in atheists, and I believe it is possible to have no belief in the divine whatsoever. God-concepts, though, like the last annoying party guest, who just won't take a hint and go home, are masters at overstaying their welcome. When this happens, and you're trying to communicate to Mr. or Mrs. Zero-Self-Awareness that the party is over, what kinds of behaviors do you employ? You might start yawning dramatically, talking about how early you need to get up the next day, or cleaning up in a flamboyant manner, just to get the point across.

I think that *some forms* of atheism function similarly to this. It is often those who are the most vitriolic in their condemnations of religion who are actually trying the hardest to get the party guest to leave. Now, again, I'm not claiming that passionate atheists actually believe in God and are hiding it, or that all atheists are somehow hurt, or mad at God. Some god-beliefs deserve to be ridiculed, and I for one count many of the "new atheists" among the greatest prophets of the 20th and 21st centuries. All I'm saying here is that the unbelief of *some* functions very much like belief. Sometimes, the party guest is still in the head of the one doing the exaggerated yawning, and their intense efforts might be as much about convincing themselves of this "god's" lack of existence as they are about helping to free others. In this case, it might not be so much about bothersome policies that are hindering societal progress, but repressed beliefs that the unbeliever is attempting to exorcise. Heck, maybe that's even why I wrote this book? Maybe I'm just yawning loudly and complaining about how early I have to get up in order to shake off my own false god beliefs? Who knows? If anyone does know, though, it most certainly won't be me. And that's the point, really, as these beliefs often function in our lives without our knowledge. Our whole shtick could be that we don't believe, but we might still live and act as though we do, even if we don't.

It's in that sense that I say modern secularism is often not truly secular. The wholly secular is often unintentionally the holy-secular, as both secular and sacred derive their identities from each another. They are protests against each other, and so are very much the same. The sacred seeks to break away from the secular, and the secular seeks to break from the sacred. You cannot define one unless you understand other, and it's in this way that Uncle Simon finds a very sneaky way of living on. Our exaggerated denial of him speaks volumes about the battle raging in our heads. If he can't exist as the object of our worship and affection, he'll settle for being the object we oppose and protest. And so we can claim unbelief and freedom, but living in vehement opposition to something only proves that the thing itself still has control over us. We can actually experience the sensation of being free from "gods," while still being completely led around and controlled by them.

To illustrate, consider the movie The Truman Show, whose main protagonist, Truman Burbank, played by Jim Carrey, is born and raised on international television, having his entire life recorded and broadcast live to audiences around the globe. It's a form of "reality TV" in which the only things that are actually real are Truman's reactions to the very unreal world created for him. He is the only one unaware that his life is one, long and continuous television show, but slowly begins to see behind the facade and realize that something is amiss.

Eventually, he realizes he must break away from the life he has known, and escape whatever forces out there are controlling him. He faces his fear of the ocean (subliminally planted in his mind by the show's creators to keep him from ever attempting an escape) and sets sail, only to face a massive, manufactured storm that threatens to capsize his boat and drown him. He presses on, however, and eventually prevails.

As the storm subsides, and Truman emerges victorious on the other side of facing his fears, he sails confidently into open waters, towards bluer skies. It seems he is finally experiencing the sensation of freedom, when, suddenly, the illusion is shattered when his boat plows into a wall that he had thought was open sky. What appeared to him as freedom was nothing more than the massive set on which his life had been filmed. It is at this point, when Truman realizes that even his sense of freedom has been an illusion, that he is afforded the opportunity to be actually free. Eventually, Truman exits the set in an ironically powerful way, and we are left to imagine what becomes of his life from there.

The point I'm trying to make is that even when Truman found himself leaving behind the world he had come to loathe, he was still a part of that world. His protest against the system that had enslaved him, and the sensation of freedom that came with that, was an illusion, as his protest was occurring from within the system itself. He had to collide with the "sky," as it were, before he could find the true freedom which only existed on the outside. No matter how detached or separated from his old life he felt, as long as that sense of detachment or separation was being had from within the system, he was a part of the system. It was only on the outside that freedom could be had. Everything experienced prior to that, though it felt like freedom, was an illusion.

This is exactly what I mean when I talk about unbelief that operates the same as belief. We might feel free from our "gods," or old ways of worshipping them, but when we live our lives in protest of these gods, and the beliefs that come with them, we are still very much their slaves. Again, it's Uncle Simon rearing his ugly head in an even harder to detect form, because conscious opposition to him creates the illusion that we are truly apart from him. If my life is lived in a constant struggle with him, though, far from being apart from my life, I show through my actions that he is still very much a part of my life.

Consider again the words of Justin Martyr, which I used in the last chapter to make the point that Christianity has an atheistic legacy:

> Hence are we called atheists. And we confess that we are atheists, so far as gods of this sort are concerned, but not with respect to the most true God, the Father of righteousness and temperance and the other virtues, who is free from all impurity. [20]

So, the early church was accused of atheism for rejecting the gods of the state and the larger culture, but what had they replaced them with? According to Justin Martyr, at least, it was with a version of God who was the opposite of the gods the culture worshipped. According to him, the idols that pagans bowed before were not just chunks of stone wrongly understood as representing real beings, but actually very real, and very existent demons. He wrote of these idols:

> we not only deny that they [idols] who did such things as these are gods, but assert that they are wicked and

---

[20] A. Cleveland Coxe, Ante-Nicene Fathers: Volume 1: The Apostolic Fathers, Justin Martyr, Irenaeus [1885]

impious demons, whose actions will not bear comparison with those even of men desirous of virtue. [21]

So, the idols of the culture were actual beings in his mind, they just weren't on the same level as God. Their actions were impure, impious and sinful, and the god he worshipped in their place was their polar opposite. He was free from all impurity and the father of righteousness, in direct opposition to the unrighteousness of these other beings. So, while claiming atheism, the truth is that he still lived as though these beings were real, and we can see this in how he understood God. God was not wholly other and removed from these beings, but was something like them, just their opposite in character and nature. He existed in the same world as they, however, and in that sense, was like them.

This is very different from how Paul dealt with the issue of idolatry in the New Testament:

> 4 Hence, as to the eating of food offered to idols, we know that *"no idol in the world really exists,"* and that *"there is no God but one."* 5 Indeed, even though there may be so-called gods in heaven or on earth—as in fact there are many gods and many lords— 6 yet *for us there is one God, the Father, from whom are all things and for whom we exist, and one Lord, Jesus Christ, through whom are all things and through whom we exist. 7 It is not everyone, however, who has this knowledge.* Since some have become so accustomed to idols until now, they still think of the food they eat as food offered to an idol; and their conscience, being weak, is defiled.

-1 Corinthians 8:4-7, NRSV (Italics mine)

Paul claims that many first century, Gentile Christians would not allow themselves to eat meat that had been sacrificed to an idol because their consciences were weak. They still thought of the world in terms of there being a plethora of gods out there, and so now that they had chosen Jesus as Lord, it would simply not be fitting for them to partake of food offered in sacrifice to one of his competitors. For Paul, however, there was one God, and all things came from him, and there was one Lord, Jesus, through whom all things came to exist. He did not think in terms of there being certain bits of the world that belonged to certain other gods, while certain other parts belonged to his god, but saw the whole of creation as being inextricably linked with and connected to the Father and the Son. Paul simply says that not everyone had this knowledge, and so still lived as though the world hosted many, many gods.

---

[21] A. Cleveland Coxe, Ante-Nicene Fathers: Volume 1: The Apostolic Fathers, Justin Martyr, Irenaeus [1885]

Now, the question I think needs asking is, why did these Gentile converts not know that there was only one God, and one Lord? I mean, you would think that would sort of be standard Christian doctrine, and that they would have been taught it, somewhere right around day one. So why didn't they know? I think the truth is that they probably did know, they just didn't *know.* As Paul says, "some have become so accustomed to idols...they still think of the food they eat as food offered to an idol." It wasn't that they'd never learned these doctrinal truths, but that they could not get these gods out of their heads. Christianity, to them, became something of a protest against their old objects of worship, instead of an entirely new way of living in which one saw all things as being swallowed up in and sustained by the person of Jesus.

This, again, was a form of belief that operated very much the same as belief. Their unbelief in idols was not a true unbelief, they had merely moved them down a few rungs on the ladder of importance, and given the space they once occupied to Jesus. For Paul, these things had no literal existence. But for the converts in question, both they *and* Jesus were real, and Christianity to them was about putting Jesus before them, not negating them altogether.

In both the cases of Justin Martyr and these early Christian converts, we have the same thing going on: unbelief is operating exactly as belief, or, to put it another way, atheism is functioning exactly as theism.

Paul's faith, however, was something else entirely. He was Truman after he had exited the studio and realized that the entire world he had been born into was an illusion. The others were Truman in the boat, mistaking their protest against certain ways of living for freedom.

You can bury nuclear waste, and pretend it no longer exists because it's out of your sight, but the seven-legged cows grazing over its burial site testify to its continued influence. Likewise, we can bury our god-concepts, believing we've gone "one god further" until "god is dead," and we're truly free from their influence, but we have our own "seven-legged cows" testifying that maybe we haven't buried our "gods" after all, but are still very much buried in "gods" ourselves. Be it our turning the person of Jesus into a figure who hates who we hate, and justifies our bad behavior, or a philosophy that does the same, or even our extreme opposition to theism of all stripes, many times these are tells, indicating the presence of a god-concept at work.

The question, then, is how do we exit the "studio"? How do we get rid of Uncle Simon 2.0, with his cane, leg brace, and endless incarnations? How do we rid ourselves of these "gods," whether they appear in sacred or secular forms? Pushing them down the stairs doesn't work, nor does pushing them up the stairs into the attic, out of sight and out of mind.

How is it, exactly, that the Gospel makes godly men godless, when these things are just so relentless, and hang on with pit bull-like tenacity?

Well, to do that, we're going to need something stronger than hack job history lessons on the origins of religion, or lay attempts at explaining cognitive science's theories on the emergence of god-concepts.

No, to take out the likes of Uncle Simon, we're going to need to do some time travelling.

3 | TERMINATING THE VOID

"…it is not enough to prove that God does not exist – the formula of true atheism is that God himself must be made to proclaim his own inexistence, must stop believing in himself."

-Slavoj Zizek

So far we've discussed Christianity's atheistic heritage as well as the origins of "gods" and the difficulty we face in trying to rid ourselves of them. But we didn't actually discuss any answers as to how the ridding is to be done. So, how do we do it? Well, I'm not so arrogant as to think I have the final answer to that question, but we'll at least begin the discussion in this chapter. First, however, I want to do a very brief review on how or why gods emerge in the first place.

We looked at just two among numerous possible answers to this question, and where we landed was that "gods" were:

1.) Cases of mistaken identity and agency over detection. That is, we mistook the workings of the natural world for the activities of cosmic beings of a similar mind as us, only on a much larger scale. They were our first attempts at answering scientific questions, and plugging the gaps in our knowledge about the natural world.

2.) "Gods" are projections of our desires to escape both the horror, and humdrum of daily existence. "Gods" are essentially our idealized selves, and represent the desire to escape things as they are and arrive at a place of mythical perfection. They represent freedom from pain, anxiety, etc., and so long as they exist in our minds, we retain the hope that we can, in fact, get beyond life, and become something more.

The first of these god-concepts was easily done away with through scientific discoveries about the natural world. One look under a microscope and we realized that it wasn't angry, unappeased "gods" who caused sickness, but germs and bacteria. When it comes to the second god-concept, though, those that represent our idealized selves, well, they're not quite as easy to get rid of. In fact, they hang on with the strength of a vise-grip held shut by a rusted-closed bear trap. This is problematic, not because we shouldn't aspire to greater things, but because when one allows these drives to become "gods" in their lives, it ceases to matter to them what earthly thing they forsake or trample on in order to get to them. Since it is not what's "down here" that matters, but only what's "up there," the "down here" can be neglected, families can be fractured, and even lives taken, if that is what the "up there" requires. So long as it gets us "there," it's acceptable.

As we discussed last chapter, even when one ceases to believe in literal "gods," the void we were attempting to fill with them remains. At that point, the void becomes a vacuum, and begins to draw into itself other things to meet the same need the "god" failed to meet. Things like money, sex, power, philosophies, ideologies, or whatever, though they make no claims to divinity, become the new hosts through which the old gods live on. And so, instead of simply being approached healthily, as the natural things that they are, all of these come to be treated by us exactly as we once treated our "gods," in addition to controlling us exactly as the "gods" once did. We will kill for these things, destroy our relationships, and trample on whatever gets in the way of us and what we think will make us complete. So long as there is void, or a vacancy, there will be a womb to give birth to that which we'll treat like divinity.

So, how exactly, does one get rid of these harmful god-concepts, then?

Well, the only option I can see is to eliminate the void, and to do away with the vacuum. We cannot kill "gods," as we've already discussed, but what if we could keep them from ever being born in the first place? What if we could eliminate the "womb" that "gods" crawl out of before they ever had the chance to crawl out of them? What if we could return to a time before these things were even conceived, and take out the matrix that conceived them? That's what I want to explore.

How would we go about accomplishing something like this? Well, it's going to require time travel, as I suggested at the end of the last chapter, but it won't require a Plutonium fueled DeLorean, nor Bill & Ted's phone booth, so you're good.

GOD IS...TERMINATED?

Since we've already brought the Twilight Zone, and robots named Uncle Simon into the mix, we might as well go full sci-fi, and throw the Terminator mythos into the mix as well. In the Terminator franchise, which, in my opinion, consists only of 2.5 movies and a television series (the nerds will understand), the future human race finds itself at war with an army of machines controlled by a self-aware computer program called Skynet. The human resistance against Skynet is led by a man named John Connor, whom the machines can't seem to take down in what, to them, is the present, and so hatch a plan to travel back in time and take him out retroactively. They send a cybernetic assassin, a Terminator, who bears a striking resemblance to a former California Governor, from 2029 back to 1984, before John Connor was even conceived, in order to assassinate his mother, Sarah Connor, to keep him from being born.

Now, sure, Skynet's logic sort of backfires on them, as the human resistance sends back a human soldier to protect Sarah Connor who ends up impregnating her, and is revealed to be John's father. Still, though, their logic was quite sound in theory: If you can eliminate the mother of your enemy, prior to them having been conceived, you should find yourself bereft of said enemy in the future. When it comes to taking out Uncle Simon 2.0, or "gods," this is precisely the route that I believe the Gospel takes.

How would you take out Uncle Simon? Firstly by bearing in mind that it isn't actually Uncle Simon that is the problem, as he simply reflects Barbara's desires. The real problem lies with "Barbara" herself, and the desire she won't let go of. She could have extricated herself from Uncle Simon's controlling grip decades before, but her stubborn insistence on inheriting his estate kept her his slave. It was her hope in something "out there" with the power to rescue her from things as they were that kept her a prisoner of things...as they were. She could have refused the inheritance, and begun a life of her own, and Uncle Simon would have withered and died, out of sight and out mind. But instead, her hope in a salvation she would never touch, became the very thing that ended up depriving her of the salvation she longed for.

You see, the death of "gods" is impossible to achieve once they've been born. They reappear in newer, more resilient forms, no matter how many times you kill them, because the "god" itself is a reflection of the desire that still lives in us. So long as the desire persists, the thing which we think can satisfy it must, by necessity, persist as well. So long as there is a void, there will be a womb through which the "gods" can be reborn. This is the "Sarah Connor" that the Gospel eliminates. It travels with us back to the time when we first dreamt up the need for our "gods," and shows us that, from the beginning, we never needed the thing to which "gods" were our solution. In this way it eliminates the void, or the womb, by keeping it from ever being formed, and thereby keeps the god-concept from ever being born.

CLAW HANDS AND REVIVAL MEETINGS

Once upon a time I was an extreme Charismatic. During that season of my life, I sought the supernatural anywhere and everywhere it could be sought, and was convinced I had found it on more than one occasion. During my teenage years, for fun, I would regularly travel in a fifteen passenger van with a pack of middle aged women to various revival meetings around the state, at which I hoped to receive a "fresh anointing" or have an experience of God. The week prior to my attendance at these meetings were always spent the same way; in fasting, prayer and pleading with God to do something profoundly powerful and supernatural in my life. These meetings, by the way, did not consist of hymn singing and listening to preachers prattle on for hours. No, these were the holy-roller type of meetings you've seen parodied on Comedy Central, complete with ecstatic laughter, rolling in the aisles, and running laps around the building. Actually, helmets were actually provided for several of the church's more rowdy congregants, in order to keep them from hurting themselves, and their designated folding chairs even had seat belts attached to them, just for added safety. And no, I'm not making this up.

After one such service, a friend and I (the middle aged ladies stayed home that night), went out to grab a bite to eat. I began to feel like I was going to black out, and began to have the strangest, tingling sensation in my hands. It literally felt like they were on fire, or charged with some kind of electricity, which I assumed, of course, was the power of God. My fingers began to be drawn together, until my hand was positioned like some weird crab claw, and I just remember thinking that, were I to lay these anointed crab claws on someone and pray, they would likely die from the raw power rushing through them. I *knew* that I knew that I knew this was the "power of God," and for years after the event, whenever I would experience doubt, I would hearken back to that moment, and recall what I felt. This sustained my faith for many years, and kept me on the path of the Charismatic pilgrim who was ever seeking deeper and higher experiences with the divine.

This all changed, though, when a friend of mine recounted the story of how he once had to call 911 when a kid he had been babysitting went into shock. The kid had apparently not eaten for 2 or 3 days, and began to experience fits. At that point in the story, all was well, but with the few sentences that followed, and with no intention whatsoever of doing so, this person sent my entire world crashing to the ground. He said, "By the time EMS got there, this kid was half conscious in the corner, with his hands drawn together like claws since, you know, that's what happens when you're dehydrated and in shock."

He had literally just described the experience I'd had years earlier, which I knew that I knew that I knew was an experience of God, only in his story, it was shock and dehydration that was causing this reaction. Minus attendance at a revival service, the dehydrated kid's and my stories were very similar, as I had spent 2-3 days in fasting and prayer preparing for the service, and by the time it had ended, I had expended a fair amount of energy. It suddenly dawned on me that I, like the young man in the story, had simply been experiencing what happens when your body is malnourished, dehydrated, and not functioning properly.

I hadn't had a "God experience" at all, I just needed some water, and maybe a hamburger.

People had tried to talk me out of my extreme Charismatic ways for years and years, all to no avail. They pointed to the craziness of the meetings I was in, the seeming smarminess of the preachers, and the overall weirdness of the atmosphere, but none of it moved me. The introduction of information seeking to disprove my experiences and invalidate my pursuits was simply not going to work. I'd felt something, and simply pointing out the fact that I'd felt it in a strange setting would move me nary an inch. In fact, the experience itself transformed the weirdness of the setting in which it occurred into something I craved more and more of. No matter what argument you came up with, I had a counter argument.

Even when the lifestyles of some of the preachers I followed were shown to be more holey than holy, I still found a way to make things work. You couldn't talk me out of this stuff, and you couldn't "kill" my "god" either. In the telling of a very simple story that was not in any way aimed at dissuading me, though, the faulty origins of my experiences were exposed, and things began to crumble on their own. It was as though that information transported me back to the very moment of the experience, explained to me the actual science behind what was happening, fully deconstructed it, and then transported me back to an altered present in which the experience could no longer rule my life.

I share this story only to say that sometimes examining the origins of a god-concept, and understanding why we hold it, is the key to ridding ourselves of the invisible overlord to whom we've become enslaved. Uncle Simon won't die, but if you recognize the origins of your relationship with him, that the logic behind serving him all these years was flawed, and that you do not need his inheritance to be happy, he will, in time, vanish from your life.

Friedrich Nietzsche, whom we briefly spoke of in the last chapter, famously proclaimed the death of God in his work, *Thus Spake Zarathustra*. He wrote of a madman, running through the streets with a lantern declaring that God was dead, and that we, humanity, had killed him. When the madman was scoffed at, and his words went unheeded, he sorrowfully concluded "my time is not yet." Writing of this madman, and his grim proclamation, atheist theologian, Leron Shults, writes:

> Claims about the death of God are deathly boring. Depending upon whether or not one is an active participant within a religious in-group, such proclamations seem either obviously wrong or wrongly obvious. The message that "God is dead" gets surprisingly little traction in our mental and social worlds...the idea of divine *genitality* is much more interesting-and disturbing-than the idea of divine mortality...The theoretical and practical relevance of this message will make it much more difficult to ignore. [22]

No one has ever killed a "god," it simply doesn't happen. Pushing Uncle Simon down the stairs is a futile exercise, but if you can expose how it is that Uncle Simon began to hold sway over your life in the first place, how he was born, so to speak, you can do away with him retroactively. As Shults says, if you can expose the *genitality* of the god-concept, as opposed to trying to take advantage of its *mortality*, you have a better shot at finding freedom from it. That is to say, if you can convince Barbara that she gave birth to the need for Uncle Simon through her greed, and that she will be much happier in rejecting the inheritance, she can be truly saved. What this amounts to is Terminating Sarah Connor, the void, and keeping John Connor, the "god," from ever being born.

My involvement with a certain brand of Christianity could not be refuted by people telling me bad things about the preachers I was listening to, or by pointing to the craziness of the gatherings I was attending, but discovering the faulty origins of the experience I'd had was enough to do the trick. The "way" of Jesus, similarly, leads us back in time, exposing the origins of the god-concepts the world, and the church, are still rife with, and in exposing their origins, affords us the opportunity to truly

[22] F Leron Shults, *Theology After the Birth of God: Atheist Conceptions in Cognition and Culture* (New York, NY : Palgrave Macmillan, 2014.)

leave them behind. In the same way that scientific discoveries exposed the faulty origins of Thor, Ba'al, or any number of "gods" from antiquity, born from the womb of our lack of understanding of the natural world, so understanding the origin of our need for Uncle Simon-like gods will prove to be their undoing.

Shults writes:

> ...after the discovery of the "birth of God," theology can now follow a radically atheist trajectory that has long been suppressed within it. [23]

Christianity, at its core, is not so much a violent opposition to false god-concepts, as it is a revealer of their faulty origins and lack of necessity. The Gospel, in revealing God to be Jesus-like (a far cry from revealing Jesus to be God-like) and thereby revealing the definitive truth about God's character, also reveals our lack of need for salvation from so many of the things we think we require it from. When we see this, we experience the disappearance of the "gods" we've created to save us from these things, but not through a violent episode that occurs in the present. Rather, it is something more like a Terminator-style assassination, in which the Gospel transcends time, and eliminates the void that birthed our "gods" in the first place.

So, how does the Gospel accomplish this termination of our "gods?"

Imagine that, from birth, you were told that all humans were universally born lacking in a key element called "hydratia," and that until one found this mythical substance and drank it, they would not be fully human and in danger of dying at any second. Now, don't bother googling the term "hydratia," as I literally just made it up. Regardless of this substance's inexistence, though, were you all your life told that you could not be whole, and were in mortal danger without it, you would no doubt develop a thirst and an appetite for it. It does not have to be real in order for you to experience cravings for it, you need only to be made to feel that, without it, you were incomplete, and in harm's way.

Now, had you been raised with this thought and this thirst burning in your imagination, how exactly would you go about quenching it? Well, there would be no actual way of quenching it, as it is illegitimate and has as its object something that isn't real. The only real way, then, to do away with it would be to deal with it retroactively. That is, to have the thirst negated by being shown that it was illegitimate from the start, and that "hydratia" was never real.

---

[23] F Leron Shults, Theology After the Birth of God: Atheist Conceptions in Cognition and Culture (New York, NY : Palgrave Macmillan, 2014.)

Similarly, from our earliest days, we have had impressed upon us this idea that there is something inherently wrong with us. That there is something higher to attain to, that the dust beneath our feet is to be fled from, and even our very humanity, if possible, needs to be jettisoned. We once sought this in "gods," and we now seek in "gods" of other forms, but it's still the same yawning chasm crying to be filled. We desperately wish to build a Tower of Babel to the heavens in order to leave behind a world of pain and meaninglessness, and search our whole lives, often times throwing them away in the process, looking for this mythical "hydratia" that we believe will quench our thirst.

The problem, though, is that this thirst cannot be quenched, because "hydratia" isn't real. Though we've been told that desire is proof for the existence of the desired, the truth is that we're capable of desiring the nonexistent. Just because we feel the need for a thing, doesn't mean that the thing itself is real, or that the need is legitimate. It also doesn't mean, though, that we won't feel it, and that we won't ruin our lives seeking satisfaction for it. So it must be responded to, and the God and Father of Jesus has, in fact, responded to it. His response, though, is not intended to satisfy it, but to enable us to set it aside.

Think of the woman at the well in John 4. She comes to gather water at an inconvenient time, likely to avoid colliding with individuals whose judgments of her and her lifestyle she'd rather not deal with, and has an encounter with Jesus instead. He asks her for water, and she exposes a soul wounded by human judgment when she responds by asking:

> 9 How is it that you, a Jew, ask a drink of me, a woman
> of Samaria?" (Jews do not share things in common with
> Samaritans.)
>
> -John 4:9, NRSV

This was a woman who had had it impressed upon her that, at least in the eyes of Jews, she was inferior and untouchable. Jesus' response, and her subsequent reply, again go to show that she carried within her a deep void that had been pulling into itself all sorts of "gods," and would be solutions:

> 10 Jesus answered her, "If you knew the gift of God, and
> who it is that is saying to you, 'Give me a drink,' you
> would have asked him, and he would have given you
> living water." ... 13 Jesus said to her, "*Everyone who*
> *drinks of this water will be thirsty again, 14 but those*
> *who drink of the water that I will give them will never be*
> *thirsty. The water that I will give will become in them a*
> *spring of water gushing up to eternal life.*" 15 The
> woman said to him, "*Sir, give me this water, so that I*

may never be thirsty or have to keep coming here to draw water."

-John 4:10; 13-15, NRSV (Italics mine)

At this point we realize that we are no longer talking physical wells, literal water, or water jars. We are talking about a deep void this woman feels within; a sense of emptiness, longing, loss, and lost-ness that drives her to continually seek satisfaction at different wells, or "gods," if you will, but all to no avail. Jesus goes on to reveal that at least one source this woman has sought satisfaction in is relationships, as she has been married five times, and was presently in a relationship with a man she was not married to. As the conversation continues, Jesus discusses religion with the woman, and she seems to express a frustration with how confusing and muddled it all is, but also expresses her hope that Messiah will make things clear:

> 20 Our ancestors worshiped on this mountain, but you say that the place where people must worship is in Jerusalem." 21 Jesus said to her, "Woman, believe me, the hour is coming when you will worship the Father neither on this mountain nor in Jerusalem. ... 25 The woman said to him, *"I know that Messiah is coming"* (who is called Christ). "When he comes, he will proclaim all things to us."
>
> -John 4:20-21; 25, NRSV (Emphasis mine)

We now begin to get a picture of a woman whose thirst has led her to not only seek relief in physical things, but in spiritual things as well. She's searched in relationships and religion; men and mountains, and still nothing. There seems to be, though, in her questions, a sense of desperation; a sense that she's tried it all, and is becoming disillusioned. Her unwillingness to commit even to the relationship she was presently in, seems to speak to this fact. She has, however, placed her hope in the coming of Messiah. When he comes, she says, all questions will be answered, and all needs fulfilled. When Messiah comes, she seems to think, her thirst will finally quenched, and will no longer need to return to the various wells she's come to frequent.

Jesus' answer to her, though, was likely not what she expected:

> 26 Jesus said to her, "I am he, the one who is speaking to you."
>
> -John 4:26, NRSV

This was clearly not what the woman expected in a Messiah! He had answered none of her questions, as at the end of their conversation she still had them, and he most certainly didn't address or help her resolve her relational issues. And yet Jesus assures her that he is the solution she seeks, even though he's addressed none of her problems. What did he address, though? When the woman leaves, and goes back to the city, she says of her encounter with Jesus:

> 29 "*Come and see a man who told me everything I have ever done!* He cannot be the Messiah, can he?"

-John 4:29, NRSV (Emphasis mine)

While he did none of the things she expected Messiah to do, he also did something she in no way expected-he told her everything she had ever done, with no apparent condemnations added. He did not speak to her felt needs, or her desires for the mythical "hydratia" of perfect relationships and a squeaky clean set of doctrines, but only revealed that he knew her, and that he loved what he knew about her. Though it did not speak to the area in which she thirsted, it apparently affected her in that very place, for before she left Jesus, we're told the non-accidental detail that she "left her water jar and went back to the city." (verse 28)

Now, the whole story began with the water jar representing this felt need, this thirst that the woman carried around within her, which caused her to constantly need to return to certain sources to find satisfaction. Relationships did nothing to quench it, and religion only made things more confusing, but when Jesus revealed to her that he knew her, and that he apparently loved and approved of what he knew, symbolically speaking, her thirst was quenched. It was not quenched, though, in the sense that it was satisfied, but in that it was set aside. He did not give her what she desired, because what she desired did not exist, but instead showed her that the very thing she was trying to escape, the "everything I had ever done," was something that he was well acquainted with, and loved. This retroactively dealt with the thirst itself, revealed its faulty origins, and satisfied it by setting it aside. He showed it to be illegitimate, and illusory, because there was nothing this woman needed to escape in order to be acceptable before God.

No longer would she need to return to the "well," but not because she'd left Jesus with a filled to the brim water jar that would never again run dry, but because she was able to leave the actual water jar itself behind; the very void that required filling. The "gods" that were once drawn to this vacuum, and then reborn through the womb that it doubled as, would be drawn no longer, but not because she'd found the right "god," but because the vacuum into which these "gods" were drawn had vanished. The void, or the vacuum, had merely been an illusion, created by a sense that her experience of life was disapproved of, but the approval of Jesus revealed the illusory nature of her thirst. She needed nothing to save her from the life she'd felt was wasted and worthless, because the only person whose opinion mattered had a very high opinion of her.

In other words, Sarah Connor, or the womb from which those pesky, controlling gods continually arose, had been Terminated. Her need for the external wells and "gods" of this world had been dealt with, and she was now free to discover a life that could actually be about living, as opposed to escaping.

When we trod the atheistic "way" of Jesus, we inevitably collide with an experience of satisfaction such as this that retroactively eliminates the need for all "gods" and idols. We come to understand that the thing we had longed to escape, that is, the life of which we are ashamed, with which we are discontented, or even that we're just terrified to live, is something that the true God says needs no escaping, that we need not be ashamed of, and that we need not fear living. He knows it, approves of it, and is fully intent on living it with us. These human concepts of "gods" as escape pods, are revealed for the things that they are, and that is mere projections of our own desires. These "gods" have only ever been us, trying to solve problems that were never real to begin with. When we behold their place of birth, however, and realize that the "gods" were only ever in our heads, something truly remarkable happens - they cease believing in themselves!

Zizek writes:

> The formula for true atheism is thus: divine knowing and existence are incompatible, God exists only insofar as He does not know (take note of, register) His own inexistence. The moment God knows, He collapses into the abyss of inexistence...
>
> To put it in descriptive terms, it is not enough to prove that God does not exist – the formula of true atheism is that God himself must be made to proclaim his own inexistence, must stop believing in himself.[24]

In other words, you and I seeing these "gods" for what they are is tantamount to the "gods" seeing themselves for what they are, because they've only ever been you and I. When this happens, the termination occurs. The void closes, and the womb ceases to be fertile. The "gods" stop believing in the "gods," and Barbara realizes she doesn't need Uncle Simon. Only a God who disavows what we think to be divine, and declares divine what we think to be un-divine, can accomplish this for us. All other god-concepts encourage us to hold on to our own reflections

---

[24] Slavoj Zizek, *Less Than Nothing: Hegel and the Shadow of Dialectical Materialism* (London ; New York : Verso, 2012.)

that we've confused for "gods," but maybe just give them a new name or carve them a new image when the old one becomes untenable. As Buber suggested, when one image fails us, we just build a new one that we will inevitably be forced to destroy as well. We continually go "one God further," eventually fooling ourselves into thinking that we've gone all the way, all the while we're still beholden to some undercover concept of "god," who has simply adopted a new name and persona. Only in Jesus, do we realize that at the bottom of the idol pile is nothing but our own desires, not that which is truly divine. Only here do we see that simply jettisoning the "gods" does not save us from them. No, they must see that their origins are faulty, the need for them illegitimate, and that they, in fact, are our own wrongheaded ideas about who and what we are.

This is where the "gods" in our heads come face to face with their own inexistence and their own lack of necessity! It is here that the need for them finally disappears! When we see that the very thing we've been seeking to escape-life-is the very thing God has approved of, we suddenly no longer need to be satisfied, nor gratified, by some imagined concept, but only to live that which we now know is approved.

This was my own experience.

I tried to be an atheist, as I've already told you, but I wasn't a good enough Christian to pull it off. But I also tried to be a Christian, but wasn't a good enough atheist to pull it off. What I mean when I say that is that, while I did, in fact, try my damnedest to be the Christian's Christian, and the man of God's man of God, I simply could not shake the idols that were inherent, both to my Christian and human experience. They hounded me, vexed me, and caused me great anxiety. For me, my desire to escape looked like an extreme desire for holiness, and transcendent experiences with the divine, and I sought these both at great cost to myself and my family. I couldn't sleep, and sometimes literally couldn't even breathe, due to panic attacks, because of my obsession with a certain concept of "god." This was anything but the "way" of Jesus, and I needed to become an atheist as far as these concepts were concerned, but I'd yet to meet the Jesus who could lead me down the path of the atheistic theist, and terminate my "gods." So, while I tried to be a Christian, I just wasn't a good enough atheist to manage it.

And so, because of the nightmarish nature of the Christianity I knew, I sought to break from it altogether. I did, in fact, try to become a literal atheist, in the popular sense of the term. I read the works of every atheistic philosopher, scientist, former preacher or laymen I could get my hands on, and desperately, desperately sought to leave behind God altogether. I was done, and wanted nothing to do with it. It was here, though, that I realized I wasn't a good enough Christian to pull off atheism, because, while I secretly disbelieved in "god," one was still very much present in my life, only now in the form of my atheism. I couldn't become truly atheistic, because my hopes for escape, which I had once placed in the hands of something divine, I had now placed in the hands of a certain type of philosophy. What I once sought from the "god" I was trying to leave behind, was still what I was seeking in the system I thought would help me do the leaving.

Paul Tillich writes of the phenomenon of atheism itself becoming "god," or what he calls "the impossibility of atheism," when remarking on the supposed "death of God" spoken of in Nietzsche's *Thus Spake Zarathustra*. A character called "the ugliest man" becomes the murderer of God in the story, but then becomes a servant of Zarathustra, who is put forth as being a sort of prophet of a secular humanity. Tillich writes:

> The murderer of God finds God in man. He has not succeeded in killing God at all. God has returned in Zarathustra, and in the new period of history which Zarathustra announces. God is always revived in something or somebody He cannot be murdered. The story of every atheism is the same.

In my case, when even my atheism failed to rid me of "god," it was Jesus who saved me from him. It was ultimately God who saved me from "god," and atheism that saved me from theism.

I realized that it was only in a God who rejected what I understood "god" to be, and who flat out refused participation in that which I imagined when I imagined the divine, that I could find salvation from the "gods" that haunted me. It was only this one, stand-alone figure of Jesus, this God who refused to be god-like, who could rescue me from my own "gods," and expose them as nothing more than wrongheaded attempts at solving a problem that needed no solving. I needed a God who himself disbelieved in "god," so that the "gods" in my head could stop believing in themselves.

I needed a *true* atheism, which meant I needed Jesus.

WHERE DO WE GO FROM HERE?

It took us a couple of chapters to get here, but I want to begin narrowing our focus now, and examine one very specific god-concept that needs termination. We've been somewhat vague up until this point, and spoken mostly just of god-concepts, and screwball ideas about the divine, without getting too specific or naming names. Here's where that all changes. What I want to begin to do now is to examine the faulty origins of the "god" of much modern Christianity, the scheme of salvation he peddles, and the threats of damnation he levies.

Now remember, I'm doing this as a Jesus-follower, as a devout Christian, and fellow traveler of "the way." It is my Christianity, and my adoration of the person of Jesus that have motivated me to do the deconstruction you'll read in the chapters that follow. My aim to see this god-concept terminated does not have as its impetus a hatred for Christianity, but rather a deep love for it and its Christ. I'm afraid, though, that the idols of yesteryear have gone underground, and lie undisturbed in so many of our cherished, "Christian" beliefs about the Father of Jesus, and so when I speak about them as I do, it will inevitably sound to some like an attack on God, and not simply a god-concept.

Be forewarned that I will use strong language when I speak against this particular concept of god, and it may be a bit shocking to some readers who are very much accustomed to these ideas, and think them sacred. I do not intend to offend, but simply feel that many of these ideas are inherently harmful and damaging, and need to be drug out into the cold light of day and shown for the things they are. Idols are notoriously good at camouflaging themselves and blending in, and so pointblank language is often necessary in order to expose and identify them. Please, especially when we get to the chapter on hell, don't jump ship simply because the language frightens you.

As an additional warning to some readers, I will use many quotes and statements from some of our generation's most notorious atheists; guys like Richard Dawkins, Sam Harris, the late, great Christopher Hitchens, and so on. I will be using these quotes, not in the negative or in order to disprove them, but in the positive, and will present them as valid critiques of certain "Christian" beliefs. This too may sit uncomfortably with some more conservative readers, who are unaccustomed to subjecting themselves to critique by those they inherently disagree with on some weighty matters.

Why I will be using these specific writer's and lecturer's words, is to show that, at its core, Christianity is an atheistic religion, and most of these critiques don't necessarily eviscerate God, but simply the "gods" that have lived in our heads but now operate undercover in popular forms of Christianity. The critiques of many of the new atheists are actually very much in line with orthodox Christianity, and serve to point us toward the Jesus-way, not away from it.

To be perfectly honest, I consider many modern atheists to be the closest things we have to prophets today. Far too many Christians are content to remain within the Constantinian system of idolatrous Christianity, without ever so much as asking a difficult question about belief, praxis, or thinking for themselves. We desperately need to hear the voices of the "godless," who are often speaking more truth to the power structures who house these "gods" than we, who are snugly sealed up within them.

Finally, and more than anything else, the following chapters contain some of the blunt, unapologetic language they contain, because I know that so many of you reading this *do*, in fact, have questions of your own, but no one with whom you feel comfortable talking about them. I know that many of you reading are neck deep, or deeper, in your own deconstruction of your beliefs, and I want to travel that path with you. I want to stand with you in solidarity, and maybe say for you and ask for you, some of the things you're afraid to say and afraid to ask. I want you to know that your questions are ok, and that even some of the anger and frustration you feel toward certain beliefs is ok as well.

In the chapters that follow, what we will do is take a look at three issues,

1.) The doctrine of Original Sin
2.) The doctrine of Penal Substitutionary Atonement
3.) The doctrine of hell as Eternal Conscious Torment

We will be examining these three subjects since they are something of the backbone of modern, Western Christianity. The reason we feel the need for the "god" of this system in the first place is because of the doctrine of original sin. It tells us we are damned to eternal conscious torment because of the sin of another, and so require a form of salvation that speaks to both the crime and the punishment. From this arises the version of the cross in which God must pour out his wrath upon Jesus in order for us to be saved, both from Adam's sin, and the punishment of eternal hell that it earned the whole lot of us.

I will start with original sin in order to attempt to show it illegitimate, and thereby showing both the punishment and its solution to be illegitimate as well. If we terminate the womb from which this "god" is born, we terminate the "god," and all that it comes to be, as well.

We must not be so foolish, though, as to think that simply tinkering with doctrine, and deconstructing bad ideas will rid us of them altogether. I know that a time travelling assassin seems like it would be the final answer to such a problem, but it actually isn't. If the later Terminator movies and television series taught us anything, it's that when you alter the events of the past, the future of which they were the seeds still occurs exactly as it did the first time, and remains unaltered. It has already happened, and there is no undoing things that have already been done. What does occur, though, is that an alternate timeline is created that exists parallel to the one from which the time traveler came. Altering the past does not change the future, it simply creates another potential one.

The parallel we can draw here is that, while we may be able to retroactively terminate dangerous god-concepts, they do not disappear altogether from our minds. Obviously, we will still continue to feel the effects of our former beliefs. Such things just don't disappear, no matter what you come to believe. What happens in Jesus, though, is that an alternative timeline is presented to you, in which you are able to see another potential future, other than the one that you previously endured under a false god-concept. While the other will not vanish altogether, you now have an alternative to choose over it.

While we will deconstruct what I think to be the faulty foundations of the Western concept of "god," as well as some of the effects of this belief, we will also explore the alternate timeline. After each deconstructive chapter, I will offer an alternative understanding of the concept we have deconstructed. What does, for example, original sin look like once the false god-concept is terminated? Does it have any relevance? Is there anything redemptive in this view that we should hold onto? Or how about the cross? What does it say to us and to the world once we remove the "monster god" who demands blood payment and human sacrifice from the picture? Or what of hell? When we deal with this most dubious of doctrines, what's left on the other side? How do we live if we remove this belief from our systems?

Those are the things we will examine in the next 6 chapters.

So let's continue our journey, and, hopefully arrive together at a place of Godly godlessness, and of godless Godliness; a place of atheistic theism

4 | THE TOTAL DEPRAVITY OF ORIGINAL SIN

"I was blinded by the devil, born already ruined, stone-cold dead as I stepped out of the womb…"

-Bob Dylan

"These two things are distinctly to be noted, that is, that, being thus in all parts of our nature perverted and corrupted, we are now, even for such corruption, only holden worthy of damnation, and stand convicted before God, to whom nothing is acceptable but righteousness, innocence and purity."

-John Calvin

"We must question the story logic of having an all-knowing all-powerful God, who creates faulty Humans, and then blames them for his own mistakes."

-Gene Roddenberry

In the last chapter we began to discuss how it is that we do away with harmful god-concepts, and I suggested that it can only be done by having them retroactively terminated, via the Gospel. I have argued that Jesus exposes the faulty origins of these beings in which we seek salvation, causing us to come face to face with their inexistence. In order to be rid of a god-concept, we must identify its birthplace, or the need that gave rise to it, and expose the need itself to its own illegitimacy in light of the truth about God revealed in Jesus. When this happens, we cease to believe in it, it ceases to believe in itself, and it eventually disappears.

When it comes to the "god" of modern, Western Christianity, its birthplace is not difficult in the least to identify. The doctrine of *original sin*, or, the idea that human beings have inherited the guilt, and therefore the due penalty, of the sin of Adam and Eve, has, in one form or another, been with the Church for most of its existence, but owes its present form mainly to the influence of Augustine of Hippo. Augustine basically taught that humankind was the heir of their primordial parents' sin, and that only the Christian could achieve and walk in righteousness through the work of the Holy Spirit and divine grace.

In Calvinist doctrine, the idea that all human beings are born corrupted by the first sin, and incapable of living a righteous life, is called *total depravity*, and is what the *T* in the famous acronym, *T.U.L.I.P.*, stands for. While its basic purpose is to establish that man cannot choose God on his own, what gets transmitted in the process is that there is a fundamental taint in man's nature that not only compels him to live in a disgustingly discordant way, but also makes him appear as vile and unacceptable in the eyes of his Creator. In modern evangelicalism, these two doctrines of Original Sin and Total Depravity, often get conflated together to form one larger, slightly more complicated and, slightly more destructive, hybrid, and while less fundamentalist strains of Christianity will not be found teaching them as heavy handedly, or even as obviously as some, it still lies at the heart of most Western forms of Christianity, forming the basis for their doctrines of salvation.

It is precisely this idea that gives rise to the "god" of the most popular forms of Christianity. It is this doctrine that creates the illusion of thirst in us, and creates the womb out of which this god-concept crawls. It is the tale we are told, or at least the idea we have impressed upon us since birth, that convinces we need to partake of the mythical "hydratia" in order to be complete, and fully human. We can see this ache, and this longing in Augustine himself, in these very well-known words of his:

> Thou hast made us for thyself, O Lord, and our heart is
> restless until it finds its rest in thee.[25]

---

[25] Augustine, Saint Bishop of Hippo.; E B Pusey; Marcus Dods; J J Shaw,

Now, I don't think any theist would argue against the beauty of his words, nor even the sentiment behind them. However, when we understand the state Augustine believes the human is in prior to an experience of salvation, it becomes clear that the restlessness he refers to here might not be the loveliest of things.

He writes:

> No one is free from sin in your sight, not even an infant whose span of earthly life is but a single day... The only innocent feature in babies is the weakness of their frames; the minds of infants are far from innocent. [26]

In Augustine's estimation, humanity is born corrupted to the core by original sin. Even the baby, he says, is guilty of sin in their thoughts. What could a baby possibly be guilty of? Well, we have old Augustine's thoughts on this as well:

> What then was my sin at that age? Was it perhaps that I cried so greedily for those breasts? Certainly if I behaved like that now, greedy not for breasts, of course, but for food suitable to my age, I should provoke derision and be very properly rebuked. My behavior then was equally deserving of rebuke. [27]

His view of adolescence wasn't anymore cheery, as he writes of his own:

> From the mud of my fleshly desires and my erupting puberty belched out murky clouds that obscured and darkened my heart until I could not distinguish the calm light of love from the fog of lust. [28]

To Augustine, the whole experience of being human was one of being driven along by uncontrollable lusts and selfishness. We were born with the power of sin at work in us, leading us and driving us to do terrible things, which, no doubt incurred the wrath and displeasure of God. It's not difficult to see how, if one has it impressed upon them in infancy or youth, that they were born in sin, hopelessly bent toward evil, and on a collision course with behaviors that would invite the flames of God's wrath, they would experience a restlessness, a thirst, and a desire for salvation. The problem presented by Augustine's concept of original sin

---

The Confessions ; The City of God ; On Christian Doctrine (Chicago: Encyclopaedia Britannica, [1955, ©1952])

[26] Ibid.
[27] Ibid.
[28] Ibid.

creates a void within us that demands a "god" of a very particular shape. He must answer the problem of the sin itself, as well as the punishment said sin deserves. And that is precisely what the "god" of Western Christianity is.

My contention is that it is the idea of original sin, as opposed to original sin itself, that we need saving from. It is, I believe, at least in this form, a horrid concept that hides the true nature of the God revealed in Jesus, destroys the human spirit, and leads us deeper and deeper into the very sort of darkness it claims we are born in, and purports to be able to save us from.

Let's look a bit more deeply at the idea in order to get a handle on why it is I think it so problematic, and the god-concept it gives rise to so worthy of termination.

In the *Formula of Concord*, an authoritative Lutheran statement of faith, here's what we are told of the doctrine of total depravity, which is very much linked to original sin:

> First of all, it is true that not only should Christians regard and recognize as sin the actual violation of God's commandments in their deeds, but they should also perceive and recognize that the horrible, dreadful, inherited disease corrupting their entire nature is above all actual sin and indeed is the "chief sin." It is the root and fountainhead of all actual sins. Luther calls this a "nature-sin" or "person-sin," in order to indicate that even if a human being thinks, says, or does nothing evil (which is, of course, after the fall of our first parents, impossible for human nature in this life), nevertheless, our entire nature and person is sinful, that is, totally and thoroughly corrupted in God's sight and contaminated by original sin as with a spiritual leprosy. Because of this corruption and on account of the fall of the first human beings, God's law accuses and condemns human nature and the human person. [29]

What exactly could I find disagreeable in this statement? I mean, it contains all the basic elements of an evangelical salvation message, right? Yet, here I am, suggesting that it hides the true image of God revealed in Jesus, and destroys the human spirit.

---

[29] Theodore G Tappert, *The Book of Concord: The Confessions of the Evangelical Lutheran Church* (Philadelphia : Fortress Press, ©1959.)

So, what's wrong with it?

Well, let's begin with this line: "*...even if a human being thinks, says, or does nothing evil...nevertheless, our entire nature and person is sinful, that is, totally and thoroughly corrupted in God's sight and contaminated by original sin as with a spiritual leprosy. Because of this corruption and on account of the fall...God's law accuses and condemns human nature and the human person.*"

In order to illustrate where I see a problem, let's talk about Mike.

Mike's, as you've probably guessed, is a tragic tale, or else I wouldn't be using it to illustrate the nature of doctrines I find problematic. It is also *only* a tale, and as far as I know, does not contain any elements of truth, so feel free to not feel too outraged as you read.

Mike comes from a single parent home and carries a fair amount of baggage, both emotional and psychological. This is due mostly to the extreme amount of physical, emotional and psychological abuse he experienced at the hands of his father. Since this abuse came from his father, and since I already mentioned Mike was from a single parent home, you've probably deduced that his mother was out of the picture. It is, in fact, her absence that lay at the heart of Mike's story, and serves as the impetus for all he would come to endure from his father.

Mike's father had absolutely adored his wife and had practically worshipped the ground she walked on. Needless to say, when she died giving birth to Mike, he was utterly and completely devastated. Pushed to the edge of sanity, he unfortunately, fell from it, and became a heavy drinker and abuser of various substances, all aimed at expiating his grief and anger. One day it dawned upon him, though, that there was a more effective way of dealing with his pain. His son, Mike, was the real problem after all, and so he came to find great release and relief in laying a daily beating on him. Why should he harm his own body when he could harm his son's? He *alone* was the cause of his beloved wife's death, after all, and he alone deserved to be punished for it.

Daily, Mike was savagely beaten as payment for the sin of "murdering" his mother, and was intermittently reminded during these beatings that he was a killer. Little Mike was told over and over again that he was *born* a murderer, and deserved to be treated the way that murderers are treated. His very first act as a human being, so he was constantly told, was murder, meaning that he was an evil, wicked child, who was actually getting off easy in only having to endure a daily beating or two. Or three. Or five.

Would it surprise you at all to know that young Mike grew up to be a very angry and abusive adult? Probably not. Would it surprise you if you were told that he actually did become a murderer? A serial murderer, in fact?

If it would surprise you, it probably shouldn't.

Mike was told by the most important and significant figure in his life, his father, that his first act as a living, breathing person was that of murder. He was violently and savagely beaten as punishment for this action, in addition to being constantly reminded of his crime and murderous nature. Now, obviously, young Mike did not murder his mother. Sure, his birth had been the indirect cause of her death, but to say that he murdered her and was guilty of a crime is just absurd. Mike was as innocent of his mother's death as she herself was. In fact, if one used Mike's dad's twisted logic, *he* was just as guilty of his wife's death as his son. He was, after all, responsible for Mike's existence, and if Mike was responsible for his mother's death, then he, the father, was just as responsible, if not more so.

Regardless of these seemingly logical truths, young Mike was told from infancy that he was a murderer by nature, and deserved every bit of suffering that came his way. If young Mike grew to be a serial murderer, no one should be surprised. He was only living up to what he was told was in his nature.

How does this tie in with the doctrine of total depravity and original sin?

Very closely, actually, for the "god" of these doctrines is exactly like Mike's father. He blames us for a sin we were not even present to commit, and punishes us for the same. We had no control over whether or not a naked couple in an idyllic garden ingested a piece of forbidden fruit, and yet this doctrine serves as a constant reminder to us that God holds us accountable, and sees us as corrupt to the core, and beyond hope. We are born sinners, and, according to Augustine, even as babies are guilty of thought crime. From our earliest moments we have an expectation of sin, disobedience, and total depravity impressed on us by this "god's" representatives, and it should serve as no surprise to anyone if we grow to live accordingly.

This original sin, this inherited total depravity, is what the popular Christian message offers us salvation from. God creates us, presumably with the knowledge that sin will one day become an issue, and then holds us accountable by punishing us eternally for a problem he clearly saw coming. It all sounds rather absurd when you say it that way.

Standup comedian, Bill Burr, rather crassly but humorously remarks on the idea's basic problems:

Dude, you made me. So this is your f--- up. Let's not try to turn this around on me. You give me freedom of choice...you have me suck at math, and you don't think this thing is gonna go off the rails? You set me up to fail...If I built a car and it didn't run, I wouldn't burn it forever... I'd troubleshoot![30]

Singer songwriter, David Bazan, articulates the same problem, albeit more poetically, in a song called *When We Fell:*

What am I afraid of? Whom did I betray?

In what medieval kingdom does justice work this way?

If you knew what would happen and made us just the same,

Then you, my lord, can take the blame[31]

Sometimes we need the comics and the poets to strip our cherished beliefs bare naked in front of our eyes so that we can clearly see the silliness that too often gets a free pass, because it hides behind theological jargon. God made us, knowing that we'd become the broken creatures we are today, and also saw fit to create a place of eternal punishment in which we would forever pay for a sin that, in all honesty, is more his fault than our own. As Burr riffed, "If I built a car and it didn't run, I wouldn't burn it forever...I'd troubleshoot!" Surely, if anyone is to blame, it's not the creation, but the creator! And only an insecure creator would be so ashamed of the failings of his handiwork that he would bury them deep inside an eternal fiery furnace. As Star Trek creator, Gene Roddenberry, has said, "We must question the story logic of having an all-knowing all-powerful God, who creates faulty Humans, and then blames them for his own mistakes." And that's coming from a man who knows a thing or two about "story logic."

The late Christopher Hitchens, one of the most eloquent and outspoken atheists of our generation, has said:

Once you assume a Creator and a plan, it makes us objects in a cruel experiment whereby we are created sick and then commanded to be well,[32]

---

[30] Jay Karas and Bill Burr. 2014. Bill Burr: I'm Sorry You Feel That Way.

[31] Bazan, David. "When We Fell."

[32] This quote comes from a debate between Christopher Hitchens and Tony Blair. The full debate can be seen here:
https://www.youtube.com/watch?v=xFnSjmQCGDM

While we don't come right out with it, that is precisely the message that gets transmitted to the masses through popular Christian preaching. We tell them that they are born broken, through no fault of their own, and despised enough by God to warrant their eternal torture; born sick, and commanded to be well, or else face hell.

WHO COMES UP WITH THIS STUFF?

I've heard well-meaning parents remark that they didn't even require scriptural evidence for original sin, since, from birth, their children were selfish, disobedient and rebellious. What that means is they screamed in response to the trauma of being plucked from a warm, dark womb, forced to use their eyes and lungs for the first time, and made their discomfort known when their only source of nourishment was severed. And, if it was a boy, they likely screamed when a portion of their genitals were hacked off. That is a very Augustinian condemnation of infantile behavior, but is it warranted? Is such behavior actually sinful?

I had one man tell me that the only evidence he needed was a glance in the direction of his grandchildren, who, apparently, argued and even (gasp) fought with each other sometimes. It definitely had nothing to do with the fact that they were just kids who had yet to fully learn how to control their emotions. Again, who is telling us that actions like this are sinful? That kids being kids, and having yet to learn to control themselves, are sinning? It seems to me that calling such banal things sinful will only impress upon our children an expectation for worse behavior, in which case it all becomes a self-fulfilling prophecy.

I once even heard a very popular Calvinistic preacher suggest that, were infants a hundred pounds heavier, they would beat us to a bloody pulp, take from us whatever they wanted, and crawl over our shredded corpses, laughing and smiling from ear to ear. While I agree that an adult-sized baby would be more than a little bit frightening, it would only be because of its lack of motor skills, combined with brute strength. Yeah, sure, that's scary, but not because the baby was a totally depraved monster.

Seriously, you have to stop and wonder what kinds of minds come up with this stuff!

Sadly, all too often it's well educated, and spiritually inclined minds, encased within frames that bear titles like Pastor or Reverend that "come up with this stuff," leaving many to conclude that, regardless of how absurd it sounds, it must actually be reasonable. The minds whose opinions the Christian ought to be most interested in when it comes to this stuff, though, are those we all too often ignore. The writer of Psalms 139, for example:

> 13 For *you created my inmost being; you knit me together in my mother's womb.* 14 I praise you because *I am fearfully and wonderfully made; your works are wonderful*, I know that full well. 15 My frame was not hidden from you when I was made in the secret place, when *I was woven together in the depths of the earth.* 16 Your eyes saw my unformed body; all the days ordained for me were written in your book before one of them came to be. 17 *How precious to me are your thoughts*, God! How vast is the sum of them!
>
> -Psalms 139:13-17, NRSV (Italics mine)

This man, writing long before Jesus or any Protestant notions of salvation were contemplatable, and long before any doctrine of original sin had been imagined, asserted that it is God who knits a child together in the womb, and that he makes us in a manner so wonderful, that it ought to inspire reverence and awe. The Psalmist is not speaking of some intended, pre-fall state, but of his own self, an untold number of centuries after the supposed fall occurred. Apparently he missed that all-important memo detailing the human race's inheriting of a fallen and damnable nature that made them the targets of God's wrath. He didn't seem to understand children as being incapable of goodness, nor hopelessly bent in the opposite direction of righteousness. Rather, for the Psalmist, all of humankind had been fearfully and wonderfully fashioned by the creative hand of God, and he therefore insisted that God's thoughts concerning them were both precious and vast.

The concept of a fallen and alienated creation is not native to Judaism, from which Christianity springs, and would likely not have even been in the Psalmist's theological or anthropological tool box. Philip J. Lee writes:

> The Old Testament asserts that the Creation itself cannot be faulted. One is able, in facing the cosmos, only to offer a prayer of thanksgiving, "The earth is the LORD's and the fullness thereof." Humankind, far from being an "abortion," is the direct product and responsibility of a loving God: "For thou didst form my inward parts, thou didst knit me together in my mother's womb."[33]

This is not, however, how a great number of Christians, both past and present, have seen things, and, sadly, our theology has been less

---

[33] Philip J Lee, *Against the Protestant Gnostics* (Oxford University Press 1987.)

informed by guys like the Psalmist and Lee, and more by those with different takes on the issue. Consider the following quote from famed Puritan Author, Arthur Hildersham:

> ...all infants are sinners, and deserve damnation...many infants have been vessels of wrath, and firebrands of hell![34]

This lovely chap would have us think that, simply because they have had the misfortune of exiting the womb, all infants, universally and across the board, are considered "sinners" by God and deserve damnation. Others, Hildersham insists, have actually been specially chosen by God (lucky them) as vessels of wrath who will eventually become "firebrands of hell," whatever that means. According to Hildersham, God has specially fashioned certain helpless and choice-less babies to be damned to a fiery, Christ-less eternity, just because it pleased his twisted heart to do so.

Jonathan Edwards once suggested the same thing about the election of infants as "vessels of wrath." He said:

> Reprobate infants are vipers of vengeance, which Jehovah will hold over hell, in the tongs of his wrath, till they turn and spit venom in his face!

Let's set aside the fact that the Jehovah envisioned by Edwards, like a serial killer or CIA interrogator, has a tool in his possession called the "tongs of wrath," and move on to the more relevant matter. This famed revival preacher actually states that certain infants are elected by God to be tortured forever in a lake of fire.

Again, you have to stop and wonder what kind of minds come up with this stuff, but again comes the disappointing and disturbing answer: highly educated and spiritually inclined minds, like Hildersham and Edwards. Edwards, for example, was not a backwards, uneducated savage, but *extremely* well-educated, having studied in fields ranging from religion to philosophy and psychology. He was no ignorant brute, but a brilliant and well-respected theologian, and yet this didn't stop him from imagining little babies being actively tortured by a god who toted a bag full of aptly named torture-tools to aid him in his misery-making. How could one so bright be so duped? It matters not how intelligent a person is, once the belief in original sin takes hold, and someone is devoted enough to follow it through to its logical conclusion, this is where they will always end up.

---

[34] Arthur Hildersham, CLII lectures upon Psalm LI : preached at Ashby-Delazovich in Leicester-shire (Early English books, 1641-1700, 942:7.)

Elsewhere, Edwards wrote of how he thought Christian fathers, who made it to heaven despite their children being damned, would react upon seeing them in hell:

> The sight of hell torments will exalt the happiness of the saints forever…Can the believing father in Heaven be happy with his unbelieving children in Hell…I tell you, yea! Such will be his sense of justice that it will increase rather than diminish his bliss.[35]

Not only will some infants, due to their total depravity and inherited sin, be chosen to roast in hell forever, but their own parents will have their "bliss" increased by the sight of God holding them over flames! Sounds slightly more Hitlerian than holy, and just ever so anti-Christ, but this is what famed and respected theologians have handed down to us as sound, biblical doctrine.

What was it again that these little babies spoken of by Hildersham and Edwards did to deserve such horrific treatment at the hands of God? I mean it must have been something pretty horrible, if even their own parents are blowing kazoos and waving pompons upon seeing them in hell! So, what was their crime exactly?

Oh, that's right.

They were born. And then after birth, according to Augustine, they sometimes cried too loudly to be nursed or some such nonsense.

One commenter on an internet forum I was perusing concerning this very subject wrote: "From the moment cells come together to form a child in the womb, they are instantly enemies of God because of their violation of the Law through Adam. They are guilty, defiled abominations, for they ate of the forbidden fruit through Adam, their forefather."

How do these words, or those of Hildersham, or Edwards, or Augustine, in any way agree with the Psalmist's declaration that man is fearfully and wonderfully made? How is a child, fashioned in the womb by God Himself, deserving of punishment for its nature? How can the Psalmist's words and those of Edwards, Hildersham, and random internet commenters all be true?

They can't.

One is wrong and one is right, and when it comes to judging between the opinions of Psalmists and internet commenters, I usually fall on the side of Psalmists (though not always).

---

[35] From a sermon entitled, *The Eternity of Hell Torments*, the full text of which can be read here: http://www.jonathan-edwards.org/Eternity.html

The Westminster Confession of Faith seems to agree with Mr. internet-commenter, however, stating of Adam and Eve:

> They, being the root of all mankind, the guilt of this sin was imputed; and the same death in sin, and corrupted nature, conveyed to all their posterity descending from them by ordinary generation.[36]

In other words, since they were the original root of humanity, Adam and Eve passed their corruption and sinful defilement on to the rest of us.

What is the result of being born thus corrupted? *The Confession* gives this answer:

> Every sin, *both original and actual*, being a transgression of the righteous law of God, and contrary thereunto, does in its own nature, bring guilt upon the sinner, whereby he is bound over to the wrath of God, and curse of the law, and so made subject to death, with all miseries spiritual, temporal, and eternal. (Italics mine)[37]

It's claimed that, since infants inherit the sinfulness of Adam and Eve, from conception and from birth, they, just as much as the Nazi war criminal or the serial killer, are "bound over to the wrath of God and...made subject to death, with all miseries spiritual, temporal, and eternal."

What would these "miseries eternal" look like for the innocent child who'd had the misfortune of being born in sin? What would its eternal fate look like on account of this inherited sin? Once more, here are the words of the Westminster Confession on the matter, just so we know we're getting it straight from the horse's mouth:

> ...the souls of the wicked are cast into hell, *where they remain in torments and utter darkness*... (Italics mine)[38]

So, according to the Westminster Confession, a child, from its earliest moments, perhaps even while still in a cellular state and lacking consciousness, is deserving of "torments and utter darkness." *Why?* Because within this Augustinian framework, they are defiled and counted guilty of a crime they played no direct part in committing.

How could this be considered "just" in any universe, and how could such an unjust brand of "justice" be attributed to a God of Whom it is said,

---

[36] John Macpherson, *The Westminster Confession of Faith* (Edinburgh : T. & T. Clark,)

[37] Ibid.

[38] Ibid.

"unto thee, O Lord, belongeth mercy: for *thou renderest to every man according to his work*."? (Psalms 62:12, KJV)

While the Psalmist declares that God is merciful in that he does not impute the guilt of one man's sin to another, but holds individuals accountable for *individual* actions, many Christians would have us believe that God, in His justice, has counted the entire world guilty of the first man's sin and has chosen to see every human being, from the developing fetus to your great grandfather, as sin-infected monsters, who deserve wrath-tongs and eternal conscious torment. Nowhere in the good old U.S. of A. would any human judge be able to get away with making such prejudiced rulings. And if they were, you'd better believe that Christians from all walks of life would be in the streets protesting. Yet, when we attribute this same type of behavior to God, calling it "holiness," many Christians will not only excuse it, but call it perfect. Sure, we're not allowed to get away with similar behavior, but this is one of those *His-ways-are-higher-than-our-ways* situations, I guess.

It's funny though, because many believers, apologists in particular, like to claim that the only reason we humans have any sense of morality or justice to begin with is because we've inherited this trait from our creator. In more than one atheist vs. theist debate, I've heard it argued that there *must* be a God, based on the fact that human beings have a sense of justice. This, they insist, results from the imprint the creator has left upon his creation. Yet his version of justice and ours could not be more diametrically opposed to one another.

I also find it interesting how many American Evangelicals like to speak of the U.S. Constitution as though it were a divinely dictated document, and yet, in its opening line, it completely contradicts the foundational doctrine of their entire worldview. How exactly do you square "All men are created equal and are endowed by their creator with certain unalienable rights," with all men are "bound over to the wrath of God, and curse of the law, and so made subject to death, with all miseries spiritual, temporal, and eternal?"

In speaking of things like the Constitution as though they were divine, what we actually show is that we, human beings, have risen above the one we call creator in things pertaining to morality. We understand that one cannot have a civil society in which it is assumed that certain of its citizens are born contaminated and worthy of death or enslavement, and yet the very creator we claim as the source of our morality is one we claim sees all mankind, not as equally deserving of "unalienable rights," but of endless agony.

We hold ourselves to a much higher and responsible standard of justice, and would never imagine implementing anything reflected in the doctrine of original sin in a court of law. At least in the United States, we demand one be presumed innocent until proven guilty, but the God we claim as the source of our justice declares us guilty before we even have a chance to show him otherwise. I just can't help noticing how un-American and decidedly un-constitutional America's "god" really is. Countries whose legal systems resemble him are what we call *dictatorships*, actually. We use words like *draconian* to describe the way they operate, and often protest their cruelty to their citizens to the point of calling for war. Yet, when it is God acting the same way, we suddenly fall in line and our protests go silent.

The real question for a Christian, though, isn't whether human justice is congruent with beliefs about divine justice, but whether or not the scriptures, and the Christ whose name we claim, are in agreement with these ideas. Did Jesus think of human beings as being born tainted by Adam's sin, bearing the guilt of his decisions, and damned from conception? When the little children came to Jesus, did he see them as being soiled by the Adamic transgression, and incapable of doing anything good or holy? Was Jesus disgusted by the sight of them, and feel a sort of inexplicable urge to burn them with eternal fire? I obviously say no, but if one believes Jesus to be the son of the wrathful "god" of Western Christianity, and also believes that all humans are born tainted by original sin, Jesus would have had to have seen things this way.

And yet, does that in any way square with what we know to be true of Jesus? Jesus did not walk around, after all, condemning children or pointing out a need to be cleansed from Adam's transgression. Rather, he speaks of children as innocents whom we should strive to emulate. In fact, He even goes as far as to say that the Kingdom belongs, both to children, and to those who emulate their innocence. Hildersham had a slightly different take:

> It is evident that God hath witnessed his wrath against the sin of infants, not only by hating their sins, but even their persons also...And not only inflicting temporal punishments upon them, but even by casting them into hell.[39]

Would Jesus shout "amen" and dance a Pentecostal jig in response to this drivel? Would he shake Hildersham's hand and say, "Good preaching, son?"

I think not:

> 2 He called a child, whom he put among them, 3 and said, "Truly I tell you, unless you change and become

---

[39] Arthur Hildersham, CLII lectures upon Psalm LI : preached at Ashby-Delazovich in Leicester-shire (Early English books, 1641-1700, 942:7.)

like children, you will never enter the kingdom of heaven. 4 Whoever becomes humble like this child is the greatest in the kingdom of heaven. 5 Whoever welcomes one such child in my name welcomes me. 6 "If any of you put a stumbling block before one of these little ones who believe in me, it would be better for you if a great millstone were fastened around your neck and you were drowned in the depth of the sea.

-Matthew 18:1-6, NRSV (Italics mine)

The humility of a child, Jesus tells us, should be the hallmark of our lives. That which they naturally do, ought to be the state we seek to return to, and so protective is he of this quality of theirs, that he warns His disciples that those who put stumbling blocks in their way, hindering their belief and ability to come to him, would be better off drowned with a millstone tied to their necks.

In other words, there is something valuable that we're born with, but that we lose as we grow, not the other way around. Those who would prematurely rob a child of this innocence by putting a stumbling block in their path are spoken of in not so flattering terms. The problem is not the child's nature, but things placed between them and the reality of their innocence.

What are these stumbling blocks, I wonder? Perhaps they're doctrines like those of original sin and total depravity, which teach our children that no matter what they do, even if it's "getting saved," they'll never be worthy or deserving of God's love? Maybe it's the infectious and lethal viruses of guilt and shame that we ladle into them each time we suggest that they deserve hell and eternal torture? Maybe these "stumbling blocks" are concepts like little children needing to be "saved" in the first place, since they're so sinful that God can't even have a conversation with them, unless he beholds them through the lenses of atonement?

THE AGE OF ACCOUNTIBILITY

Some would raise here the issue of the "age of accountability," which is the idea that a child only becomes judgment-worthy after reaching an age where they are able to see the sinfulness of their own actions, and are able to make a personal decision to follow Jesus. The problems with this idea are so numerous, it would take several chapters to break them all down, but the most glaring of these problems is the fact that the bible's authors do not so much as breathe a whisper about it, and so it's almost a moot point.

While we're on this, though, when exactly does a child become capable of understanding their sinfulness, their need for God, and thus become accountable? Ten? Twelve? Thirteen? What if that child has a learning disability, do they get an extension? When, exactly, does one cross the line from unaccountable to accountable? And what if someone is *never* really able to grasp the message that so many call the gospel? Are they then forever unaccountable? It seems that such an important issue shouldn't be mired in so much subjectivity. I mean, if we are talking about burning in hell forever, you would think the instructions would be a little bit clearer.

If it is true, though, and a child cannot go to hell if they're not able to rightly make a conscious "decision for Jesus," it would seem that seeing to it they suffer a traumatic brain injury before reaching their early teens would be the easiest way of ensuring they make it to heaven. Even more disturbingly, going the way of a woman like Andrea Yates, who drowned her five children in the name of keeping them from going to hell for eternity, would actually be a moral choice within the framework of this worldview. Now, I know that is a sick and disgusting thought, and I apologize for even bringing it up, but this idea has actually been used by Christian apologists to gloss over some of the more disturbing Old Testament accounts of God ordering the slaughter of children.

MERCIFUL INFANTICIDE?

The following quotes come from two different, but similar, popular Christian apologetics websites that pride themselves on providing Christians with easy answers to hard questions. These particular quotes are attempts at answering the question of why God commanded the Israelites to wipe out whole people groups, including the children:

> ...the death of a child might be a very merciful thing because had the child grown up in the sin of the Amorite culture, it would surely have suffered the eternal wrath of God. If the "age of accountability" notion is correct, then God delivered them into His hands; and it is possible that by this they were spared eternal damnation.[40]

And:

> ...most importantly, God may have provided for the salvation for those infants who would not have otherwise attained salvation if they had lived into adulthood. We must remember that the Canaanites were a barbarous

---

[40] https://carm.org/why-did-israelites-destroy-cities-and-kill-all-people-inside

and evil culture. If those infants and children had lived into adulthood, it is very likely they would have turned into something similar to their parents and been condemned to hell after they died. If all infants and young children who die before an age of moral accountability go straight to heaven (as we believe), then those children are in a far better place than if God had allowed them to live and grow to maturity in a depraved culture.[41]

I don't think I really need to dig too deeply into why this is troublesome. I mean, it's literally the same rationale used by a woman whom everyone in their right mind considers to be out of hers, and whose actions are universally condemned. Somehow, though, it's ok when it's God who's doing it, and everyone and their brother will strain credulity in order to make sure he doesn't look bad. I mean, come on! But, if someone truly believes that a child may possibly go to hell, but are guaranteed heaven, so long as they die before a certain age, they would almost be forced to admit that there's some kind of sick wisdom in the words of these apologists, and even in the actions of a woman like Andrea Yates.

Just think about this, the doctrine of original sin, the implications of which unavoidably condemn infants and children to hell, is likely what inspired the doctrine of the age of accountability. We were understandably troubled by the child-condemning words of men like Edwards, Hildersham, and John Calvin, who claimed that there were "babies a span long in hell," and so sought to remove this stumbling block, and came up with a view in which children weren't culpable until they could actually understand the difference between morality and immorality. This was a move on our part to do away with the uglier implications of what has become core Christian doctrine, but it actually opened the door for even more vile thoughts to be had. It actually gave us a way justifying exterminations of whole people groups, including children, because, in this view, those children went straight to heaven, whereas, were we working within a framework that took original sin seriously, those same children would have gone straight to hell. So, vile, then, are the implications of the doctrine of original sin, that they necessitated a "kinder" alternative, in which infanticide, or the killing of children, actually appears as moral.

When I looked into the eyes of my first child, I began to experience extreme cognitive dissonance concerning this doctrine. How could one so pure and innocent also be, according to the Westminster Confession, "utterly indisposed, disabled, and made opposite to all good, and wholly inclined to all evil," and therefore "bound over to the wrath of God, and

---

[41] https://www.gotquestions.org/Old-Testament-violence.html

curse of the law, and so made subject to death, with all miseries spiritual, temporal, and eternal?" Such beliefs are easy to hold from a distance, but not so much when you're holding your newborn son or daughter. And so, I suppose the idea of an age of accountability is a comfort, because nobody wants to imagine babies in hell. I think the fact that we did come up with the idea shows that our moral scruples are superior to the "god" of original sin's, but the implications of this doctrine are as problematic as those for which we're looking for a solution.

The other problem here is that most who believe in an age of accountability also hold to some version of original sin, and as far as I can tell, these ideas are in complete disharmony with one another. Original sin, teaches that humans are born guilty of the first transgression, defiled by it, and worthy of its punishment. It is not because of anything they will grow to do on their own that they're in this state, but because of the actions of another. The age of accountability idea cannot be harmonized with this, since original sin teaches that it is our natures that make us the object of God's wrath, not the choices that we make. Personal accountability and the ability to choose between good and evil shouldn't even figure into the equation if God's justice is offended by who we are, as opposed to what we will come to do. If God *must* judge sinners precisely because they are born sinners, and for no other reason, then these born-sinners must be hell-worthy from their earliest moments, regardless of cognizance, or the ability to decipher right from wrong. One cannot rightly be said to have been born in sin, and yet to only become a sinner once they are able to understand what sin is. No, you're either born a sinner, or you become one, but we can't have it both ways. And if certain Christians are correct, and it is the nature of humanity that God hates, a child who dies prior to understanding, and therefore being "accountable," would have to be on a collision course with divine wrath.

Interestingly, the apologetics sites quoted from above, who both stated it was merciful for God to order the murder of children since the age of accountability would ensure they made it to heaven, both say in their statements of faith that they see man as being utterly corrupted due to the sin of Adam and Eve. If God must judge sin, and we are all born over our heads in the stuff, how in the world can it matter if we've reached an age of moral accountability or not? These two ideas are absolutely incongruent, and one must make up one's mind whether they believe children are born damnable, or if they become that way through their own actions. If we go for what's behind door number two, the doctrines of total depravity and original sin begin to unravel, but if we go with door number one, we are forced to confess belief in a god who punishes children because of something done to them, as opposed to something done by them. Children would be liable to hellfire and judgment in this "God's" universe, not because they chose evil, but because evil was chosen for them. I think that the thoughtful Christian sees the inherent problem here, and so grabs on to the idea of an age of accountability, simply because, even if it makes nonsense of your statement of faith, it at least doesn't force you to confess belief in a God who engages in victim-blaming, even if killing them to ensure their salvation remains within the realm of possibilities.

Honestly, while I think the age of accountability idea shows that we're trying, and that we have our wits about us a bit more than some of our theological forefathers did, I just don't think one can claim a belief in both it, and original sin at the same time. If a person is going to believe in original sin, they must, in order to be consistent, affirm that infants, and even developing fetuses, are totally depraved and deserving of hell. There's no getting around things by inserting an age of accountability. There is simply no way to embrace the Augustinian concept of original sin, without confessing that babies deserve damnation.

Consider this resolution by the Dutch Reformed Church at the Council of Dort on the subject:

> Such as man was after the fall, such children did he beget,-corruption by the righteous judgment of God being derived from Adam to his posterity-not by imitation, but by the propagation of a vicious nature. Wherefore, all men are conceived in sin, and are *born the children of wrath, unfit for every good connected with salvation, prone to evil, dead in sins, and the servants of sin*; and without the Holy Spirit's regenerating them, they neither will nor can return to God, amend their depraved nature, nor dispose themselves for its amendment. (Italics mine)[42]

In a critique of this resolution, Aylette Raines, wrote more than a century ago:

> ...if they will be consistent, [they] must also hold the doctrine of infant damnation! The council at Dort declares that we "are born the children of wrath;" and Calvin says that original corruption only makes us worthy of damnation; and that, in consequence of this corruption, we stand convicted before God! Infants, then, stand convicted before God, and are worthy of damnation! Reader, you must-yes, we say, you must either reject total hereditary depravity, or else go the

---

[42] The Canons of Dort can be read here: https://carm.org/canons-of-dort

whole length of the doctrine, premises and consequences, with Calvin and the council at Dort.[43]

The author goes on to, in a snarky 19th century fashion, rework Jesus' famous words, "Suffer the little children to come unto me, and forbid them not, for of such is the Kingdom of Heaven," to read: "Suffer the little 'totally depraved' 'children of wrath' and heirs of 'damnation,' to come unto me, and forbid them not, for of such is the kingdom of heaven."

He continues:

> That is, the inhabitants of the kingdom of heaven are totally depraved! And are children of wrath! We rather think that our Lord intended to teach infantile innocence in this verse! [44]

If one embraces Original Sin and Total Depravity, and is to remain logically consistent, they must, as Raines suggests, admit to serving a God who, at any given moment, is inflicting misery upon the souls of infants. Now, there's no rule saying they need to be logically consistent, and many aren't, but if they wish to be so, then there's no real way around this problem. God would be the judge, not simply of the original sinners, but of those affected by their sins. It would not just be the offenders who were made to suffer, but those they offended. After all, no child put in a request to be conceived in a sinful state, and if things actually work this way, God would be like Mike's father, who blames an innocent child for an injustice they suffered, which was actually more the fault of the father than his child. It would be like a judge sentencing to prison, not only a rapist, but also his victims; like locking the abuser and the abused in the same cell, and somehow mustering up the gall to call it justice.

Jesus, on the other hand, seemed to reserve judgment for those who would speak to children this way.

VICTIM-BLAMING

How is it just for a victim to be punished with the same punishment as the perpetrator? The "fall," after all, is not something anyone asked for. It is reckoned as being something invited by one of our number, sure, and while we certainly may have made the same mistake had we been there,

---

[43] Aylette Raines, *A Refutation of the Doctrine of Total Hereditary Depravity* (Dayton : Van Cleve & Comly, 1833.)

[44] Aylette Raines, A Refutation of the Doctrine of Total Hereditary Depravity (Dayton : Van Cleve & Comly, 1833.)

the fact is that we *did not* and we *were not*. Sin, in the context of the original sin argument, is something that happened *to* us, not *because of* us. Yes, we now must deal with the fallout and the aftermath, but the original fault does not lie with us. At the end of the day, sin, whatever it is, is the victimizer, and we its victims. And if God really created the world in a way where things could go awry like this, it would actually be his fault, not ours. As Bazan sings, "you, my Lord, can take the blame."

St. Athanasius wrote in the 4th century:

> Was He [God] to let corruption and death have their way with them? In that case, what was the use of having made them in the beginning? Surely it would have been better never to have been created at all than, having been created, to be neglected and perish; and, besides that, such indifference to the ruin of His own work before His very eyes would argue not goodness in God but limitation, and that far more than if he had never created men at all. It was impossible, therefore, that God should leave man to be carried off by corruption, because it would be unfitting and unworthy of Himself.[45]

There were those in the early church, like Athanasius, with a very different view of sin than we have today, and therefore very different views of how God responded to it. Sin was more than just the transgressing of a law to Athanasius, as he states in the next paragraph:

> Had it been a case of a trespass only, and not of a subsequent corruption, repentance would have been well enough... [46]

What Athanasius saw was that had the "original sin" been nothing more than a case of rule-breaking, God could have simply called Adam, and those born after him, to repent. The problem, according to Athanasius, was much deeper, though. There had been a literal corruption that had taken place, leading humanity into deviant behavior, in addition to causing them to literally, physically die. Athanasius sees the answer as lying in the incarnation, and vicarious humanity of Jesus, whose death essentially becomes Adam's, and whose resurrection becomes the recapitulation of humanity.

Now, I'm neither agreeing nor disagreeing with Athanasius, but just want to draw our attention to the sense of injustice he perceived in the idea that God would count us guilty of sin without stepping in to help. He saw *humanity*, not God, as the true victim of sin, making it incumbent on God to save us from it. Had God simply watched sin run rampant and destroy

---

[45] Athanasius, *On the Incarnation of the Word of God* (London, 1944.)
[46] Athanasius, On the Incarnation of the Word of God (London, 1944.)

us, it would argue for limitation in his nature, not goodness. He goes as far as to say that it would have been better to have never been created at all than to find ourselves in such a state, and that for God to not act, upon seeing our misery, would speak against his goodness. In other words, God would be unjust were he to allow corruption to swallow us up, since it was he who created us, and therefore he, who was responsible for us.

Imagine then, how incensed one like Athanasius would be at the idea of God not only allowing sin and corruption to victimize creation, but then purposefully distancing himself from, and punishing for an eternity, sin's victims, including babies! If, in the mind of Athanasius, God allowing corruption to flourish unchecked equaled limitation and evil, how much more, then, would victim-blaming, and victim-damning? It would certainly have been better had God never created us in the first place than for us to find ourselves in such a state.

SOUR GRAPES AND FORBIDDEN FRUIT

Back to the idea of divine just now. I want to ask-is there any biblical basis for this notion that guilt can somehow be transferred from person to person, from one generation to the next, and that humans inherit the sinful disposition of other humans? Or is this an idea so warped that even Old Testament prophets addressed it, and were careful to distance themselves and their God from? Let's see:

> 1 The word of the Lord came to me: 2 "What do you people mean by quoting this proverb about the land of Israel: *'The parents eat sour grapes, and the children's teeth are set on edge'*? 3 "As surely as I live, declares the Sovereign Lord, you will no longer quote this proverb in Israel. 4 *For everyone belongs to me, the parent as well as the child—both alike belong to me. The one who sins is the one who will die.*

> -Ezekiel 18:1-4, NRSV (Italics mine)

Israel was apparently in the habit of quoting a certain proverb which Ezekiel saw as maligning the character of God. The idea behind it was that a child could, or must, pay for the sins of its parent. In his critique of this way of thinking, Ezekiel stated quite clearly that the sins of one do not transfer to another. Individuals are accountable for their *individual* actions, not anyone else's. He makes it clear that God is not in the business of putting the taste of sour grapes eaten by a parent into the mouths of their children, meaning that God does *not* hold one generation accountable for the mistakes another has made.

It is actually thought by some that Ezekiel is correcting and annulling a principle set forth in Torah, stating that God, in his mercy, would punish only up to 3-4 generations of children for the sins of a parent. We find this in Exodus 34:6-7, where we're told that God is:

> 6 "...merciful and gracious, slow to anger, and abounding in steadfast love and faithfulness, keeping steadfast love for the thousandth generation, forgiving iniquity and transgression and sin, yet *by no means clearing the guilty, but visiting the iniquity of the parents upon the children and the children's children, to the third and fourth generation.*"

> -Exodus 34:6-7, NRSV (Italics mine)

This is a bit different from what we're told in Exodus 20:5, and Deuteronomy 5:9, both of which say essentially the same thing about the 3-4 generations, but contain the very important, and differentiating line: "of those who reject me." In these instances, it isn't just that God is holding 3-4 generations accountable for their parent's actions, but that it is specifically those who continue to walk and live as their parents, in their rejection of God. All of this is intended to appear as merciful, as Exodus 34 indicates, since it suggests that punishment of children for parent's sins will not continue indefinitely, as was thought to be the case with the priest Eli, whose house was said to be cursed forever, without any 3-4 generation, or "those who reject me" caveats. In his mercy, God was said to only punish a small number of a person's descendants for their sins, and even then, it was only if they continued to reject him.

According to the Talmud, however, when Ezekiel makes his claim that God will not allow children's teeth to be set on edge because of the grapes their parents eat, he is actually annulling Moses' words about God holding subsequent generations responsible for parental sins:

> ..."Moses made four decrees upon Israel which four prophets came and canceled...Moses said: "He visits the iniquity of the fathers on the children." Ezekiel came and canceled this: "The one who sins will die.""[47]

So, let's just break this down for a second. Even if we go back to the harshest "sour grapes" sort of punishment ever said to have been doled out by God, in the case of Eli's house being cursed forever, the curse began with him, and his unwillingness to deal with the actions of his sons. It did not start in Eden, but with Eli. If he were already cursed by the actions of Adam and Eve, what more could he be cursed with? But moving on from there, we have a few updates given on how God handles

---

[47] B.T. Makkot (24a)

this matter, and it's no longer the case that he will curse an entire family line, regardless of how that family lives, but, mercifully, only up to 3-4 generations, and even then, only those who continue to walk as their parents. Then Ezekiel comes along and simply says "Nope, God doesn't do things that way at all!"

So, are we really to believe, then, that a God who distinguishes himself as one who, in his mercy, will not allow punishment of children for parent's crimes to continue indefinitely, and who is later said to not punish children for parent's crimes at all, is holding the entire planet guilty for the sins of Adam and Eve? If God won't behave like this on the micro level, are we really to believe that he does on the macro? Is he really going to have the whole scheme of sin and salvation resemble something that he has specifically distanced himself from?

Are we really to understand God as condemning infants for sins committed by the "first human," when, even if we were living under the Torah, the 3-4 generation statute of limitations would have already run out? Are we to believe that, while we're innocent of things done by our parents, just decades ago, we are *guilty* of Adam's forbidden-fruit faux-pas, that occurred God knows how long ago? Are the sour grapes plucked from Eden's vines setting our teeth on edge too? Does God see us as guilty and flawed in our genetic makeup, all because of someone else's crimes?

This just isn't consistent with what we read of God in scripture. Even when we look at the Genesis story itself, nowhere does God indicate to Adam and Eve that billions upon billions of people born after them are going to be born in a sinful state, and bound over to the wrath of God because of their "sour grape" eating. Peter Enns, an Old Testament scholar, writes:

> All three parties [Adam, Even, and the serpent] are cursed by God...and those curses have lasting consequences for the human drama.
>
> Fair enough, but note the consequences for Adam. From now on (1) growing food will be hard work, and (2) death will be a fact of life.
>
> Note what is not said: "And a third thing, Adam. From now on all humanity will be stained by your act, born in a hopeless and helpless state of sin, thus earning my

displeasure and making them all objects of my wrath." If Genesis did say that, it would clear up a lot.[48]

What Enns says here is not something to be rushed past. At the very moment "original sin" is thought to have become...original, God says nothing of it. Not a word is breathed about humanity, as a whole, becoming infected by a disease they'll never be able to overcome, but will constantly be being overcome by. Nor is there even a whisper of an incurred wrath that all subsequent generations will be heirs of. On the contrary, the three parties involved incurred individual curses: snakes are going to crawl, pregnancy and childbirth are going to hurt, and work is going to be difficult. No total depravity, no universal sin, no inheriting of the wrath and displeasure of God. We simply have three characters, in a story, who are all three held accountable for their specific actions. It is nowhere insinuated that anyone is being blamed for the actions of anyone else, but rather quite the opposite

Nahum Sarna, a Jewish scholar, has written:

> The Garden of Eden incident is thus a landmark in the development of the understanding of the nature of man, his predicament and destiny. Man is a free moral agent and this freedom magnifies immeasurably his responsibility for his actions. Notice how each of the participants in the sin was individually punished. Freedom and responsibility are burdens so great for man to bear that he is in vital need of discipline...man is free to disregard the moral law, should he wish to, though he must be prepared to suffer the consequences. In short, we are being told by the Garden of Eden story that evil is a product of human behavior, not a principle inherent in the cosmos.[49]

In other words, what we learn from Adam, Eve, and the serpent, is that humanity has moral autonomy, and is able to choose to disregard the good if that's what they want to do. However, they must be prepared to face the fact that actions have consequences, and we will each be the individual recipients of the consequences for our individual actions, as shown in the story. Evil is not "inherent in the cosmos," or some force by which we are possessed, born into, and helpless to resist, as is the case in much pagan myth, but a choice. No one is born with that choice having

---

[48] http://www.patheos.com/blogs/peterenns/2013/02/5-old-testament-reasons-to-rethink-original-sin/

[49] Nahum Sarna, *Understanding Genesis* (New York, Jewish Theological Seminary of America [1966])

been made for them, but must choose for themselves if that's the way they desire to live.

Put simply, if what Sarna says here is correct, we've understood the implications of the story, precisely...backwards. God does not judge one person for anyone else's actions, but the consequences that come to the individual is all the punishment there is. Additionally, God does not see to it that all subsequent humans inherit a genetic bent towards evil, but it remains a choice one has the ability to make, not one that's been made for them, regardless of how they live. The Garden of Eden story does not alleviate the human of the responsibility of choice, replacing it instead with one made for them by Adam, but reinforces the power of choice and individual autonomy. Sure, individual choices can bleed outward, and have corporate implications, but that isn't because God is punishing all for the sin of one. And don't get me wrong, the corporate consequences of human sin *is* a massive deal, and I'm in no way minimizing that. In fact, that's one of the reasons it's a bad thing. My point here, though, is simply to say that, in the creation story, it is not a magical, cosmic, universal choice made by one for all that is being highlighted.

ADAM AFTER THE FALL

How we can read the Eden story, and come away with the idea that God holds all humans guilty for the sin of Adam, and that all subsequent generations are damned because of it, is beyond me. One might argue that it is only in the New Testament that this is revealed to us, but if it were going to be laid out anywhere, it seems like right after it happened would have been a good place to do it. But alas, it is absent. Additionally, after the "fall," Adam almost disappears from the Old Testament completely, and the subsequent sins of humanity, beginning with Cain's, and extending all the way through to the actions of Israel condemned by the prophets, are never connected to "original sin" or to Adam. Israel's constant and continual breaking of covenant with God is always laid squarely at their feet, never at someone else's, as are the consequences they incur. Nowhere, anywhere, in the whole of the Old Testament, is anyone said to be being punished for the actions of Adam. As Ezekiel stated oh so plainly, "The one who sins is the one who will die." (Ezek 18:4, NRSV)

So what of the idea that the New Testament is where we are introduced to the idea of original sin? Well, for starters, Jesus' own ancestry is traced back to Adam in Luke 3, and while it is Joseph's line that is being traced, logic would have us reason that Mary's ancestry would have traced back to Adam as well. Yet, are we to believe that Jesus was born guilty of, or tainted by, original sin? Some might argue that, since Jesus was conceived by the Spirit, no such nature or condemnation would have been inherited by him. Yet, does this not conflict with the writer of Hebrews' assertion that Jesus was, "like his brothers and sisters in every respect, so that he might be a merciful and faithful high priest"? (Heb 2:17) If he was made like us in *every* respect, would this not have entailed being the heir of Adam's guilt, and vile, corrupt nature? Yet which of us is ready to confess such things of Jesus? Any takers? Anyone?

This concept is, in point of fact, as utterly absent from the New Testament as it is from the Old. In the writings of Paul, Adam *does* emerge as a key player in the history of humanity, however. Even then, though, the standard, Western interpretation of Paul's approach to Adam is not necessarily the gold standard, nor is it even necessarily representative of Paul's intent. Again, Peter Enns writes:

> Paul's understanding of Adam's role in the human drama has had a very influential interpreter, at least for Western Christianity-Augustine (354-430)...in its bare outlines, Augustine understood that in Adam and Eve's transgression, the state of humanity was transformed. From then on, the depraved and guilty nature of the first couple was transmitted through sexual union to their offspring and consequently to all humanity. Augustine even goes so far as to say that all of humanity was present in the some sense in Adam's transgression, and so all humanity shares in Adam's guilt. [50]

As Enns points out, it is *not* from the Garden of Eden story that we find the idea of inherited sin and guilt before God, but rather in Augustine's interpretation of Paul's use of the story to speak to the problems of sin and death, and Christ as the solution. Paul does, indeed, speak of Adam as a literal person, and he does, indeed, also see Adam as the source of these problems. What is glaringly absent, though, is any evidence that Paul understood God as holding all humans guilty for his actions. Rather, in Romans 5 and 1 Corinthians 15, Paul uses Adam to explain how it is that humans became enslaved to sinful behaviors and to physical death. He did not, however, have anything to say about humans becoming universally depraved to the point that God would sooner condemn an infant to hell than spend eternity in its offensive presence.

Enns, in his book, *The Evolution of Adam*, is making the case for a non-literal Adam, but one need not even make that jump in order to agree with his comments on Paul's theological use of Adam. He continues:

---

[50] Peter Enns, *The Evolution of Adam: What the Bible Does and Doesn't Say About Human Origins* (Grand Rapids, MI: Brazos Press, ©2012.)

A literal Adam may not be the first man and cause of sin and death, as Paul understood it, but what remain of Paul's theology are three core elements of the gospel:

The universal and self-evident problem of death

The universal and self-evident problem of sin

The historical event of the death and resurrection of Christ

These three remain; what is lost is Paul's *culturally assumed* explanation for what a *primordial* man had to do with *causing* the reign of death and sin in the world. Paul's understanding of Adam as the cause reflects his time and place. Although Paul interprets this story in his own distinct way and for his own distinct purposes, the Israelite tradition handed to him still provides the theological vocabulary by which he can express his unique theology. There is no hint of modern arrogance (or heresy) whatsoever in a modern reader's making that observation.[51]

Perhaps even more importantly, Enns writes:

Israel's story, including Adam, is now to be read in light of its climax in the death and resurrection of Christ. In other words, Paul's understanding of Adam is shaped by Jesus, not the other way around.[52]

Approaching the issue from this perspective is, I think, the healthiest way of doing so. Firstly, the Adam of Paul is a theological device, intended to explain the origins of sin and death, though he undoubtedly saw him as an actual historical figure. What is most important, though, isn't Adam's actual historicity, but what Paul uses Adam to address: the problems of sin and death, and their solution in the resurrection of Jesus from the dead. Secondly, we also must understand that, for Paul, the whole of the Old Testament has its climax in Jesus, and it is never Jesus who is understood by Paul in the context of Adam, but Adam who is always understood, and sometimes re-understood, in the context of Jesus. In light of this, Enns concludes:

...[We] can still point to Christ, the Alpha and Omega, the one whom Christians confess was from the

---

[51] Ibid.

[52] Peter Enns, *The Evolution of Adam: What the Bible Does and Doesn't Say About Human Origins*, (Grand Rapids, MI : Brazos Press, ©2012.)

foundation of the world-before Adam, before hominids. Even if we cannot point to Adam as Paul does, we can, with Paul, begin with Christ and allow that reality to continue to reorient our thinking as well.[53]

To sum it up, Paul uses Adam for very specific theological reasons. He has observed, as have all thinking men and women throughout history, the very real problems of sin and death, and used, and even repurposed, images from his own culture to address their origins. More importantly, though, he understood Jesus to be before them all, and so never preached an Adam-centric Gospel, but a Jesus-centric Gospel. Even the one not embracing Adam as a historical figure can, as Enns suggests, begin with Christ, and address any problems that follow in light of him.

Now that's all well and good, and in fact, quite beautiful. What I actually want you to see is here, though, that the idea of inherited guilt and defilement before God is missing, even from Paul. Paul saw Adam as the one who introduced sin and death to the human experience, but humans aren't said to die because Adam sinned. Rather, in Pauline thought, humans die because we all continue the family tradition of sinning. For Paul, Adam started the mess we find ourselves in, but he did not make us damnable from conception. It is only a specific interpretation of Paul by later Christians that say these things.

Now, think back to Augustine's claims about himself as being guilty of sin from infancy. He literally interprets even his most basic instinct to cry for his mother's breast in order to nurse, as a form of sinful selfishness, for which he deserved to be rebuked. That is like faulting sea turtles for instinctively crawling towards the brightest light in the sky, and thus making their way to the ocean, or upbraiding birds for migrating to warmer climates during the winter months! A child's cry is not a sinful action, but one of the most natural, normal, and even healthy things in the world. Imagine, though, believing that even this most innocent, most instinctive and natural thing about you was evil, and deserving of divine rebuke! How much more would every other one of your actions, desires, or habits be more so! While utterly brilliant, Augustine was also a man with a very warped sense of what humanity was, as well as of who humanity's God was. And, sadly, his thoughts on this matter became the salt that created the thirst which necessitated the "god" of modern, Western Christianity.

As we covered in the last couple of chapters, "gods" are often projections of our idealized selves, meaning that they represent our ideals of what perfection is. For someone like Augustine, who came to faith in Christ after having lived quite the rowdy, and debaucherous lifestyle, the god-

---

[53] Ibid.

concept he overlaid onto the face of God, was one that looked like the opposite of everything he once was. His "god" then became one whose definition of sin was very narrow, and very specific: "Sin is an utterance, a deed, or a desire contrary to the eternal law." While there might be a little bit of play and flexibility in his definition of it, again, it is going to be his own past and history that informs his understanding of "eternal law," and what a violation of it would be.

When we imagine our "gods" as our idealized selves, at first they appear as our saviors. They are what we aren't, but they afford us the opportunity to escape what we are, and to attain to what *they* are. These savior figures, however, soon become our tormentors, for once they become externalized, and now observe of us from above, the perfection we imbued them with, and imagined them as possessing, seems to hover over us disapprovingly, constantly reinforcing things about us we already suspect to be true. We are not good enough, holy enough, or righteous enough. We are disapproved of and despised. When this happens, and we imagine a cosmically significant observer, who sees us as less than and sinful, it affects us on a very deep, deep level.

Leonard Mlodinow, in his book, *Subliminal: How Your Unconscious Mind Rules Your Behavior,* tells of several studies conducted which, to me, speak volumes to how a god-concept that observes evil in us, and expects behaviors matching it, literally changes us into the thing we're seeking to be saved from. Such god-concepts actually become the very things that empower and promote the evil behavior that they also condemn us for.

He writes:

> One of the most revealing studies of human nonverbal communication was performed using an animal with which humans rarely share their homes, at least not intentionally: the rat. In that study, students in an experimental psychology class were each given five of those creatures, a T-shaped maze, and a seemingly simple assignment. One arm of the T was colored white, the other gray. Each rat's job was to learn to run to the gray side, at which time it would be rewarded with food. The students' job was to give each rat ten chances each day to learn that the gray side of the maze was the one that led to food and to objectively record each rat's learning progress, if any. But it was actually the students, not the rats, who were the guinea pigs in this experiment. The students were informed that through careful breeding it was possible to create strains of maze-genius and maze-dummy rats. Half the students were told that their rats were the Vasco da Gamas of

maze explorers, while the other half were told that theirs had been bred to have no sense of direction at all. In reality, no such selective breeding had been performed, and the animals were effectively interchangeable, except perhaps to their mothers. The real point of the experiment was to compare the results obtained by the two distinct groups of *humans*, to see if their expectations would bias the results achieved by their rats.[54]

While one would think it silly to believe that the expectations of observing humans could actually affect a rat's ability to find food, the truth is actually quite befuddling:

The researchers found that the rats the students thought were brilliant performed significantly better than the rats believed to be on the dumb side. [55]

But why did it work this way?

The researchers then asked each student to describe his or her behavior toward the rats, and an analysis showed differences in the manner in which students in each group related to the animals. For example, judging from their reports, those who believed their rats to be high achievers handled them more and were gentler, thereby communicating their attitude...They essentially repeated the experiment but added an admonishment to the students that a key part of their task was to treat each rat as they would if they had no prior knowledge about its breeding. Differences in handling, they were warned, could skew the results and, by implication, their grade. Despite these caveats, the researchers also found superior performance among the rats whose handlers expected it. The students attempted to act impartially, but they couldn't. They unconsciously delivered cues, based on their expectations, and the rats responded.[56]

These rats, all of them equal in their abilities and breeding, responded to the expectations of their observers. If they were expected to perform poorly, the unconscious cues of their observers moved them to underachieve and perform poorly, while those expected to perform

---

[54] Leonard Mlodinow, *Subliminal: How Your Unconscious Mind Rules Your Behavior* (New York : Pantheon Books, ©2012.)
[55] Ibid.
[56] Ibid.

optimally were likewise moved to do so by their observer's expectations. Mlodinow goes on to tell of a similar experiment that was conducted with children, though, for obvious, ethical reasons, didn't involve mazes with food at the end. Relative to the experiment, though, the results were nearly identical, showing that unconscious expectations don't only affect animals, but humans as well.

With this in mind, I wonder what we're doing to our children and to one another when we observe them through the lens of *original sin*? How does it affect society when we look upon it as a moral cesspool, inhabited by degenerates who aren't capable of doing anything good, moral or loving? Could it be that the very "sins" we loathe are things we, on some level, encourage, if not create, in the lives of those we condemn?

Even if we aren't actively condemning anyone, but simply viewing them, on an unconscious level, as totally depraved, we will be constantly giving off signals and cues that communicate to them that there's something wrong with them. Honestly think about what it does to a child's mind to have it suggested to them, while they're still in diapers, that they need to be saved from a God who will otherwise burn them forever. If rats are affected by an observer's belief that they are genetically inferior, how must it affect a child when they're observed as having been, as Dylan sang, "born already ruined," and "only holden worthy of damnation," as Calvin mused?

Beyond that, what are we doing to ourselves, our children, and our world, when we release these ideas into the atmosphere in "aerosol form," as god-concepts? What was once a long-dead theologian's conclusions about human nature, has since come uncoupled from the man himself, and become the very image we have in mind when we say "god." It now, like a virus, is carried by all who embrace this Western model of Christianity, whereas before, one would have had to have gone "into the lab," so to speak, where the virus itself was being engineered in order to catch it, it is now a part of mainstream thought, even among the irreligious, and most are infected without even knowing it.

Culture has become so saturated by these once strictly theological concepts, that nearly everyone you'll ever meet will go through life feeling unclean, unworthy, unloved, and all of the other "uns" that destroy the human spirit. Among the religious, the general feeling is that there is a massive, disapproving "eye in the sky," that watches their every move, and shakes its head in disgust far more often than it smiles approvingly. Among the irreligious, the "eye in the sky" might simply be the collective opinions of society, but still, most will carry around this sense of being disapproved of. And, just like the rats in the experiment, these unseen, but deeply felt expectations, lead to all manner of dysfunctions and maladies, and ultimately creates a thirst, which necessitates a form of salvation that looks nothing like what the person of Jesus Christ offers us.

Once upon a time I found the sight of children responding to an altar call for salvation beautiful. I would marvel at their innocent heart's response to the "gospel" message, until it dawned on me what needed to be suggested to a child in order for them to respond: they weren't, in fact, innocent at all, but were so bad that God would have to punish them forever if they did not respond to the "good news." Many children who grow up in homes where such beliefs are regularly reinforced, struggle their whole lives with issues of identity, as well as crippling guilt and shame for simply being human. They were, after all, told that just being born was enough of a crime to warrant hell, so God only knows what awaits the pubescent teenager with access to the internet!

How can you ever be good enough for this God? What could you possibly ever do to please or make him happy? If you're born on his bad side before you've even had a chance to try, how easy must it be to *stay* on his bad side? Again, the question comes: How can you ever be good enough for this God, and what could you ever do to please or make him happy?

The answer that Protestant Christianity has offered for centuries has not been a very helpful one, as it answers both questions with a flat *nothing.* That's right, in this God's world, there is literally nothing you can do to please or make him happy. Jesus, in this type of thinking, is the only one capable of pleasing the Father. Our part is to believe on what Jesus has done, and God is said to offer us the good works and merits of Jesus as something of a "robe of righteousness," which really amounts to a cloaking device, that hides our sins from his sensitive eyes.

Now, I understand that this is a gross oversimplification of the doctrine of imputed righteousness, and I don't at all intend to launch into a deconstruction of it here. What I mean to point out though, is that, in many streams of Christianity, the doctrines of sin and salvation alike damn us as worthless and incapable of being pleasant to God. The idea of being saved from sin, far from communicating that God is somehow pleased with us, in the Protestant tradition anyways, only reaffirms his displeasure with us. After all, the only part of us he loves and adores is the part that looks like him. It's not us that he's pleased with, but the Jesus costume he's asked us to dress in whenever we're in his presence.

When you grow up hearing this over and over again, what gets communicated is that no matter what side of salvation you find yourself on, you'll still never be good enough. The figure whose observations matter to you the most, God, only sees you as dirty, worthless, and depraved. You, in yourself, are so warped, damaged and stained by original sin that he can't even look at you out of costume. Sure, we're told that at some point in the future, in the sweet by and by, all of this will be rectified, but for now, we're stuck as Jacob dressed like Esau. Just a few inches beneath our disguise, we're loathsome and unwanted, and any acceptance we think we feel is nothing more than an illusion.

Here's the bottom line of the message: *You're* not accepted, and *you* never will be. *Jesus* is, though, and as long as you're covered in his "scent" and dressed in his clothes, the Father will have to treat you like something you're not. George MacDonald, perturbed by this concept, writes that a truly converted soul would, "rather sink into the flames of hell than steal into heaven and skulk there under the shadow of an imputed righteousness." This idea that we're saved from our defective nature by being granted to appear before God as something we're not, while at first appealing to the heart that's been trounced and trampled by religion, eventually leaves you in the same place you were before believing it. As a "sinner" you were the unsalvageable scum of the earth, and as a "saint," you're the same. There's nothing about you that God loves, only the "him" that he sees in you. Again, it's an initially tempting idea, since it will at least let you feel some momentary relief from the guilt and shame that the church has so often heaped upon you. But once you really begin to ponder the concept, you quickly realize that, while perhaps "eternally" you're set, in the present moment, you're still so revolting to God that he has to dress you up in order to even look upon you.

In the case of the rats, it was the expectation of their observers that determined their behavior. They couldn't help but pick up on the unconscious cues and signals of those tasked with judging their performance. What happens to us, I wonder, when our God, whether real or imagined, is thought to observe us as so horrifically evil, that even as tiny infants, we deserve torture? What changes occur in us as a result of believing that the only figure whose opinion ultimately matters, sees us as so sickeningly scarred by sin, that salvation amounts to him providing us with a mask to keep our appearance from moving him to violence?

Well, what happens to us is that we begin to thirst, and a truly thirsty person will drink from almost any stream, regardless of how polluted or bacteria-laden it is. Likewise, the Augustinian thirst created in us by the doctrine of original sin has left us with the same restless soul the bishop of Hippo himself spoke of. We wander about in anguish, searching for something, anything, that can quench our thirst and give us rest, and because it is a direct response to this thirst, the modern Gospel seems to fit perfectly. And of course it does fit perfectly, but only because it was created in response to the thirst. That it answers it, or fits over it like a glove, is merely an illusion, as is the thirst itself. We don't need to have the "sour grapes" of Eden picked from our teeth, because we never ate them. God does not disapprove of us, and he certainly does not do so from the moment cells come together to form our bodies. That is a myth, a bald-faced lie, but a very convincing lie, nonetheless.

I know I've spoken in a very crude and crass way of a doctrine that has been written of and presented so eloquently elsewhere, but all of the flowery rhetoric of theologians can't erase the disapproving and disappointed scowl that beliefs like this paint on the face of the God we worship. No matter how technically you present it, what this belief leaves us with is a deity who looks upon and observes even the most innocent among us as horrible creatures that deserve to die and be punished eternally. This doctrine can only create in us an illegitimate thirst that gives birth to an illegitimate "god" as the solution.

I say no to this "god."

And it's not just because I've embraced some liberal brand of theology that I feel this way. It's because I'm convinced this is how Jesus felt. I think it's precisely teachings such as these that Jesus identified as stumbling blocks. I think it is precisely ideas like this, that teach our children that the most significant "observer" in their lives, sees them as little more than genetically inferior rats, predisposed to sin and loathed by God, that are the stumbling blocks that angered Jesus. These ideas rob our children of their innocence, keep them locked in states of fear and guilt, and turn them into maladjusted adults, who've never even learned to love themselves, let alone the world around them. They grow up hearing of "god," but the "god" they hear of does not, because he cannot, accept them as they are. Instead, he demands they make mental assent to certain truths, at which time he will provide them with a covering that will keep his pure and virgin eyes from having to look upon their true, disgusting nature.

Heartbreakingly, the most original of human sins, that is, the sin we're most likely to first engage in or be engaged by, is that of self-hatred, and it is all too often reinforced by religious teaching. Jesus called such teaching stumbling blocks, and condemned those who peddled them, but we've called them gospel, and embraced them as orthodox.

For thousands of years we've imagined *salvation* as being found in reacting to the Augustinian thirst by drinking from the fountain of the "gods," but perhaps it is actually found in our refusal to drink. Perhaps it is in realizing that we do not need to be saved in that manner, and so "drinking" in what we imagine salvation to be will only damn us further, that we are saved. Perhaps true salvation lies in an unwillingness to pursue the salvation offered in response to the Augustinian thirst, and perhaps until we realize we don't need saving in that way, there will be no salvation?

Are we perfect? *Heck* no. Are we born deserving to be roasted while gripped tightly in God's "tongs of wrath?" *Hell* no. Do we need to be rescued from some terrible patterns in our behavior? Of course! Do we need to be saved from the divine, juridical consequences incurred by the behavior of another? Come on now.

Surely, if there is a God who has the ability to speak to our deepest needs, it's not the one we've been discussing in this chapter. This "god," who accuses us of murder in the womb, can only make us into murderers. This one who claims to desire to transform us, but whose expectations deform us, cannot be our salvation.

So again, I say no to this "god."

But is there one worth considering saying "yes" to?

5 | JESUS DIED FOR NOTHING

"Nothingness lies coiled at the heart of being like a worm."
-Jean-Paul Sartre

"to open their eyes and turn them from darkness to light…"
-The Apostle Paul

"…the glad good news brought by the Gospel was the news of original sin."
-G.K. Chesterton

One accusation I have hurled at me continually, is that the message I preach negates the need for salvation. Since I don't emphasize concepts like hell, judgment and the wrath of God, and dismiss as tenuous the traditional understanding of total depravity and original sin, I'm often asked, "Are you saying that Jesus saves us from *nothing*?"

In the name of clearing the air and putting rumors to rest once and for all, I want to answer this question as plainly and as bluntly as possible. So here goes:

Yes, I do, in fact, believe that Jesus saves us from *nothing*.

Now, allow me to explain.

I'm about to ask you a question that is going to require all of your Sunday school knowledge.

Ready?

I want you to think back to the ingenious and innovative *flannelgraph*, the paper cut outs of bible characters, the animal crackers and apple juice, the bleary eyed, oh-so-enthusiastic teacher, the puppet shows, the songs, and all of their hand motions; I need you to call upon all of it!

Are you ready? Here goes:

On which day of creation was *darkness* created?

Think really, really hard. Think Genesis 1 and 2. Think "in the beginning."

Anything?

If you're coming up short, it's probably because there is no record in either of the biblical creation stories of darkness being *created*. In Genesis 1, the first of two creation accounts, we read of God's initial, creative command of "Let there be light." We're told of God creating the sun to rule the day, the moon to rule the night, as well as of the creation of "lesser lights" (stars) being made to fill the night sky. We have ancient cosmology at its finest, but no mention of the *creation* of darkness.

Now, this would seem to make perfect sense, as darkness is not an actual, substantial *something,* but rather *nothing.* It is not the presence of anything, but the lack of something, namely light. Darkness is not something that can be bottled up, projected, or measured, simply because it is not *anything.* Therefore, it would make sense to not see it spoken of as having been created, since, being *nothing,* it would not require a creation. That which lacks ontology, or being, needs no genesis.

What we actually read is that darkness was present before the process of creation began:

> 1 In the beginning *when God created* the heavens and
> the earth, 2 the earth was a formless void and *darkness*
> covered the face of the deep...
>
> -Genesis 1:1-2, NRSV (Italics mine)

As I said, darkness was present prior to any creative words being spoken. But then, that's not really a proper way to speak of darkness, now is it? To call darkness "present" would suggest that it were something, but as we've already mentioned, it isn't. It's nothing. It's nonexistence. Nonbeing. Lack. It requires no creation, because there is nothing to create.

In Isaiah 45, however, we read these words:

> 7 I *form light* and *create darkness*...
>
> -Isaiah 45:7, NRSV (Italics mine)

Now, allow me to admit upfront that my treatment of this passage is going to be wholly creative (no pun intended), as my treatment of the Genesis creation story has been as well, and I am in no way suggesting that this is how you properly exegete a text. That said, notice the writer's words that God *creates* darkness. While the account of darkness's creation is absent from the Genesis story, and while it seems like a rational omission since darkness is *nothing*, Isaiah tells us something else. He tells us that God forms light and *creates* darkness.

Now, remember, in Genesis 1, darkness was present prior to any creative act. Light is spoken into existence, but darkness was there prior to. And yet Isaiah tells us that darkness *was*, in fact, created, as surely as light was formed. Darkness exists prior to the creation of anything, as darkness is what you get when you have nothing; it's a lack of light or matter of any kind. However, when light is formed and pierces the nothingness, the nothingness itself begins to, in a sense, exist as a *something*. Don't get me wrong, darkness does not come to take on a substantial form, but the creation of light causes darkness to be contrastable with something else. Darkness has now gone from being nothing, to being the opposite of something, whereas prior to light's creation, darkness was non-existence. In "light" of light's existence, darkness begins to exist as a *concept*, even though it continues to lack any being or essence.

Perhaps the insertion of the words "and as a direct consequence," in the middle of Isaiah's proclamation, would help give some insight into what I'm trying to say here. This would cause the passage to read:

> *I form the light, <u>and as a direct consequence</u> create darkness...*

In other words, darkness continues to be a substance-less nothing, but it is no longer alone. The inexistence that is darkness has now become a part of existence, and so can be understood to be the opposite of that which exists. In this sense, it gains definition and *something-ness,* though, in reality, it remains *nothingness.* The entrance of light causes darkness to go from *nothing* to *something.* Until light breaks in, there was no way to define darkness, since it was all that there was, and all that there was, was nothing.

As Terry Pratchett writes in the novel, *Reaper Man:*

> Light thinks it travels faster than anything but it is wrong. No matter how fast light travels, it finds the darkness has always got there first, and is waiting for it. [57]

---

[57] Terry Pratchett, *Reaper Man* (London : Victor Gollancz, 1991.)

No matter how light comes into being, darkness will always have preceded it. But again, even speaking of darkness as something that can precede something else is an improper way of speaking of it. Darkness is not a thing that has an existence of its own, but only exists as a concept when in the presence of that which does exist. So, in every corner of the universe where light has yet to travel, darkness is present, but not as a substantial thing, or even really as a concept that could be understood. If one were an inhabitant of that particular part of the universe, darkness would still not even be definable, as there would be nothing to define it against. It is only the interaction of nothing (darkness) with something (light) that causes the nothing to become a something. Light makes darkness apparent, and in that way, grants it existence.

As human beings, we function in a very similar way.

The French philosopher, Jean-Paul Sartre, once wrote, "Nothingness lies coiled in the heart of being-like a worm."[58] If I'm reading Sartre right (and that's a big *if*), he is suggesting that nothingness, or non-being, is essential to the experience of being; that inherent in the experience of being a conscious *being*, is the experience of *not being* all other beings. Therefore, non-being, or nothingness, lies coiled at the heart of being.

How does this work, exactly?

Well, just imagine if you were unable to distinguish between yourself and others. Life could get really complicated, really fast. Essential, then, to the experience of being you, and all that it entails, is the experience of not being everyone else. You *must* be able to distinguish between yourself and others in order to function healthily in the world. Therefore, to truly know that you *are,* is also to know that you are *not*. You are you, but you are *only* you. You are not your mother, your father, your brothers, sisters, or the guy across the street. You are you, but this is not something you can be fully in touch with if you are not aware of what you are not. Nothingness, then, or what it is that you're not, always lies coiled at the heart of being, at the very center of our understanding of that which we are.

Now, this nothingness that stands between you and everything and everyone else in the world, is much like the darkness that predates the creation of light. It is always there, in the sense that I am always not you, and in the sense that you are always not me. This does not become apparent to the point of being an actual experience on non-being, however, until we encounter one another. My not-you-ness only comes to exist as a substantial thing when I experience you. And likewise, your not-me-ness only comes to exist when you encounter me. Again, like the

---

[58] Jean-Paul Sartre, *Being and Nothingness: An Essay on Phenomenological Ontology* (New York : Philosophical Library, [1956])

darkness, it is always "there," but it is not something that I actually notice until I encounter my lack of you-ness through an experience with you.

In my encounters and experiences with others, the them-ness that I lack begins to condense, congeal, and solidify, and that which is nothing quickly becomes something. Now, sometimes my lack of you-ness can be a cause for celebration. Maybe I don't want to be you, and the revelation that I'm not comes as a most welcomed discovery. However, we often find our encounters with others solidifying the darkness, or our lack of them-ness, into shame, jealousy, envy, remorse, anxiety, and a host of other emotions that can weigh quite heavily on the heart.

Consider how easy it is to feel content with a modest lifestyle until you are forced to interact with someone whose lifestyle isn't quite so modest. Before the encounter, you were not comparing yourself with this individual, and so weren't experiencing your lack of them-ness as a something. The entrance of "light" into the "darkness,", however, causes that coiled-like-a-worm nothingness to rear its ugly head, and take on physical qualities. As much as you try to simply be happy for the person, and assure yourself that what you have is more than enough, you can't help but feel exposed, vulnerable even, and as though there is a noticeably large, gaping hole in your being.

Or think of times in your life when your wallet was a bit on the empty side. While the lack of money is not the presence of anything, but quite literally a lack, walking through the shopping mall, and coming face to face with all of the things you cannot afford sure makes that nothing feel like something. Again, the problem is a literal *nothing*, but it soon solidifies and manifests itself when it becomes apparent to you. The nothing of an empty wallet or bank account can come into existence as depression, anxiety, or even as a strong motivation to work hard and succeed, but the fact remains that you began with nothing and ended up with something.

This is how "darkness," or *nothing*, is "created," and comes to exist as *something*. It never truly ceases to be *nothing*, but the presence of that which it is not gives it definition, and grants it existence.

What I want to suggest is that this sense that we lack something, that we've come unhitched from a source we are now separated from, and that there is something inherently wrong with us which we must rectify at all costs, is what God, in Jesus, seeks to save us from. So I here reaffirm the position I took at the start of this chapter, that Jesus saves us from nothing, but this *nothing* from which we are saved has become a cancerous *something,* that is destroying and tearing the world apart.

To illustrate, let me introduce you to *that* couple.

You know the couple I'm talking about, right? *That* couple?

The couple who always looks as though they stepped right off the cover of Healthy Living Magazine, and whose children are as well dressed, and well behaved as the mannequins in the window of GAP kids? You know the couple, right? They spend their days at the gym, while also managing to both be CEOs of major corporations, wherein they make more in a month than you make in twelve? Yeah, *that* couple. Their elementary school aged children are already studying law at Harvard, while also playing every sport known to man, as well as the cello. And despite their work and gym schedule, their parents somehow manage to drive them to every practice and game, while also maintaining a relationship so romantic, they make Jack and Rose from Titanic look like Spongebob and Squidward. Their children's birthday parties are catered and held at city hall, and their specially bred dog has better health insurance than you and your family.

That couple.

We all know them, and, sadly, we all hate them. We bond with our spouses by ripping them to shreds with our words, and take comfort in the knowledge that we're somehow different, or better. But why do we hate "this couple" so much? The answer might be a bit more complicated than I can cover in a few paragraphs, but put simply, we hate them because we're not them. And we rejoice in not being them precisely to keep ourselves from experiencing the heartbreak that grasping our not-them-ness would cause us. Our not-them-ness becomes painfully apparent whenever we're in their presence, and the nothing that separates us soon solidifies into the something of rivalry, hatred, and, sometimes, even violence.

The flipside, which very few ever take the time to consider, is that "*that* couple" may be just as jealous of your family and your lifestyle as you are of theirs. I mean, it typically takes an extreme over achiever to attain such mythical success in all areas of life, meaning that they're probably very well acquainted with the exhaustion and fatigue that accompanies overachievement. And, contrary to popular belief, romance doesn't typically thrive where high levels of stress are involved, and when no one ever sees or talks to each other. So, the Nicholas Sparks-esque romance you imagine they have is probably more fiction than fact. I could go on, but I think you get the point. They may very well look at your lifestyle, which is perhaps a bit more lax, and wish they could be more like you. This power couple might long to return to simpler days, before all of the stress and isolation, when they were just a simple family who loved and spent time with each other. But we who dwell on the outside, poisoned by a sense of lack, likely never take the time to consider this.

And so, a good majority of humans, all of us bringing one another's darkness, or nothing, into existence, secretly loathe one another. We feel exposed, vulnerable, and as though the gap we sense within us is visible to all. This is what leads us to destroy one another.

Now, in a "civilized" day and age like the one we presently occupy (there was some subtle sarcasm intended there), our nothingness-become-something-ness might manifest as jealousy, passive aggressive behavior, or something similarly benign in the big scheme of things. But you take this back a few hundred, or a few thousand years, and the something crawling out of humanity's collective nothing looks a whole lot more brutal. In fact, one does not need to time travel to discover this fact, but simply look at things on a macro level. When the *nothing* of nations and governments becomes a tangible *something*, it usually looks like war.

In the book of James we read:

> 1 Those conflicts and disputes among you, where do they come from? Do they not come from your cravings that are at war within you? 2 You want something and do not have it; so you commit murder. And you covet something and cannot obtain it; so you engage in disputes and conflicts...
>
> -James 4:1-2, NRSV (Italics mine)

In other words, an inward sense of lack leads to covetousness, and this felt void of separation, or of nothingness within, leads to conflicts, disputes, and murder. War within always leads to war without. Nothing becomes something, and that something is always deadly.

It seems to me that, perhaps, the writer of Genesis understood something of how this works when they wrote of humanity's sudden awareness of their nakedness:

> 8 They heard the sound of the Lord God walking in the garden at the time of the evening breeze, and the man and his wife hid themselves from the presence of the Lord God among the trees of the garden. 9 But the Lord God called to the man, and said to him, "Where are you?" 10 He said, "I heard the sound of you in the garden, and I was afraid, because I was naked; and I hid myself." 11 He said, "Who told you that you were naked? Have you eaten from the tree of which I commanded you not to eat?" 12 The man said, "The woman whom you gave to be with me, she gave me fruit from the tree, and I ate." 13 Then the Lord God said to the woman, "What

is this that you have done?" The woman said, "The serpent tricked me, and I ate."

-Genesis 3:8-13, NRSV (Italics mine)

Notice, first, Adam and Eve's realization that they were naked caused them to hide from God, and cover themselves in order to keep his eyes from viewing their more sensitive members. The thing is, though, according to the story, they were created naked. I can't imagine God had formerly needed to be accompanied by angels who held up little black squares to cover up the couple's naked forms. No, he created them naked, and was fine with them in that state. Their nudity was, a non-problem, a *nothing* in God's sight.

Interestingly, it was their attempt to fix the perceived problem by putting on clothing that actually became the problem. Adam and Eve's donning of clothing, though appearing to be an addition to their naked state and a solution, was actually a subtraction from the state in which they were created, and now necessitated a solution. The more they attempted to address the non-problem of their nakedness, the further they walked from their original design, and the more *nothing* became *something*.

The appearance of God in the story, the sound of his walking in the garden in "the cool of the day," instantly created a fear inside the man and woman, and they hid from his presence. When sought out, and asked why they were hiding, they confessed to fearing his presence because of their nakedness. Never before had God's nearness evoked such feelings. Never before had his presence exposed an absence in their lives. But now, suddenly, after having begun to operate in another form of knowledge, God became something else to them. He became an exalted version of their former selves; one who, perhaps, possessed everything they now felt they lacked, and so his sudden appearance gave definition to the darkness, or nothing, they now perceived in themselves. The non-problem of their nakedness suddenly became something that warranted hiding from God, as God had become someone, or something, altogether different in their minds.

God became to them what we've already spoken of in prior chapters. He became the idealized, perfect version of them, who now only reinforced the terrible suspicions they had about their state. He went from a loving Father and Creator to one who is keenly aware of the difference between good and evil, and who makes judgments of us based on this knowledge. Their nakedness, or original state, became an evil in their eyes, and therefore in the eyes of their "god" as well. Of course, this "god" is not the one who lovingly crafted and exhaled them into existence, but a larger, and ultimate version of themselves. What they've come to believe about themselves is what they now assume "god" believes about them. God becomes "god," or an idol crafted in their own image, who represents the ultimate example of everything they are not. Thus their new instinct to hide from him. His presence now brings their "darkness" into existence, making something out of nothing.

Interestingly, when confronted on whether or not they had eaten from the Tree of the Knowledge of Good and Evil, they respond by throwing one another under the bus: *The woman made me do it! The serpent made me do it!* And again we see how their attempt at a solution actually became a problem. Their newfound feelings of dread toward God ("god") led them to accuse, blame and go to war with one another, perhaps in an attempt to shift "god's" disapproving gaze from them momentarily, and onto something or someone else.

In the very next chapter of Genesis, we find, in symbolic language, how this sense of lack jumps from the micro to the macro, and how the resultant problem of blame and accusation turns deadly, in the story of Cain and Abel:

> 2 ...Now Abel was a keeper of sheep, and Cain a tiller of the ground. 3 In the course of time Cain brought to the Lord an offering of the fruit of the ground, 4 and Abel for his part brought of the firstlings of his flock, their fat portions. And the Lord had regard for Abel and his offering, 5 but for Cain and his offering he had no regard. So Cain was very angry, and his countenance fell. 6 The Lord said to Cain, "Why are you angry, and why has your countenance fallen? 7 If you do well, will you not be accepted? And if you do not do well, sin is lurking at the door; its desire is for you, but you must master it." 8 Cain said to his brother Abel, "Let us go out to the field." And when they were in the field, Cain rose up against his brother Abel, and killed him.
>
> -Genesis 4:2-8, NRSV (Italics mine)

Professor Christine Hayes interprets the Cain and Abel story somewhat differently, suggesting that it's not meant to be read as a case of God accepting one sacrifice over another, but of God approving of one way of life while rejecting another. She writes:

> The story of Cain and Abel has been cited as evidence of the tension between settled, civilized areas and the unsettled desert areas of the nomads in biblical culture. Abel, the keeper of sheep, represents the nomadic pastoralist while Cain, the tiller of the soil, represents settled urban life. When Yahweh prefers the offering of Abel, Cain is distressed and jealous to the point of murder. Yahweh's preference for the offering of Abel

valorizes the free life of the nomadic pastoralist over urban existence.[59]

Hayes posits that the story represents two different cultures seeking validation for their way of life. When one is preferred to the other, it doesn't lead to a change of heart on the part of the one rejected, but to feelings of jealousy and rage. Abel's "darkness" becomes apparent, and that which is nothing becomes something. In this instance, however, it doesn't simply manifest in finger pointing, but in fratricide. The yawning chasm "created" in Cain's soul through his comparison of himself to Abel, comes to exist in the form of hatred and murder.

In the aftermath, we're told that Cain is driven from his home and settles east of Eden with his wife, and in the course of time, builds the first city mentioned in the biblical narrative. Human civilization, then, according to the Genesis story, was founded by a man moved to murder his brother because of an inward sense of lack, rejection and separation. In the story, this trait apparently grows, until Cain's ancestor, Lamech, is recorded as calling for vengeance seven times stronger to come to his enemies than that which came to Cain's (Gen 4:).

In a purposely creative reading of this text, what I see occurring is a literal *nothing* (nakedness) becoming a terrible, terrible *something*. What humanity came to believe of themselves they projected onto God, rendering him an idol bearing their image. His presence no longer comforted or refreshed, but terrified them, and caused their sense of lack, or darkness, to come into being. This *something* evolves from coverings with which they hide their nakedness, to accusations against one another, and external conflict. The problem then jumps to another level when Cain's sense of lack leads him to murder, which leads to the founding of a world that functions in this same Cain-like manner. We have a world at war without, because we have a world at war within. The nothingness, that is merely our distinct *us-ness*, is constantly leading us into destructive places where we wage war, on both micro and macro levels, with those who remind us of our lack.

It is ultimately our understanding of God as the disapproving "eye in the sky," constantly judging our every move, that brings our darkness into existence. No matter where we go, or how deeply we isolate ourselves, the spectral presence of this "god" is always felt. And much like the rats observed as inferior, this imagined disapproval leads us to behave in ways we normally would not. We throw one another under the bus, constantly needing a scapegoat whose sin is "worse" than ours, which we can use to feel as though we are diverting "god's" attention from us to

---

[59] Christine Elizabeth Hayes, *Introduction to the Bible* (New Haven : Yale University Press, [2012])

them. Sometimes it looks like nothing more than accusation and the pointing of fingers, but other times it looks like death and murder. One thing is for sure, though, it *always* looks us against them.

For a contemporary example of how one's god-concept can exacerbate a sense of lack, leading to destruction, consider ISIS, or the Islamic State. This is a group of radical, religious zealots, who behead and crucify children, rape young girls, and leave a trail of blood and terror wherever they go. And this they do all in the name of their concept of "god." They no doubt behave this way to prove themselves his most zealous and devoted followers, but this zeal does nothing but prove how inadequate and impoverished they feel in his sight. The inadequacy they seek to do away with via their devotion, this *nothingness*, has sadly become the source of all sorts of hideous *somethings*.

To show just how, at the heart of their actions, is *nothing,* consider this illustration: Let's say that ISIS was able to devise a missile targeting system that would allow them to target and destroy all non-ISIS sympathizers. They turn it on, arm their weapons, and launch. The only problem is that they configured the targeting system backwards, and instead targeted *only* ISIS sympathizers. Within seconds of the launch, every person on the planet who harbored even the slightest bit of sympathy for the group is wiped out, and ISIS becomes nothing more than a memory.

Now, you won't be able to scour through the rubble and find some black, tar-like substance that represents the evil that existed in their hearts. In their destruction, the evil that manifested itself in their actions is also destroyed, proving that it was not a substantial *something,* but literally *nothing.* At the same time, though, their very destruction and extinction as a group is proof enough that that which did not exist as something substantial, did take on a substantial form. In one event, both the *nothing* and *something* of evil are displayed, and they're shown to be one and the same thing. The lack of approval their perception of "god" created within them became a problem big enough that they sought its resolution. The resolution they sought, however, turned into terror and violence, and thus they gave existence to that which, properly, does not exist.

To a great deal of humans throughout the millennia, "god" has been nothing more than this ultimate example of everything that we're not, and his name and presence does nothing but expose our lack of devotion and god-likeness. And so we strive like madmen to attain it. There is no actual problem, only an imagined lack of approval, and the sensation of separation, but this sense gives rise to substantial evil as we desperately try to claw our way out of our present state and into a higher one. *Nothing* will always become *something* in the presence, or at the invocation of the name of this "god," and that something will always lead us to harm ourselves, and eventually others. The real problem, then, lies not simply in what it is we believe we lack, but in the image of the "god" we seek to emulate in order to fill that lack. The real problem isn't the existence of a substantial evil, but a nothing that becomes substantial when we understand "god" in a certain way.

So stop and think for a moment about how you imagine God. Who is he? What is he?

If you grew up in Christianity, a string of "omni terms" will likely come to mind: God is omnipotent, omniscient, and omnipresent. He's a sort of ultimate us, only very far above us, and in possession of everything we lack. Just one of these three terms, *omnipotence,* or the possession of all power, speaks to everything humans can typically be found in pursuit of. We want influence, authority, dominance and control. Sometimes that manifests in dictatorships, and sometimes it manifests in overbearing parenting. Either way, it goes back to the same thing: we want control. We want power. "God," to us, is the perfect example of this power, and our pursuit of it, even if it's secular in nature, is little more than an ancient pursuit of imagined god-likeness.

So long as we imagine a "god" who exists as the ultimate example of all that we are not, we will never find refuge from the disapproving "light," whose ubiquity is constantly turning our *nothing* into *something.* Even if we turn this "god" into nothing more than a lofty ideal for which we shoot, its ghostly presence will haunt us, and this will *always* lead us to scapegoat one another, and seek for one worse than us, whose faults we can use to shift "god's" eyes from us onto them.

This is the "god" of *original sin* and *total depravity,* but interestingly enough, it is also this "god" who is the cause of what I would actually be comfortable calling our "original sin." It is our belief in such a being that actually leads us to behave in the "totally depraved" ways we seek a "god" to rescue us from. This deity who blames us before our parents even name us, and sentences us to hell before we've even taken our first breath, is actually at the heart of the actual problem humanity struggles with, and desperately needs saving from. This "god" who disapproves of us, condemns us, and finds us so loathsome that he cannot even bear to look in our direction, is the very source of that which we call sin, evil, and depravity, for he reaches into the heart of *nothing*, and from it fashions a world of violence.

Remember the rat story from last chapter? Remember how behaviors not native to either group of rats were elicited from them, simply by their observer's expectations? Imagine how unconsciously affected we are by the belief that we are under the constant surveillance of a perfect being who considers our very existence to be a crime! Again, even if we've attempted to secularize this portrait of "god," and seek only self-improvement for self-improvement's sake, there is still some unseen, spectral figure motivating us to do so. We are seeking to escape our very existence, our "nakedness," if you will, precisely because someone or something's expectations and observations have turned our non-issues into issues we will seek to rectify, no matter who we hurt or leave behind in the process. This someone or something can be a disapproving parent, even one who is long dead, but whose disapproval we still feel breathing down our necks. It could simply be society as a whole, and the values of the Western world which constantly remind us that we aren't working hard enough or that we aren't smart enough. But whatever it is, it is a presence that we feel constantly. Its disapproval lives through us and animates us, destroying our sense of worth and taking our relationships down with it.

There can be no true freedom from the curse of *nothing* that becomes *something* until we deal with the disapproving observer, the "light" which gives definition to our "darkness." It must be terminated if we are to ever be free. In Christianity, our answer has simply been to domesticate the observer, and insist that, while he does indeed require god-like perfection, he has satisfied this need through the work of Jesus. George MacDonald, rightly baffled by this concept, calls it "confusion", and "an inversion of right and wrong." And truly it is just that! To declare that "god" is the being the first couple imagined him to be, and that in Jesus, God is simply telling us that we had things mostly figured out, it was just that we weren't able to offer a big enough sacrifice to satisfy his needs, is simply ridiculous. But this *is* precisely what we've taught.

The millions of souls who worshipped violent, sacrificial deities, and sought to do away with their sins and assuage the anger of their gods through violence, were actually quite enlightened, if we take this view. They were just worshipping the wrong gods and offering the wrong types of sacrifices, but their understanding of the divine, and how it functions, was right on the money. God is, in fact, the all-perfect, everything-that-you're-not, omni-being, and he does, in fact, demand from you a perfection you cannot ever possibly attain! So they were right in seeking to offer him perfect sacrifices and such, it was just that they couldn't possibly hope to meet his standards by shedding the blood of livestock and virgins. No, God is so picky that only his own perfection would do.

In Christian circles, we often claim that God sends Jesus to live a life that is perfect according to the standards of the Mosaic Law (something we're assured only God himself could do), who is then capable of meeting God's perfect, sacrificial standards. Never mind the fact that Paul, a mere human, tells us he lived a life that was blameless in light of the Law (Php 3:6), we insist that no human could ever possibly meet that impossibly high standard. After Jesus is ritually murdered, the expectations of the divine are finally met, and now, provided we pray the right prayer and recite the right creed, God will accept us, in spite of the fact that we are but filthy and unworthy worms in his sight.

While this view may help to alleviate fears concerning hell, eternal judgment and the like, it still very much keeps "god" alive and enthroned in our imaginations. It is merely a response to the Augustinian thirst, but not an elimination of the thirst itself. Regardless of whether or not we think God's need for perfection has been satisfied, he still remains a being who needed perfection in order to be satisfied. He remains the ultimate example of everything we're not, and his presence will still turn our non-issues into the worst of issues. Even when we hear the name of God in the context of a grace-laced message of forgiveness and mercy, *because* that forgiveness and mercy needed to be *literally* purchased by perfection, that name will ultimately bring our darkness into existence, and leave us feeling the same void we sought refuge from in the message of grace. Our problem is "god," and we do not simply need doctrines that domesticate him or satisfy his needs so that we won't have to. We need for him to vanish. To be done away with. To be terminated.

In the Gospel story, I believe we have what amounts to the most potent cure for this curse.

In Isaiah 53 we have the song of the suffering servant, which we often interpret prophetically as speaking of Christ. In some of its opening lines, we read:

> 2 For he grew up before him like a young plant, and like a root out of dry ground; *he had no form or majesty that we should look at him, nothing in his appearance that we should desire him.* 3 He was despised and rejected by others; a man of suffering and acquainted with infirmity; *and as one from whom others hide their faces* he was despised, and we held him of no account.
>
> -Isaiah 53:2-3, NRSV (Italics mine)

Now, what we have to remember here is that, for the Christian, Jesus is not merely representative of one of God's character qualities, but is the distillation of all that God is. Literally, for the Christian, God finds full definition in the person of Jesus. And it isn't merely in some mystical or nebulous sense that God is revealed in Jesus, no, it is in his flesh and blood existence where the fullness of deity was made known, once and for all:

> 9 For in him *the whole fullness of deity dwells bodily,*
>
> -Colossians 2:9, NRSV (Italics mine)

This is, perhaps, made even more powerful when we consider what Paul said just one chapter earlier:

> 19 For in him all *the fullness of God was pleased to dwell,*
>
> -Colossians 1:19, NRSV (Italics mine)

And even more pointedly:

> 15 He is *the image of the invisible God…*
>
> -Colossians 1:15, NRSV (Italics mine)

So this being we've been attempting to imagine for centuries, this one onto whom we've projected our own likeness and imagined as being the ultimate version of all that we wish we could be, has come to be fully and finally revealed in the flesh and blood existence of one single individual. Jesus Christ is the image of that which is invisible; a human life in which the invisible fullness of that which we call God is *fully* and *completely* on display for all the world to see.

If God were to ever be fully manifested, the last place we would imagine it could be done is within a frail human frame. If, somehow, God *were* to reveal himself in a human, that human would need to be a genetic purebred, free of all defects, physical imperfections, and the like, and surely he would be so different from us lowly creatures that we'd scarcely even recognize him as human. Isaiah tells us a different story, though. The suffering servant, whom the early church associated with Jesus, is not some bronze god of a man, with a face carved from marble, and free of any physical imperfections. No, on the contrary, we're told that this one who gives image to the invisible, who fully and completely unveils, in his physical person, the reality of God, was nothing to write home about. No one would have stopped him on the street to stare at his beauty and marvel at his perfection. There was nothing jaw-dropping about his appearance, or probably even all that captivating about how he delivered his messages. He was a plain, ordinary human being, and, taking it a step further, Isaiah tells us he was like one from whom people purposely hid their faces. Far from being an attractant, Jesus' appearance seemed to have actually been a repellant.

And yet, in this plain, ordinary, nothing-to-write-home-about human being, whom people went out of their way to avoid, the full reality of God was displayed.

In this single human life, every human notion of the divine as something "up there," "out there," or looming over us in unapproachable perfection, is completely contradicted. According to the Christian tradition, God was not revealed in the form of a glistening warrior, descending from the heavens on a war horse, nor as some luminescent, saintly creature, but rather as an itinerant, Jewish peasant, with nothing in his appearance that caught the eye, activated envy, or reminded us of what we weren't. "God," the "up there," "out there," everything-that-we're not "god", whose perfect brow is ever furrowed, and whose fiery eyes scowl disapprovingly at us, is shown to be a fraud. God is simply not *that* kind of perfection. He's painfully easy to overlook, unattractive by human standards, and lacking in all of the traits and qualities that turn our *nothing* into *something*. The attributes we have ascribed to him are attributes he lacks, or at least chooses not to possess, and this causes the problems we see in ourselves to once again become non-problems. God's full embrace of that which we try so desperately to escape, reveals our "nakedness" as something we need not be ashamed of. At the same time, the things we've thought to be solutions are revealed to be the problems, as God himself rejects the high state of god-likeness we pursue at the expense of others.

Paul speaks of this same reality in the first chapter of 1 Corinthians, when he writes:

> 22 For *Jews demand signs and Greeks desire wisdom,*
> 23 *but we proclaim Christ crucified, a stumbling block to Jews and foolishness to Gentiles,*

> -1 Corinthians 1:22-23, NRSV (Italics mine)

This is a most interesting move the apostle makes here, as he states that the Gospel does not meet us in the place of our felt needs. It does not speak to those things which we desire, but to something much, much deeper. Jews, Paul asserts, desire wisdom, which he later equates with *power*, while Greeks, so he claims, desire wisdom. If the divine were to ever speak or manifest itself directly, a first century Jew may have expected it to look like a sign of divine power, whereas the wisdom-obsessed Greeks may have expected for it to look like a certain brand of philosophical wisdom. The Gospel, however, speaks the exact opposite of both. Those who desired a powerful, sign-wielding king, were met with the weakness of the corpse of a Roman execution victim, and those seeking wisdom were met with the foolishness of the same. Neither group found their desires confirmed in the Gospel, but contradicted. The concept of God they'd held so tightly to was completely subverted and turned upside down in the person of Jesus.

The God of the Gospel is not a powerful, warring tyrant, but a plain, weak teacher, who can be killed by the very government they were hoping he'd help them overthrow. Neither is he some wise sage whose very life and existence is a veritable fountain of practical wisdom, but in many ways, the antithesis of conventional wisdom. He is simply none of the things we've imagined him to be.

This will naturally elicit one of two reactions from us:

1.) We'll reject both the God of this message and the message itself, or

2.) We will be forced to rethink our God concepts, and everything we thought we knew about the world.

If we opt for number 2, the implications will be deep and penetrative, and the consequences traumatic, for we will not simply be forced to reconfigure our understanding of the divine, but to do what will feel like leaving it behind altogether. Losing one's understanding of "god" as God is traumatic, because it tells us that there is no well from which we can draw satisfaction to quench our thirst. The thirst, the thing that exacerbates it, and the thing which we believe can satisfy it, are all illusions. None of them exist. And, for the Christian, it is in Jesus that we see this. It's an apocalyptic moment in which all we knew of the divine and of the world crumbles, but what rises from these ashes is something far greater than we could have engineered on our own.

When we encounter this radically different, and in many ways, "undesirable" God, the anxiety and fear our former thoughts about the divine elicited from us, eventually cease. While it was traumatic to let go of, and embrace that "god's" inexistence, and while it was equally traumatic to watch the collapse of our old world, their destruction and dissolution pave the way for something much greater. To see God is no longer to see our lack, to no longer feel the need to escape our humanity and scramble for higher ground. The engine driving us to climb to some place of transcendence stalls, and we gradually begin to get a sense of just how sacred what we are already is. We are granted permission to embrace the dirt beneath our feet, and to sink into the skin in which we live, and life can finally begin.

To truly see God as Jesus reveals him is to no longer need a scapegoat, whose sins we can use to divert "god's," or whatever we've put in that place, attention away from our own, and to instead see all of humanity, beginning with ourselves, represented in God's humanity. Suddenly, everyone appears accepted, loved, and as those with whom you share some sacred, familial bond, even if you've yet to really comprehend it. When we see the traumatic normalcy of the God of Jesus Christ, the nothingness that the disapproving "god" of our imaginations constantly turned into a substantial something, reverts to its natural state of non-being, and the problems created by its judgmental gaze begin melting away.

Until, though, the image of the displeased, angry observer is done away with, we will continue to be stalked and harassed by the felt presence of someone, or something, that finds us disappointing. We might not call it a "god," and may not even imagine it as anything resembling one, but something will always have its disapproving, judgmental eyes on us.

Ever notice how, even when we're alone, we feel embarrassed when we cross some line society says we ought not cross, or when we make some misstep that, if done publicly, we'd be mocked for? I mean, we're alone, so why feel embarrassed? We feel it because, as much as we might claim to not believe in a "god" of any sort, the very expectations and opinions of the world we live in have become a sort of ghostly presence that we always feel, but can never find. Something higher than us, bigger than us, more powerful than us, is always lurking in the shadows, turning our nothing into something.

In Jesus, the very concept of such a higher, greater and more powerful presence is negated. For if God himself is no such power, then no such power exists. If God himself rejects the concepts of greatness by which we judge ourselves, then our very reasons for pursuing them are dismissed as nonsensical. Our attempts at divorcing ourselves from the normalcy of human existence are exposed as utterly ungodly, and embracing the life from which we seek an escape is shown to be the most God-like thing we can do. In fact, in order to truly follow the God Jesus reveals, one *must* forsake "god." The God Jesus reveals is not in the transcendent business, and those who follow him must resign from it as well. To follow Jesus is to abandon the pursuit of god-likeness.

Paul writes:

> 5 *Let the same mind be in you that was in Christ Jesus*, 6 *who, though he was in the form of God, did not regard equality with God as something to be exploited*, 7 but emptied himself, taking the form of a slave, being born in human likeness. And being found in human form, 8 he humbled himself and became obedient to the point of death—even death on a cross. 9 *Therefore God also highly exalted him* and gave him the name that is above every name, 10 so that at the name of Jesus every knee should bend, in heaven and on earth and under the earth, 11 and every tongue should confess that Jesus Christ is Lord, to the glory of God the Father.

> -Philippians 2:5-11, NRSV (Italics mine)

The apostle tells us that, as Jesus-followers, we are to embrace the same mindset Jesus embraced. That looked like a forsaking, and a letting go of, all hopes of being or becoming some divine super-creature, who wields god-like power and authority over others, and to instead embrace, and, in fact, empty oneself into, the world we've been given. While embracing this world, however, we follow Jesus in absolutely rejecting the principles around which we have structured it, for the world we have constructed is one that drives us to leave the world behind through success, power, and god-like accomplishments.

When I say that *there is no "god,"* and that *you should follow him*, this is precisely what I mean. The sorts of "gods" we have imagined simply do not exist, and Jesus, as God, is the proof of this. In fact, Jesus is the God who refuses to be "god," and he calls us to follow him in this forsaking of idolatry. This means not grasping at, or seeking to forcefully lay hold of, a status that elevates us above the "human." As Dietrich Bonhoeffer has written: "The Christian is not a *homo religiosus* (meaning a religious creature), but simply a man, as Jesus was a man..." In other words, the Christian is not called to seek upward ascent, and a life resembling that of the inhabitants of Mt. Olympus, but to follow the ungodly God, who defines himself in the utter humanness of Mt. Calvary.

Even more intriguing, Paul claims that God has given to Jesus, *the name that is above every other name*. Now, what is that name, exactly? While we typically just think it's a reference to the name *Jesus,* however, the apostle tells us that Jesus was given this name in response to his life, and *after* he'd already been called *Jesus*. What then is this name? Leron Shults explains:

> A name that is "above every name" is beyond the finite categories of naming, and this "name" was reserved for YHWH in the Hebrew Bible. In the New Testament, however, it becomes clear that the Father shares the divine name with the Son. "Therefore God also highly exalted him and gave him the name that is above every name..."[60]

The words "name above every name" speak of the high esteem in which the sacred name of Yahweh was and is held by Jews of all eras. Paul's statement here, that the Father has bestowed this honor upon Jesus, and elevated his very common, very human name-a name that was, in fact, one of the most common names of that era-to the same status as the sacred name, is absolutely revolutionary. It is not, after all, in response to the Son's behaving as the warrior Yahweh does in certain places within the Hebrew Bible that he is given this name, but rather in response to his utter humanness, and unwillingness to lay claim to any god-like powers or abilities. Interestingly, there is some very solid evidence suggesting that Yahweh was a name once associated with a Canaanite deity that was adopted and modified by ancient Israel, and there can be very little doubt that, in many instances, Yahweh was

---

[60] F Leron Shults, *Reforming the Doctrine of God* (Grand Rapids, Mich.: W.B. Eerdmans Pub. Co., ©2005.)

118 | THE ATHEISTIC THEIST

envisioned in much the same way as other nations envisioned their "gods." Jesus comes along, though, and presents Yahweh, His Father, as one who bears no similarities to these deities, and who, in his holy homeliness, sets the image of the divine free from all of the trappings of idolatry and human gods that it had come to be associated with.

The sacred name, and the very average name, *Jesus*, are now forever conflated, so that one cannot be spoken without the other being spoken. In Jesus, the figure of Yahweh, the God of Israel, has finally found a definitive representation, and in this definitive representation we find none of the things we normally associate with deity. None of the things that cause us to shrink and tremble before the "gods" of our imaginations are present in him, and instead we find a God who looks an awful lot like us, and who, far from condemning us for what we are, embraces it, and eternally attaches the sacred to it.

That God exalts Jesus in response to his self-emptying, is often used to suggest that our motivation for "going low" should be the promise of "getting high." That is, God will exalt you, granting you all of the lofty things you've desired and felt insignificant for lacking, but only after you first humble yourself. This type of Christianity often becomes nothing more than another version of the same game we've always played. God is still "god," who is "up there," "out there," and everything we're not, only, instead of directly seeking out such things, we are to indirectly seek them through their opposites. We do this unconsciously, I'm sure, though often consciously as well, all in the hopes of being rewarded and liberated from our lowly estate. But the exaltation of Jesus is God declaring that the life Jesus embraced is how God has chosen to define and express himself. The attachment of the "name that is above every other name" to the person of Jesus, and to that which we consider "below," is not about him having paid the price to go higher, but God making a statement about himself. He does not look how we assume he looks, but like the very things we feel the need to escape.

In 1 Timothy 3:16 we read:

> 16...He was revealed in flesh, vindicated in (or, *by*) spirit...
>
> -1 Timothy 3:16, NRSV (Additions mine)

The flesh and blood existence of Jesus was vindicated as a true revelation of God by the Spirit, or through resurrection. His exaltation, therefore, is not meant to communicate that humanity has an escape hatch, but that God endorses, approves of, and stands behind the flesh and blood, un-godlike existence of Jesus.

I bring this up in the first place to answer some questions undoubtedly raised by the last chapter, in which I called us to reject the concepts of original sin and total depravity as we've traditionally understood them. I don't want to leave you in any way with the impression that I see us as having been saved from nothing, in a literal sense, simply because I reject those ideas. No, on the contrary, I believe that Jesus saves us from something very real, and that *something* is *nothing*. As Paul states, the Gospel calls us to turn from darkness, nothingness and non-existence, to something very real:

> 18 to open their eyes and turn them from *darkness to light...*

> -Acts 26:18, NRSV (Italics mine)

The distance we sense between us and all others, which is little more than the sign of a well-functioning brain with the ability to discern where it ends and all others begin, is something we have interpreted as a chasm that divides us from that which has the power to lift us up, fulfill us and save us. This felt distance lies dormant within us, like darkness at the dawn of creation, until it encounters that from which it perceives itself as being separate from. Upon such an encounter, this nothingness, this literal non-issue, suddenly becomes a very big issue. What is nothing more than positive distinction between all creatures and objects, becomes something we feel extreme anxiety, frustration and sorrow over.

Naturally, as I've said, we create god-figures, be they humans we idolize, societal constructs, or actual deities we imagine, and seek escape through these. What actually occurs, though, is that the thing in which we sought salvation comes to taunt us, simply reinforcing that we will never be all we desire to be. The heroes, ideals, and deities mock us from their ivory towers, and much like the rats in the experiment recounted by Mlodinow, we respond to their imagined observations of us in terrible, and terrifying ways. Like Adam and Eve, Cain and Abel, Republicans and Democrats, or ISIL and the rest of the world, we blame one another, heap shame on one another, and wage war with one another in order to escape our own anxieties and insecurities.

This is our problem as a species. It isn't that we are born with some Adamic taint in our nature that turns God's stomach and forces him to judge us. No, a "god" who behaves that way is a part of the problem, not the solution, and any "god" we dream up that shares traits with him will only widen the imagined chasm. Even when we dream up a type of being who solves what we believe to be the problem, the problem remains unsolved. So long as a "god" of that type exists in our minds, our problems will persist, because its inherent and unattainable perfection will constantly be at work, turning our nothing into something.

The only solution to the problem is to do away with this concept of "god" altogether, but as with Uncle Simon, it can only be done away with when we realize that the salvation it offers us is illegitimate and unnecessary. Jesus does not reveal that God is so high and holy that we offend him in our humanity, but that the "gods" we've pursued are at the root of all of our problems. And I want to be clear here, that there is, in fact, a problem. In doing away with the traditional concept of original sin, I in no way mean to suggest that humanity needs no saving. No, as I've stated, we do need saving, and it is *nothing* from which we need to be saved.

Relationships are fractured, factions are created, blood is shed, and lives are lost when *nothing* becomes *something*. When we have a conception of "god" that is perfect in the way we're trained to understand perfection, it harasses and haunts us, making us feel small, inadequate, and desirous to prove ourselves. This is what leads us to hate and destroy one another, and it is this that I think we can rightly call original sin, once we've dealt with and left behind the former, odious view.

The problem is that that one, singular view, has so tainted our understanding that even mentioning original sin, or suggesting that humanity has a problem, triggers thoughts of the Augustinian sort, and keeps us from thinking through the matter, or discovering a better way. The temptation is to either leave the concept behind altogether, or to cling to that of Augustine. Once that "god" has been terminated, though, and no longer haunts and harasses our souls, we are freed to discover the alternate timeline, as it were, and rediscover humanity's real problem and God's solution to it.

Kallistos Ware, in, *The Orthodox Way*, writes of original sin:

> Original sin is not to be interpreted in juridical or quasi-biological terms, as if it were some physical 'taint' of guilt, transmitted through sexual intercourse. This picture, which normally passes for the Augustinian view, is unacceptable to Orthodoxy. The doctrine of original sin means rather that we are born into an environment where it is easy to do evil and hard to do good; easy to hurt others, and hard to heal their wounds; easy to arouse men's suspicions, and hard to win their trust. It means that we are each of us conditioned by the solidarity of the human race in its accumulated wrong-doing and wrong-thinking, and hence wrong-being. And to this accumulation of wrong we have ourselves added by our own deliberate acts of sin. The gulf grows wider and wider. It is here, in the solidarity of the human race, that we find an explanation for the apparent unjustness of the doctrine of original sin. Why, we ask, should the entire human race suffer because of Adam's fall? Why should all be punished because of one man's sin? The answer is that human beings, made in the image of the

Trinitarian God, are interdependent and coinherent. No man is an island. We are 'members one of another'(Eph. 4:25), and so any action, performed by any member of the human race, inevitably affects all the other members. Even though we are not, in the strict sense, guilty of the sins of others, yet we are somehow always involved."[61]

Here we find an explanation of humanity's problem that has not been tainted by the Augustinian thirst. Our problem is simply that it's hard to be a human sometimes. We are born into a world in which we feel inadequate, small, needy, worthless, even, and then search for ways of expiating this pain. We look to the "gods" we create in our desperation, but eventually find them not to be saviors, but things that exacerbate and deepen our pain. We then seek out others whose sins are "worse" than ours, that we might find solace in the "gods" approval of us over them. Yes, as we said last chapter, these are individual actions on our part, for which no one else is guilty or held accountable, but as Ware points out, our interconnectedness as a species means that none of us escape unscathed when one of us chooses evil over good. We are, after all, all of us, our brother's keeper, but, as in the case of Cain, this is something that is quickly forgotten and tossed aside when we are being driven along by an agonizing sense of lack and unworthiness.

When we are thus driven, we are often led to do terrible, terrible things to our fellow humans, and all in the name of solving a problem that isn't even there. At the heart of all of this is *nothing*; there is no *actual* problem we are reacting against, and Jesus is the revelation that the something we're reacting against is, indeed, nothing. In this sense, I can agree with G.K. Chesterton, who has written that, "There is a bias in man…and Christianity was the discovery of how to correct the bias and therefore hit the mark. There are many who will smile at the saying; but it is profoundly true to say that the glad good news brought by the Gospel was the news of original sin."[62] Indeed, the Gospel identifies the reality that something, somewhere has gone wrong, and that there is a deep, deep problem that requires fixing. Sadly, we never seem to get the taste of Augustine out of our mouths long enough to think beyond notions of inherited guilt and sinfulness. Once, though, we encounter the God who refuses to be "god;" the God who heals our anxiety by revealing that there is no God in whose presence we need feel anxious, we are able to take a fresh look at all of this, and discover a better way of approaching the subject.

---

[61] Kallistos, Bishop of Diokleia, *The Orthodox Way* (Crestwood, NY : St. Vladimir's Seminary Press, ©1995.)

[62] G.K. Chesterton, *The Collected Works of G.K. Chesterton* (San Francisco : Ignatius Press, ©1986-<©2012>)

Richard Dawkins, who is not only an avowed atheist, but also a brilliant, evolutionary biologist, has said:

> I do not wish to live in a Darwinian world. The world of nature is a Darwinian world... [and] it is a very unpleasant world...not the kind of world we would wish to live in. So let us understand it so that we can construct the kind of society in which we'd wish to live...a society that departs from Darwinian principles...a society that was based upon Darwinian principles would be a ruthless, free market economy in which the rich trample the poor...[63]

Here we have one of the world's most prominent atheists essentially identifying the actual problem of original sin. It has nothing to do with inherited guilt or sinfulness, but with the way we've developed as a species. Our sense of lack and inadequacy, and the burning desire to be first, has led us to create a brutal, barbaric, and bloody world, in which we trample one another in order to succeed, and reach a god-like state. What must happen, is that the way we have naturally developed must be challenged at its core. That which is at the center of why we became this way must be terminated, in order that we might discover an alternative, less god-like, and more Godly way of existing. And this is precisely what I contend occurs in Jesus.

The Jewish Philosopher, Emanuel Levinas, was asked: *"Does going towards God always require that we go against nature?"* To which he responded: *"God cannot appear as the cause or creator of nature...God does indeed go against nature, for He is not of this world."*[64] Now, Levinas has something different in mind here than what I'm proposing, but I agree wholeheartedly with the sentiment. To follow God is to go against the way that we have naturally developed as a species, which is to be me-first, self-gratifying survivalists. As Dawkins has said, we don't want to live in a Darwinian world where things continue on exactly as they developed.

Elsewhere Dawkins has stated that what we need is:

> ...a truly anti-Darwinian society. Anti-Darwinian in the sense that we don't wish to live in a society where the weakest go to the wall, where the strongest suppress the

---

[63] This quote is taken from a discussion between Richard Dawkins and Wendy Wright. The entire discussion can be viewed here:
https://www.youtube.com/watch?v=-AS6rQtiEh8
[64] Richard A Cohen, *Face to Face With Levinas* (Albany, N.Y. : State University of New York Press, ©1986.)

weak, and even kill the weak. We — I, at least — do not wish to live in that kind of society. I want to live in the sort of society where we take care of the sick, where we take care of the weak, take care of the oppressed, which is a very anti-Darwinian society.[65]

It is in this sense that we must go against nature in order to "go towards God." God is truly not of this world, Levinas rightly says, nor can God "appear as the cause or creator of nature." In other words, though God is creator, he is not the creator of the way things are presently ordered. The natural world is his creation, but its structure is ours. So, although God is not of this world, the way that he shows us this is by becoming of this world. He literally takes upon himself the very stuff you and I are made of, and not in some pure, untainted form. No, he becomes *us*. Killable, defile-able, tempted, doubtful us. And in doing this, in becoming what we are, even when he could easily lay hold of what we desire to be, he shows that what we pursue at the expense of others is not only not worth pursuing, but not real. If God rejects a thing, after all, one must imagine that such a thing ceases to be, in a sense. Were we, then, to ever get to the top of the "Tower of Babel" we're always working so hard to construct, we would find it abandoned, and at its base, we would find God himself, fleeing the transcendent, and embracing the ordinary.

The way that we "go against nature" is not by despising where and what we are, but by recognizing that our natural bend toward evacuating where we are, and escaping what we are, is a naturally developed evil that moves us to even greater evil. The only way to escape this, the only way to truly go against this, is to embrace the one thing that is what we want, *God*, who, through his actions, shows us that what we want does not exist.

At the end of the last chapter I claimed that we *must* say no to the "god" of original sin and total depravity, but also asked if there was one worth saying "yes" to. To answer my own question, I say *yes*, there is, in fact, a God worth saying "yes" to, but it isn't a being who saves us from an inborn flaw or taint in our nature, and therefore from his own disapproval of us. He isn't a being who views sweet little kids and serial killers as being equally sinful in light of his own righteousness, nor is he a being who works on an economy of exchange, saving us from the *something* of our imperfection with the *something* of his own perfection.

The God worth saying "yes" to is the God Jesus reveals. He is not the high, lofty, Lord of Creation, whose perfection disqualifies us from

---

[65] These comments were made during a conversation with Richard Dawkins at Kennesaw State University, on November 21, 2014. The full video can be seen here: https://www.youtube.com/watch?v=TdFC7iQuHLw

participating in his life, but the incarnate One, who embraces and empties himself into our existence and calls it "good." He is the God whose name, when spoken, does not evoke shame or fear from us, and whose holiness does not motivate blame, accusation or murder, but acceptance, inclusion and radical empathy.

The God I say "yes" to is the one who reveals my nakedness to be a non-issue; who calls my attempts at solutions problems, and my problems non-problems. The God I say "yes" to is the God who saves me from my own darkness and nothingness, which, through constant comparison and contrast, has become a very literal *something* in my life. And he doesn't save me from this *darkness* by paying off a deity with blood, but by revealing the darkness to be nothing more than my unique me-ness. The fact that there does exist a separation between myself and others means nothing more than that I'm unique, and not that I'm traumatically separated from something which has the power to fulfill me.

The God I say "yes" to is the God who leaves nothing as nothing, darkness as darkness, and non-issues as non-issues. His name, nature and presence do not result in shame, blame, or bloodshed. On the contrary, his "traumatic" normalcy reveals the acceptance of all, and that we are most like him when we are most human. It is the God who announces the "good news of original sin," and liberates me from that which is natural, precisely by embracing it.

The God I say "yes" to, finally, is the God I can say "no" to, and still remain a distinct, and valuable person. It is this one, and this one only, who can save me from a concept of salvation that ultimately leads to my destruction. In this one I am saved, not from my humanity, but so that I can be truly human, as he is. To the "god" who considers my very existence to be a criminal offense, though, the "god" who must save me from the disgusting *something* of my very being, I say a hearty and emphatic "no." But to the One who saves me from *nothing,* and from all of the *something* it becomes, I say "yes."

And to all others, no matter what names they claim for themselves, or what forms they take, may I forever remain an atheist, and may they stay in the darkness, where non-existent things belong.

6 | WITH A SAVIOR LIKE THIS,
WHO NEEDS A SATAN?

"There ain't no devil, there's just God when he's drunk."
-Tom Waits

"The nonviolent God of Jesus comes to be depicted as a God of unequaled violence…Against such an image of God the revolt of atheism is an act of pure religion."
-Walter Wink

You're just 6 years old, sitting alone in your dark room, unable to sleep because you know that, at any moment, your father will return home, drunk out of his mind, and needing someone to vent his rage on.

That someone is you.

Just a little bit after midnight, you hear the front door slam. You bury yourself beneath the covers, willing yourself to either disappear, or be magically transported to a real home, in which fathers don't disappear for hours, and then return to beat their children.

Unfortunately, once again your will has failed you, and you hear your father begin hobbling his way up the stairs like the intoxicated ghost of Jacob Marley. His uncoordinated, alcohol-inhibited journey takes much longer than it should, as he must stop periodically to regain his balance, which gives your little mind ample time to imagine the terrible beating that lay just moments in your future – barring the possibility that he falls down the stairs and passes out, which has happened before.

Most nights he does not fall, though, and you pay for it.

The lumbering, Frankenstein-like footsteps suddenly cease, as he's standing directly outside your door. Your six year old heart feels as though it will beat its way out of your rib cage, straight through your chest, and you're positive that your father, even in his inhibited state, can hear it pounding. You sink beneath the pile of blankets and stuffed animals layering your bed, hoping they will be enough camouflage to keep you hidden.

The door creaks open.

He's in your room now, headed your way, and just like every other night, your blankets and stuffed animals fail as camouflage.

Just as you begin your normal routine of begging through tears, "Not tonight, daddy! Please don't hurt me, I love you!" you hear the booming voice of your older brother bellow out from across the hall. He manages to lure your father away from you and toward himself, as he shouts, "Pick on someone your own size, old man!" Enraged, your father charges your brother with the force of an EF5 tornado.

You jump out of bed and race towards the two of them, but there is nothing you can do. You simply stand mortified in the hallway, watching the horror unfold, as your raging father beats your heroic, older brother within an inch, nay, a centimeter, of his life.

After what seems like hours, your father tires, and the beating ends. Then, hovering over your brother's now limp body, his face takes on a terrifying glow of contentment. His lips begin to curl upward into a smile of satisfaction, and he lets out the type of sigh one would normally heave after eating their fill at a buffet. He stands up straight, cracks his neck, blinks his eyes a few times, and turns to you with a smile: "Boy, I sure do feel better," he says, with your brother's blood staining his hands and his shirt, "do you maybe want to go get some ice cream or something, son?"

Would you tempted to take him up on this offer? Would you run into his arms, squealing with glee? Would you be able to put out of your mind the vile thing he had just done in order to achieve the sweet disposition he suddenly came to possess? Would you be able to ignore the fact that he had been prepared to beat you, a defenseless child, senseless, only to nearly kill your brother who heroically stood up for you?

Probably not.

It's more likely that you would want to run as far away from this unstable man as your little legs could carry you, never to return. Surely, you cannot trust a man who must use violence against one son in order to interact lovingly with another. The father in this story is the very antithesis of what a father ought to be, and *safe* is something his presence *would* most certainly *not* make you feel.

Of course, such a dreadful tale has little power to move one's heart to sympathize, or fall in love with, the father. It has quite the opposite effect, actually, moving us to hate him, but to feel for and sympathize with both sons. And yet, this is nearly the exact scenario (minus a few details) that many Christians have used for the last several centuries to describe the effect of the death of Christ upon God the Father. We call it *atonement*, but, to the honest soul, it more closely resembles abuse than anything admirable, or worship-inducing. To the outsider, who is not schooled in the ways Christians think, this version of the "gospel" seems utterly repulsive. If one is not primed to love the "god" of the story, and fear his wrath, it would likely never dawn on us to identify him as anything other than the story's antagonist, and certainly not its hero. We'd hurt for the little brother, hope that he could leave behind this dysfunctional family and make something of himself, and we would cheer on the older brother for his bravery in the face of pure evil. But the father we would hate and revile, and rightly so.

If the fathers in both the opening illustration, and the version of the "gospel" I allude to here are both clearly recognizable as villains rather than heroes, how would we ever find in their actions anything imitable, or worth following? Do you see in the actions of the father in my illustration, anything that you, as a father, might want to employ in your fathering? Anything at all? His unreasonableness? His violence maybe? Anything? I didn't think so. Now what about the "Father" presented to us in popular versions of the "gospel?" Is there anything imitable in his actions? Anything that we can duplicate in our parenting, or other human relationships, that would not land us in jail?

That's precisely what I want to think through with you in this chapter, for if there is nothing worth emulating in the actions of a "god" that a particular religion calls us to worship, than neither the religion, nor its "god," are worthy of our attention, not to mention our worship. Worship is following, and if I can't follow a deity-if I cannot live just as they live, and have it translate into me being a better father, mother, son, daughter, citizen, or human, than I will not worship that deity. I care not how much it or its worshippers threaten me, or how many curses or anathemas they hurl in my direction, such a being will never receive from me the bent knee of reverence, but only the upraised fist of revolution.

So let's talk about this popular view of the atonement. Is there a "way" present in it? Is there something, anything, follow-able about its "god?"

Can I do just as he does, and have it result in humanity being bettered? These elements *should* be present, because this whole "atonement thing" is supposed to represent God's absolute best. It is supposed to be the way that God solves the salvation problem, and how he makes his nature perfectly known to his creatures. So, if ever, anywhere in all of the universe, there is to be found a "way" worth following, we should be able to find it at the cross!

So what does the cross look like in this particular theory of the atonement, which also happens to be the view whose mouthpieces have the largest platforms at present? Before we get there, first thing you need to know of it, is that it *is* simply *a* view. There is no *one* view of the atonement, nor has there ever been. Throughout church history, there have been numerous views, from the Christus Victor view of many early church fathers, to the Moral Influence view laid out by Peter Aberland, to the Penal Substitutionary view, which is the particular view we'll be looking at in this chapter.

Being simply *a* view, it has a traceable origin, and we can pinpoint when it began to gain traction and popularity, and why. In the name of saving space, time, and not losing your interest, I will not give an exhaustive history of this doctrine's origins, nor even a short, though thorough one. I simply want to bring up the point that it is but one in a sea of views. In fact, up until around a thousand years ago, anything smacking of the Penal Substitutionary view of the atonement, which will henceforth be abbreviated as PSA, was unheard of, at least on a large scale. The earliest views present the cross as something of a trap that God set for the devil in order to undo the curse of death. In some of these views, God allows Satan to swallow up Jesus in death as though he were a worm on a fish hook, but then pulls a fast one on him in raising Jesus from the dead, thus undoing the curse.

Others had Jesus descending into hell and engaging in fisticuffs with the devil and his minions, only to rise victorious in resurrection. In fact, most early views have something, or someone, other than God as the problem needing to be solved. In the PSA view, however, all of that changes, and God himself becomes the thing standing between us and salvation, making him the very thing from which we need to be saved. The purpose of the cross becomes to save us from wrath which God himself has declared we deserve to be partakers of. It is not sin, Satan, or some other evil, external force that God is rescuing us from, but himself.

In this view, God has a problem, and it's us, but he also has a solution, and it's the cross. Augustine stated quite explicitly what God's problem was, and it was that he hated us:

> ...in a wonderful and divine manner, even when He hated us, He loved us; for He hated us, in so far as we

were not what He Himself had made; and because our own iniquity had not in every part consumed His work, He knew at once both how, in each of us, to hate what we had done, and to love what He had done.[66]

According to Augustine, God loved the bits of us that he'd directly created, but hated the nature we had come to possess because of sin. While his love kept him from hating us completely, his perfection demanded that he at least partially hate us, and eventually do us great harm in hell. To save us, then, God had to find a way to do away with his own hatred for us. To do this, God, in love, would need to absorb his own hatred into himself. As one pastor has written: "...Christian propitiation (which, in this pastor's understanding, constitutes PSA) is the work of God to absorb his divine anger toward sinful man."[67] John Stott, a well-known American theologian, has written similarly, "If it is God's wrath which needed to be propitiated, it is God's love which does the propitiating."[68] So, it would seem that what God has accomplished in Christ, then, in this view, is that, in his love, he has dealt with his own hatred for us. Stott is careful to say that this is not what he has in mind, though I think his explanation makes little difference:

> If it may be said that the propitiation "changed" God, or that by it he changed himself, let us be clear he did not change from wrath to love, or from enmity to grace, since his character is unchanging. What the propitiation changed was his dealings with us. "The distinction I ask you to observe, wrote P.T. Forsyth, "is between a change of feeling and a change of treatment...God's feeling toward us never needed to be changed. But God's treatment of us, God's practical relation to us-that had to change." He forgave us and welcomed us home.[69]

Now, I'll be honest, Stott's clarification does sound a heck of a lot better than a God who straight up hates us from the start. Still, though, his understanding of the cross is rooted in the idea that there was something keeping God from treating us lovingly, even though deep inside that's precisely how he felt about us. You might not call that hatred, and you might be able to come up with all sorts of theological reasons why it can

---

[66] Augustine, Saint Bishop of Hippo, *Tractates on the Gospel of John* (Washington, D.C. : Catholic University of America Press, 1988.)

[67] http://www.desiringgod.org/articles/the-god-centered-cross-of-love-inexhaustible

[68] John R W Stott, *The Cross of Christ* (Downers Grove, Ill. : InterVarsity Press, ©1986.)

[69] Ibid.

be harmonized with a God who is perfectly loving, but I don't see it. A God who must treat us like he hates us, even though he loves us, but can only treat us the way he actually feels about us after having his son murdered, is no better than a God who hated us. That sort of love is not the follow-able sort, nor is it the sort we would ever accept from another human. Call it what you will, but at the end of the day it still looks like hatred being propitiated, not love being manifested.

According to PSA, Stott's comments notwithstanding, God could not, or would not, simply set aside his hatred, nor would he simply forgive and forget. Someone was going to have to shed some blood if we were to ever be more than wrath-magnets. And so the cross, God's supposed best, devolves into a bizarre event in which God, becomes the victim of his own hatred, in order to save us from it. Even though it isn't the original offenders who pay the price, someone will still have paid it, and God will consider it to be enough. John Calvin wrote of this idea "...God was our enemy before he was again made favorable to us by Christ's death..."[70] In other words, we weren't always on God's good side, only the one specific part of us he had directly crafted. There was that other part, though, the part Augustine suggested God hated, that needed to be dealt with, and crucifixion did the job.

GOD BECOMES SATAN

What this view effectively does, is turn God into the "satan," or humanity's adversary, and the "devil," or our accuser. It is he who accuses us of wrong, and then stands adverse to us in his wrath. As discussed in a previous chapter, this "god" sets rules that he knows we can't keep, and then condemns us for living up to his very low expectations. Then, after having ensured our failure, condemns us to hell for the very failure he ensured. Maybe Tom Waits was right when he sang, "there ain't no devil, there's just God when he's drunk."[71] What I mean is, while the early church fathers imagined God as saving us from some nefarious, external force, like the devil, demons, or death itself, modern theories, like PSA, make God into that nefarious, enemy force. He becomes the wrath-drunk devil from which our souls require saving; the accuser that necessitates a bloody day of reckoning, as well as our deliverance from it. As the old saying goes, "with friends like these, who needs enemies?" and, if I may, with a savior like this, who needs a Satan?

---

[70] John Calvin, *Institutes of the Christian Religion* (Philadelphia, Westminster Press [©1960])
[71] Waits, Tom (Heartattack and Vine.)

For the believer in a powerful, omnipotent, omnipresent, and omniscient God, what could be more terrifying than the thought of him being mad as *literal hell* at you? And if you believed God to be that way, what sort of theories would you need to come up with in order to get him to back off your back? After all, the belief that God is angry at us for original sin is what gives rise to doctrine like PSA in the first. The Augustinian thirst necessitates a well, and PSA is but one of many such wells we've come up with. Jonathan Edwards, in his most famous of sermons, speaks of the problem as he sees it:

> The God who holds you over the pit of hell...abhors you! ...You cannot stand before an infuriated tiger even; what then will you do when God rushes against you in all His wrath?[72]

Edwards' "god," or at least how he depicts him here, is no loving father, but a being intoxicated by his own wrath; a devil whose posture towards us makes angry tigers, with bloodlust in their eyes, look like baby kittens. No wonder then, in speaking of the atonement, or the way in which he imagines "god" dealing with his wrath toward sinful humans, he says:

> Thus it pleased the Father to bruise him [Jesus] and put him to grief. God dealt with him as if he had been exceedingly angry with him, and as though he had been the object of his dreadful wrath.[73]

In another sermon, while speaking of the agony he imagines Christ experiencing on the cross, he writes:

> He had then a near view of that furnace of wrath, into which he was to be cast; he was brought to the mouth of the furnace that he might look into it, and stand and view its raging flames, and see the glowings of its heat, that he might know where he was going and what he was about to suffer. This was the thing that filled his soul with sorrow and darkness, this terrible sight as it were overwhelmed him. For what was that human nature of Christ to such mighty wrath as this? It was in itself, without the supports of God, but a feeble worm of the dust, a thing that was crushed before the moth.[74]

---

[72] Jonathan Edwards, *Sinners in the Hands of an Angry God* (Great Neck Pub., 2009.)

[73] Jonathan Edwards; Sereno Edwards Dwight; Edward Hickman, *The Works of Jonathan Edwards* (Edinburgh ; Carlisle, Pa. : Banner of Truth Trust, 1974)

[74] Ibid.

For Edwards' "god," and that of many modern Protestants and Evangelicals, simple forgiveness is not an option. God's heart is filled with hatred, fury, and divine magma, and it cannot just be set aside. It *must* find a target if it is ever to be done away with, and until it *is* done away with, there can be no peaceable communion between God and his creatures. Thus, this "god" is man's main impediment to eternal peace and joy. In fact, it is his very existence that necessitates our salvation in the first place. Just look at how Edwards imagines "god's" relation to Christ's human nature: *"For what was the human nature of Christ to such mighty wrath as this? It was...but a feeble worm of the dust."* For Edwards, "god" was so averse to our humanity, to our very natures, that even the sight of his perfect Son bearing it forced him to "deal with him as though he were exceedingly angry with him." This "god," who views us as tainted from the womb, and deserving of torment, this being who cannot stand the sight of us and is provoked to charge us like an angry tiger, is the problem the PSA view sets forth. He is the accuser, and the punisher of the accused. He is the devil, and it is him from which we need saving.

Sure, in this same theory he also becomes the solution to the problem, but why on earth demand such a gory and torturous solution in the first place, if the problem is all on your end? If you love humanity and desire not to punish them, why not simply let go of the need to have your wrath satiated? Why hold on to a need for vengeance when that need is going to cost someone dearly? Why use violence to solve your problems, when you could, presumably, just as easily let the whole issue go? In *The God Delusion,* Richard Dawkins asks:

> If God wanted to forgive our sins, why not just forgive them, without having himself tortured and executed in payment? ...who was God trying to impress? Presumably himself — judge and jury as well as execution victim.[75]

While anything coming from the likes of Dawkins is usually dismissed by those inhabiting the Christian world, his question is valid, and worth pondering. In a world plagued by violence, why would God put forth, as his best, what would constitute us at our worst? And while some may accuse Dawkins, and even myself, of simply putting forth a strawman argument, consider how one of the more popular "grace" preachers of our day has spoken of the atonement:

> When the Messiah comes, He's going to bear your sins. The warfare will be over because your sins will have been paid for. God the Father will have put twice as much wrath upon His Son-

---

[75] Richard Dawkins, The God Delusion (Great Britain, Bantam Press, 2006)

the Lord Jesus Christ-as the entire human race was worthy of receiving.[76]

He then follows up with, "Jesus bore our sins and now the warfare is over...the war is over. God's not angry with you anymore. Sin isn't an issue. Jesus has paid for your sins."[77] Though this man is attempting to portray God as loving and gracious, the "god" he is proclaiming is one who could not, and would not, simply forgive humanity of her sins, but had to literally crush and shed the blood of his own Son first. Beyond just that, this guy even goes as far as to claim that God punished Jesus twice as harshly as we originally deserved to be punished! Who is God trying to impress, indeed, Mr. Dawkins! I mean, what would be the purpose of such a show of brutality? Not only is there no forgiveness in this scenario, as "god" still gets to pounce on the human nature he so hates like a tiger, it's also a bit of overkill, if you ask me.

Thankfully, the author of that quote is no theologian, and so his "twice as much wrath" theory is not one that anyone other than himself holds to, as far as I know. Still, though, the problem remains, that in PSA, humanity is not forgiven of her perceived crimes, but fully and completely punished through Jesus. Not to mention the fact that "god" is not relating to us mercifully because he is inherently merciful, but only because he has fully vented his hatred for us onto another. Consequently, the image of God itself is not redeemed from the clutches of human mythology and idolatry in the PSA view, but rather, the mythological and idolatrous view of God is vindicated, as Jesus satisfies the wrath of just such a "god."

Consider these words, from a very well-known and beloved Christian writer from yesteryear: "The cross is the lightning rod of grace that short-circuits God's wrath to Christ so that only the light of His love remains for believers."

Pay close attention to the language here. Prior to Jesus, there is a problem, there is something we need to be saved from. It isn't the devil, death, or some metaphysical evil, but the wrath of God. We are saved from it by Jesus who, acting as a lightning rod of sorts, draws the lightning of God's anger and wrath to himself, so that the only thing remaining for us is love. Now, apart from the obvious reasons why I find this statement problematic, notice that, contrary to the stated mission of Jesus, which was to reveal the truth about God which we had not formerly seen or understood, this view presents Jesus as one who confirms everything we've always suspected to be true about the divine.

---

[76] Andrew Wommack, *The War is Over: God is Not Mad, So Stop Struggling With Sin and Judgment* (Walsall: Andrew Wommack Ministries - Europe, ©2008)
[77] Ibid.

All of our mythological, sacrifice-demanding deities are supported, not contradicted in this view. It simply claims that that "god" has been sacrificially satisfied once and for all. Jesus has dealt with the problematic aspect of our gods-concepts, but has not abolished their existences. All of the pagan archetypes of divinity still live in this model of the gospel, they simply have Jesus as their solution, and therefore also as their vindication.

Consider carefully the language used by the writer of the quote in question: Christ is a lightning rod, short-circuiting what we can only imagine to be the lightning of God's anger. Really? Is god really an angry, lightning bolt wielding deity, who must be placated by blood sacrifice? Of all of the idols ancient Israel is rebuked for turning toward, the Canaanite god, Ba'al, is near the top of the list. And who is Ba'al, exactly? Well, he was a Canaanite storm god, usually depicted as holding a lightning bolt. If you wanted to stay on this god's good side, you offered him sacrifice. Or how about the chief deities of the Greeks and Romans, whom early Christians were called atheists for refusing to worship? Who was their chief god? It was Zeus for the Greeks, and Jupiter for the Romans, and both were storm gods, typically depicted as wielding lightning bolts. If you wanted to be on their good side, you offered them sacrifices.

Now, listen, my problem isn't really with the archetypal figure of a deity wielding a lightning bolt. Ba'al, Zeus, Jupiter, or whoever, are pagan deities, and we should expect nothing less from human religion than gods who look this way. My problem is with the fact that this same language has wormed its way into the very message that was supposed to reveal all such gods to be false. Instead, it maintains that the divine looks exactly the way humans have always imagined, but offers us Jesus, instead of the continual offering of sacrifices from our own hands, as the solution. This form of Christianity does not smash our idols, it simply buries them so that we can pretend we no longer worship them, when in fact, we do.

George MacDonald saw the similarities between the "god" of many Christian theologians and the idols from which the true God, and Father of Jesus, calls us to turn:

> How terribly, then, have the theologians misrepresented
> God... Nearly all of them represent him as a great King
> on a grand throne, thinking how grand he is, and making
> it the business of his being and the end of his universe to
> keep up his glory, wielding the bolts of a Jupiter against
> them that take his name in vain. They would not allow

this, but follow out what they say, and it comes much to this.[78]

Simply put, the language and imagery we use puts the God who calls us from idols smack dab in the midst of them, and as one of their number. We would never in a million years own up to, or confess this, of course, but it's true nonetheless. When we speak of the Father of Jesus as one who would hurl his angry thunderbolts earthward were it not for the sacrifice of Jesus, we are worshipping a god no better, no greater, than Ba'al, or Jupiter of old.

Jesus, according to the testimony of the apostles, is not God's lightning rod, but the "radiance of God's glory and exact representation of His being," and teaches that if we want to look like his Father, we must love even our enemies and forgive those who do us wrong. Then you have the "god" of PSA, who cannot and will not simply sheath his lightning bolts and forgive sins, but demands someone pay, even if it isn't the original perpetrator who does the paying. We have Jesus, who explicitly states in Matthew 5, that to bear His Father's image is to set aside "eye for an eye and tooth and for a tooth" in favor of a gracious, forgiving, and merciful approach to our enemies, and then a "god" who is absolutely incapable of doing any of these things. Jesus says turn the other cheek, but the "god" of PSA demands his pound of flesh. PSA presents a "god" who is hell-bent on upholding the very concepts Jesus says are opposite God's nature, and keeps alive the very idols he claimed looked nothing like his Father.

Again, George MacDonald nails it in this regard, and identifies the hidden idolatry within such doctrines:

> They say first, God must punish the sinner, for justice requires it; then they say he does not punish the sinner, but punishes a perfectly righteous man instead, attributes his righteousness to the sinner, and so continues just. Was there ever such a confusion, such an inversion of right and wrong... To lay the pain upon the righteous in the name of justice is simply monstrous. No wonder unbelief is rampant. Believe in Moloch if you will, but call him Moloch, not Justice.[79]

This "god," this incapable-of-forgiving, sacrifice-demanding deity, who can love me only because his hatred for me was short-circuited, and directed toward an innocent man in my place, is one I must, as a follower

---

[78] George MacDonald, The Complete Works of George MacDonald (Kindle Edition by O'Connor, 2010)
[79] Ibid.

of Jesus, reject with my whole being. He is, as MacDonald suggests, no better than Moloch, Ba'al, or Jupiter, and to worship him is to stoop to idolatry. There is no forgiveness in this "god," but only Moloch-like, perverted justice. One must wonder why, if the doctrine of PSA rightly represents the Father of Jesus, in all of his infinite wisdom, he failed to come up with a better way of responding to sins committed against him than resorting to violence, and behaving as the very gods he called Israel, and all of humanity, to turn from. Why not reveal to the world that it isn't just that we've gotten God's name wrong, but that we've gotten God's nature wrong as well? Why simply give us a new name, but leave us with the same nature we've imbued "gods" with from the beginning? Why not show us lost, backwards-thinking humans a better path? Why not point us to a better, higher way?

Ultimately, this is precisely why I must reject this view and its "god." It isn't just that I find it distasteful, but that it ultimately fails to do anything more than the religions of Ba'al, or any other idol, did for their worshippers. Its sacrifice is more permanent, sure, but it still upholds the image of a "god" who will not, because he cannot, forgive without first being offered violence of some kind. There is no higher way here. There is no turn the other cheek, forgive seventy times seven times, or any other Christ-like calls. There is only the muffled sounds of the beating drums of the Moloch worshippers, drifting up from beneath the floorboards where we've buried them. If I follow that "god" and his way, I do not follow Jesus. It might be the name I use when I pray, but in that case, it would have become just a name, and nothing more.

This model of atonement simply feeds Christ into a preexisting, wholly human narrative, speaking of him as though he were the ultimate ritual sacrifice, and fully agrees with all idolatrous religions of antiquity. When we attribute the violence of the cross to God, we credit him with something he desires no credit for. We superimpose base, human impulses onto the face of the one Jesus is said to represent, and end up with the very god-concept he died refuting.

I simply do not understand how we don't see the hidden idolatry in all of this, and how we have the audacity to proclaim it as "good news." We act so befuddled and shocked when those outside the church look at us like maniacs for believing this type of thing, and wonder why unbelievers aren't beating down our doors to hear it. Meanwhile, the unbeliever stands befuddled by the fact that anyone darkens or enters our doors to hear it, or finds joy in proclaiming it. The fact is that, to the outsider, this twisted version of the "gospel" sounds like incoherent nonsense. That is, of course, not universally true of all, but those it is not true of are usually those who have had some sort of Christian upbringing, and so the ideas don't strike them as completely foreign. To almost everyone else, though, there is nothing innovative, or liberating here. Just the same terrible, violent, cringe-worthy story that humans have been telling since the dawn of time.

Former Pentecostal minister, now atheist, Dan Barker, gives this apt illustration of what the "gospel" of PSA sounds like to outsiders:

> Suppose you were walking by my house one day, you'd been walking by for a long time, and I were to go up on the porch and say, "Hey, stop I've got some good news...you don't have to go down in my basement..! You've been walking by all this time, you've been ignoring me, and I deserve to be recognized and honored. [But] you've been ignoring me and it's made me so angry...so I built this torture chamber in my basement... it's horrible, but you don't have to go down there [because] I sent my son down there. And it was gruesome...but that satisfied my anger. His blood was shed, and now you're free! All you have to do is come on up here. Just tell my son you love him, hug him, and you can move in with us..!"
>
> So would you keep walking?[80]

Of course, if faced with such a scenario, right around 111% of us would keep walking. Sadly, though, this insane, "you don't have to go down in my basement" message, is actually very close to what gets passed off as the Gospel by a great number of Christians. This is nearly identical to what we proclaim from our pulpits, on street corners, and in our tracts, and we wonder why everybody seems to "keep walking."

One famous pastor and author has said of Christ's atonement:

> Christ can save us forever from the wrath of God because he intercedes forever with God. He continually puts himself between the Father and us as an asbestos shield against his white-hot anger against sin. (Italics mine)[81]

Now, bear in mind that this is not an atheist trying to reduce the PSA doctrine to absurdity, but a Christian pastor, articulating what he believes is the Gospel message. It's almost as absurd as Dan Barker's basement illustration, if not more so. As Dawkins has suggested, were it not for this doctrine's "ubiquitous familiarity which has dulled our objectivity," we

---

[80] This quote is taken from a full talk given by Dan Barker which can be viewed here: https://www.youtube.com/watch?v=dup6xkvj1S0

[81] http://www.desiringgod.org/messages/jesus-from-melchizedek-to-eternal-savior

would have no trouble seeing it as, to use his words, "barking mad." When a pastor like the one from whom this quote comes, stoops to use such crass language to describe a supposed God of love, he unwittingly reveals his "god" to be no better than the absurd caricatures put forth by its critics. Anyone outside of the fold hearing this pastor's "asbestos shield" gospel, had might as well have been approached and asked, "May I tell you about our lord and savior, Jupiter?" or told by Dan Barker that he doesn't have to go into his basement. And we wonder why people "keep walking!" We wonder why people seem to run from our message as fast as their legs will carry them! I have to be honest with you, though, I thank God they "keep walking," even when their journey ends in atheism! For those who do keep walking, and reject such a "god," are far further removed from idolatry in their atheism than they would have been had they stopped, listened, and accepted Christianity on those terms.

The late Christopher Hitchens, an avowed atheist, wrote of the view I've been critiquing:

> I find something repulsive about the idea of vicarious redemption. I would not throw my numberless sins onto a scapegoat and expect them to pass from me; we rightly sneer at the barbaric societies that practice this unpleasantness in its literal form. [82]

I believe Hitchens, a man who chose to "keep walking" when posed with the ghastly message of a deity who tortured his innocent son in our place, embraced something closer to the Gospel than what many Christians are embracing today. Though he died an ardent atheist, I believe his unwillingness to embrace these doctrines, which chaffed against the divine image in which he was created, made him more "Christian" in his views than many who embrace them. His rejection of the "god" who punishes one son in place of another was a move toward God, not away from him.

George MacDonald, again, discussing this very issue, writes similarly:

> Better the reformers had kept their belief in a purgatory, and parted with what is called vicarious sacrifice! [83]

The idea that one man could be tortured, and thereby purchase forgiveness for the rest of us, so repulsed the passionate MacDonald, that he lamented the Christian reformers' keeping of the doctrine. The idea of a "vicarious sacrifice," or as Hitchens called it, "vicarious

---

[82] Christopher Hitchens, *God is Not Great* (New York: Twelve, 2007.)
[83] George MacDonald, The Complete Works of George MacDonald (Kindle Edition by O'Connor, 2010)

redemption," was so abhorrent in his eyes that he went on to write of it in these devastatingly beautiful words:

> The device is an absurdity—a grotesquely deformed absurdity. To represent the living God as a party to such a style of action, is to veil with a mask of cruelty and hypocrisy the face whose glory can be seen only in the face of Jesus; to put a tirade of vulgar Roman legality into the mouth of the Lord God merciful and gracious, who will by no means clear the guilty. Rather than believe such ugly folly of him whose very name is enough to make those that know him heave the breath of the hart panting for the water brooks; *rather than think of him what in a man would make me avoid him at the risk of my life, I would say, 'There is no God; let us neither eat nor drink, that we may die!* For lo, this is not our God! This is not he for whom we have waited!' But I have seen his face and heard his voice in the face and the voice of Jesus Christ; and I say this is our God, the very one whose being the Creator makes it an infinite gladness to be the created. I will not have the God of the scribes and the Pharisees whether Jewish or Christian, protestant, Roman, or Greek, but thy father, O Christ! He is my God. If you say, 'That is our God, not yours!' I answer, 'Your portrait of your God is an evil caricature of the face of Christ.'[84]

MacDonald proclaimed that he would sooner give the notion of God up altogether rather than believe he was as PSA proponents say! "Rather than think of him what in a man would make me avoid him at the risk of my life," he writes, "I would say, 'There is no God; let us neither eat nor drink, that we may die!'" For MacDonald, an abandonment of "god," and an embracing of atheism would be the Christ-honoring move, if one found themselves faced with a deity claiming to have established peaceful relations by symbolically murdering the part of us he hated, by crushing his innocent Son under his wrath. For MacDonald, the Jesus-like thing to do would be to "keep walking." Saying no to "god" altogether would be better, in MacDonald's eyes, than donning the bloody, unjustly acquired asbestos shield of a vicarious sacrifice in the name of protecting oneself from an angry "god's" wrath.

To reject such a "god," even if it's the only "god" one knows of, and therefore represents a rejection of "god" altogether, is to more closely follow Jesus than some who claim his name. To reject the latent idolatry in such a message, even if it results in atheism, is to move closer to God

---

[84] Ibid.

than the one who embraces such a message in his name. But MacDonald didn't choose atheism, but a form of Christianity that, to the fundamentalist, perhaps, appears as indistinguishable from atheism. The Christian must reckon with the fact that following Jesus will often leave them appearing Godless to those with the biggest platforms, and the loudest megaphones. More difficult, perhaps, than the feeling of being rejected by the Christian majority, is the sense one will have that they are rejecting God by choosing to reject what the majority calls orthodox. We must embrace as reality, though, that rejecting idolatrous caricatures of God is to honor and follow God, and to do so is also to appear as an idolater to some.

For MacDonald, the fact that the actions of the "god" of PSA, if performed by a human, would cause us to avoid that person at the risk of our lives, was enough to cause him to conclude that they cannot possibly be attributable to the one Jesus called Abba. It seems clear enough to me as well, and yet still, this belief is stubbornly clung to by millions of believers worldwide, even when they are faced with its decidedly anti-Christ overtones. Why don't we "keep walking?" What is this belief's appeal? Sadly, I think we like simple answers more than we do moral answers, and ideas that don't violate the ethics of Jesus. The PSA model stands squarely opposed to everything that we consider just and moral as human beings, and yet, as with so many other troubling actions, when it is *God* said to be performing them, we, for some reason, give him a pass. I have to assume that PSA adherents have actually had to adjust and reconfigure their moral compasses in order to make this doctrine digestible. Like Hitchens and MacDonald, I have to believe that, inherently, we all understand a concept like PSA to be utterly immoral. I mean, after all, what father in his right mind would ever consider employing the tactic of PSA in the disciplining of his own children? Could you imagine what that would even look like?

While I'd like to say I couldn't, I actually can.

PSA PARENTING TIPS

As a teenager, I remember listening as one of my favorite preachers recounted how he demonstrated the "truth" of PSA to one of his children. They'd been caught committing some heinous crime like telling a white lie, and therefore needed to be punished. He sat them down, brandished a belt, and commenced to tell them of their wrongdoings. They knew what came next-the old "this is going to hurt me more than it hurts you" routine, followed by a sore posterior and a hug. But this day they were in for a treat, a real life "gospel" demonstration.

The father, instead of spanking his child, began to violently beat himself on the legs with the belt. His child pleaded, "No, daddy! Stop!" but he continued. And if we're to believe the story, he continued until his legs were red and welted, and the kid was a tearful mess. He then looked his hysterical child in the eye and said, "Always remember that today, daddy took your punishment, just like Jesus took yours 2,000 years ago." Of course, the listening congregation erupted in applause and shouts of "Hallelujah!" but I, as an impressionable teenager, who was still trying to figure this God thing out, found my stomach turning. Of course, I tried to make it seem profound. It was my favorite preacher telling the story, after all. But try as I might, I couldn't make myself feel anything but sickened by the story.

I remember thinking, *is this really our message?* Is this really what I'm called to tell people? You broke a rule, earned yourself a whipping, but God turned the whip on himself? This is no better than the absurd "you don't have to go down in my basement" message that Barker put forth. It's no better a story than that of the drunken father, whose anger is directed toward one son, so that there can be only love left for the other that this chapter opened with. And yet I was supposed to tell people that this was the best God could do? To turn the whip on himself? What about just letting the grudge go? How about dropping the whip? What about not needing to resort to violence on anyone, even if it's yourself, in order to solve your problems?

What about just...forgiving?

Walter Wink writes of the PSA model of atonement:

> ...God is involved in a transaction wholly within God's own self. But what is wrong with this God, that the legal ledgers can be balanced only by means of the death of an innocent victim? Jesus simply declared people forgiven, confident that he spoke the mind of God. Why then is a sacrificial victim necessary to make forgiveness possible? Does not the death of Jesus reveal that all such sacrifices are unnecessary?[85]

Wink notes that the Jesus we read of in the Gospels simply declared God's forgiveness as an unbidden, unpurchased reality, prior to any blood being shed on his part. He did not see a human sacrifice as being necessary before his Father could begin dispensing forgiveness, but simply declared sins forgiven. Furthermore, as Wink notes, the murder of Jesus, which would have equaled humanity's greatest sin, was not met with judgment or wrath from God, but forgiveness and mercy. So, not only do we see that a blood sacrifice was not needed because of the way

---

[85] Walter Wink, *Engaging the Powers* (Minneapolis : Fortress Press, ©1992.)

Jesus operated in life, we also see this truth displayed in his death. The fact that God responded to the violence and cruelty of men with mercy, proves that he is not an offended, sin-counting deity, who demands payment for our transgressions. If the cross was our greatest crime, and it was met with kindness, God is revealed to be nothing like the "god" PSA presents him as being.

Wink goes on to say:

> The God whom Jesus revealed as no longer our rival, no longer threatening and vengeful, but unconditionally loving and forgiving, who needed no satisfaction by blood-this God of infinite mercy was metamorphosed by the church into the image of a wrathful God whose demand for blood atonement leads to God's requiring of his own Son a death on behalf of us all. The nonviolent God of Jesus comes to be depicted as a God of unequaled violence, since God not only allegedly demands the blood of the victim who is closest and most precious to him, but also holds the whole of humanity accountable for a death that God both anticipated and required. *Against such an image of God the revolt of atheism is an act of pure religion.* (Italics mine)[86]

Truly, the beautifully subversive and redemptive message of the cross, in which God suffers at our hands, but refuses to respond to us with our own methods, is rendered unrecognizable in this model. God requires violence in order to forgive, but then, in some circles of Christianity, is said to hold those who do not respond to the "gospel" as guilty of participating in his murder. The very act he required to save us, when rejected, becomes the impetus of our damnation.

We often speak of the sin of Judas, of the religious leaders who called for Jesus' death, and of the Romans who crucified him, but how can we really accuse them of sin if they were essentially acting as unwitting priests, offering to God a perfect sacrifice they just didn't realize they were offering? I know that isn't how anyone would actually understand the crucifixion, but isn't that essentially what would be happening if the PSA model were correct? These people would have been carrying out the ultimate will of God in satisfying his wrath, and yet, we somehow find a way to speak of their actions as evil.

How does that work, exactly?

How can we accuse them of sin, while at the same time seeing them as representing the fulfillment of God's perfect will? This is a dualism I'm

---

[86] Walter Wink, *Engaging the Powers* (Minneapolis : Fortress Press, ©1992.)

simply not willing to follow, as it represents more than just a frantic attempt to keep a belief from falling apart, but is, perhaps, an unintentional, but very real attribution of violent and horrific actions to a God who goes out of his way to show his utter contempt for such things. To call the men who committed these actions *sinners*, but the God who required them in order to forgive sins, *good*, is not moral. One has to go out of their way to willingly reconfigure their moral compass in order to make that one work.

Zizek, speaking of the saying, "if there is no God, then everything is permitted," has suggested that it is actually precisely the opposite which is true, and that "if there is a God, everything is permitted[87]." What he means here, is that once a person brings God into the equation, they can validate and sacralize any action of theirs they wish. There are actions that are clearly evil and diabolical, but once one claims God commissioned them to carry it out, it becomes holy, righteous, and permitted. This is precisely what occurs in the doctrine of PSA, and why I fully agree with Wink when he says that the revolt of atheism against it is "an act of pure religion." The "god" of this doctrine is one who clouds our vision, and causes us to perceive goodness in an action that, were it to be committed by anyone else, and in the name of any other cause, we would clearly see as evil. Atheism as it concerns this picture of "god," again, is a move towards the truth of God, not away from it. To cling to it is to betray one's own God-given sense of morality in the name of religion, but to abandon it is to discover a religion that is pure and undefiled.

I know that's a strong statement, and I know that to the ardent supporter of PSA, it will also be a highly offensive one. I'm not, however, going out of my way to offend here, but simply stating the truth of where I'm at in my journey. I simply can no longer abide a doctrine that demands I call evil good, and good evil. Nor can I, in good conscience, call myself a follower of Jesus while maintaining a belief that effectively pits him against the very Father he claims to perfectly represent. As MacDonald writes of the belief: "To believe in a vicarious sacrifice, is to think to take refuge with the Son from the righteousness of the Father; to take refuge with his work instead of with the Son himself;"

Essentially, PSA declares that we are hidden *in* Christ *from* God, as opposed to being hidden *with* Christ *in* God. Abba becomes the drunk dad whom big brother wards off; the devil Jesus saves us from.

Additionally, in order to maintain the PSA position, I would have to rob Jesus of his right to claim that his Father was a non-violent, enemy-

---

[87] http://www.abc.net.au/religion/articles/2012/04/17/3478816.htm

loving forgiver of sins, prior to the offering of any blood or sacrifice. Take the Sermon on the Plain from Luke 6, for example:

> 35 But *love your enemies*, *do good*, and lend, expecting nothing in return. Your reward will be great, and you will be children of the Most High...
>
> -Luke 6:35, NRSV (Italics mine)

Here Jesus calls us to love our enemies. Pretty simple. But still some argue that though *we* are called to behave this way, God is under no such obligation. Vengeance is his, some claim, so while *we* must forgive and not seek out retribution, God is free to withhold forgiveness and dole out retribution in generous amounts. This is not what Jesus had in mind at all, though.

He continues:

> 35 ...*for he is* kind to the ungrateful and the wicked. 36 Be merciful, *just as your Father* is merciful.
>
> -Luke 6:35-36, NRSV (Italics mine)

The God Jesus speaks of and reveals calls us to live lives of enemy-love and forgiveness, not in spite of what he does, but in light of what he does. It is precisely the fact that God gives and forgives, with no expectation of receiving anything in return that is to be our motivation for doing the same. How can we claim to take seriously Jesus' revelation of the Father, and at the same time hold to an atonement theory claiming that this same Father cannot forgive without first needing to take a human life? How can we take seriously Jesus' claims of a merciful God who gives freely to all, expecting nothing back from them, while also believing that this God can only give freely and let go of his grudges after being presented with a human sacrifice? This theory of atonement makes nonsense out of the actual teachings and actions of Jesus, and is offensive in light of the revelation of God he set forth.

Not to mention the fact that it would be impossible to tell a devotee of the "god" of PSA that he must do as "god" says, but not as he does. One cannot help but unconsciously emulate what they believe to be ultimate goodness or holiness, and so, regardless of whether or not one believed it was only god who had the right to violence and retribution, they would still unconsciously follow his lead, even if they claimed to not possess the right to.

And ultimately, this is why I must reject this view.

I'm very familiar with many of the pro-PSA arguments, and can rattle off a host of proof-texts that would seem to back up the belief. I taught that brand of atonement for close to a decade, and could probably still present and argue it quite effectively. I dedicated a large portion of my first book to dealing with passages in the bible that seem to support the view, but I'm not really interested in going there in this chapter. Instead, I simply want to point out some of the moral problems I see with the view, and suggest to you that the "god" represented in it is not the Abba Jesus claims to have represented. And while I believe one can be a Christian and hold to the view, I do not think that in holding to it we are being as faithful to the person of Christ as we might think we are. Certainly, one can be a Christian while believing this way, but the belief itself is, in my opinion, anything but Christian. Taking Jesus seriously means taking his claims about his Father seriously, and those claims and the claims of PSA simply do not mesh. In this regard, following Jesus requires that, in an act of *pure* religion, we become atheists concerning the violent, contradictory, sacrifice-demanding deity of the PSA model.

VAMPIRIC CHRISTIANITY

To close this chapter out, I want to return to the idea that Christ's death serves as the final sacrifice that appeases God's wrath. As we've already discussed, this often gets spoken of in ways that suggest that while God was once angry, he is so no longer, provided that we abide in Jesus. This "no longer" is due to the fact that a final, perfect sacrifice has been offered. Nothing can be added to it, and nothing can be taken away. Paul, however, writes something most peculiar; something which seems to fly in the face of this belief:

> 24 I am now rejoicing *in my sufferings* for your sake, and *in my flesh I am completing what is lacking in Christ's afflictions* for the sake of his body, that is, the church.
>
> -Colossians 1:24, NRSV (Italics mine)

I know many Christian circles that would try a man for blasphemy were he to ever utter such words, and yet here they are, occupying space in our bibles. If Christ's work was a final sacrifice to appease God, what on earth would be lacking in it, and how could Paul's personal suffering in any way add to, or complete it?

What is revealed here is an often overlooked aspect of the cross; an aspect that finds itself in the "often overlooked" category, precisely because of positions like PSA. We have made the cross into something Jesus himself never even hinted at it being, and in so doing have covered over aspects of it that the early church clearly clung to as sacred. Among these sacred aspects is the cross as an exemplary model which, by the Spirit, the Christian is empowered to follow. According to

Paul, Christ's afflictions still lack in the sense that they do not directly affect the lives of the people in the churches he served, or, let's say, a poor beggar on a street corner. Sure, the death of Jesus reveals God's love and absolute forgiving nature to such a one, but it does nothing to put food in his stomach, shoes on his feet, or a roof over his head. It is only when you or I see in the death of Jesus a model worth following, and choose to live it out towards the poor beggar, that the afflictions of Christ take on a substantial meaning for him. Thus, in "laying down my life", even if only in the form of providing someone with shelter, meals, or finances, I complete through my own actions what is still lacking in Christ's.

This exemplary model of the atonement, or what has been called the Moral Influence Theory, was the primary way that the cross and death of Jesus was understood for the *first* thousand years or so of Christianity, and it has only been in the *last* thousand years that the way we understand atonement has begun to shift. For most of its history, the church has affirmed that the purpose of the cross was to work a profound, moral change in the heart of individuals, and even whole societies, through a demonstration of divine love and forgiveness. The replacement of this view with models like PSA has led to many missing out on the fact that the cross is meant to be understood as the culmination of all that Christ did, taught and revealed about his Father, not a contradiction of it. But sadly, the sacrificial, punitive way in which we've framed the cross has, in fact, made it contradictory to the essence of all that Jesus taught. No longer do we see an example, or an invitation into an others-centered life of love, but a sacrificial transaction that gets "god" off our case.

Paul's idea of Christ's afflictions lacking, and needing to be completed by us, makes absolutely no sense in the sacrificial, PSA view of things. This faulty understanding of the cross as something that appeases God and sets us free from his anger has, in many ways, contributed to a form of Christianity in which the whole goal is personal forgiveness and heaven, and in which we're not responsible for serving humanity. The cross has done all of that, we claim, and so we go on our merry way, not realizing that the afflictions of Christ still lack so long as our participation is lacking. Jesus' blood does not heal anyone's marriage, visit them when they're in the hospital or when they're sick, or serve them a hot meal on the streets. All of those things are lacking until we follow the example laid out on the cross, and bring them into existence.

Marcus Borg, writing of the payment, or PSA model of atonement's ability to distract us from actually *following* Jesus, says that it:

> ...makes "believing" that Jesus died to pay for our sins more important than "following" him. Christianity becomes believing that he has done for us what we

cannot do for ourselves, rather than participating in the passion that animated his life and led to his death. It creates what an evangelical critic of the payment understanding has called "vampire Christians"-that is, Christians interested in Jesus primarily for his blood, and not much else.[88]

The "evangelical critic" Borg mentions is Dallas Willard, who writes concerning this vampiric brand of Christianity:

> This "heresy" has created the impression that it is quite reasonable to be a "vampire Christian." One in effect says to Jesus, "I'd like a little of your blood, please. But I don't care to be your student or have your character. In fact, won't you just excuse me while I get on with my life, and I'll see you in heaven."[89]

Those are some pretty harsh words, but true, nonetheless. A "vampire Christian" feels an insatiable need to be forgiven, cleansed from their sins, and reconciled to an angry deity, and it is only in the blood of Jesus that they feel this need can be satisfied. The Augustinian thirst has created within their belief system the need for a well from which they can drink, and the violent death of Jesus has become just such a well. The doctrine of PSA becomes, then, little more than a vampiric feeding session that alleviates their craving, but leaves Christ in the place of the victim who satisfies it, since he's the same victim who has satisfied "god." There is not, in this form of atonement or Christianity, a drive to follow Jesus in cruciform love, and certainly no "way" to speak of, but only a need to feed. The cross starts and ends with what it does for us, and gets us on the track to heaven, but does not extend out into our relationships with others. There is no need to complete, through our own actions, what is lacking in Christ's, since his only goal was to alter the angry disposition of the man upstairs.

The early church simply did not see the cross in these terms. They saw an ultimate, exemplary act of love on the part of God toward humanity. Upon seeing it, it wasn't a profound relief that they were off the hook that they felt, but a deep, and profound sense of love, that then moved them to see the world in ways they hadn't prior to.

Consider some of these New Testament admonitions regarding the cross as exemplary, and what our response to it should be:

---

[88] Marcus Borg, *Convictions: How I Learned What Matters Most* (San Francisco: HarperOne, [2014])

[89] Dallas Willard, *The Great Omission: Reclaiming Jesus's Essential Teachings on Discipleship* ([San Francisco, Calif.]: HarperSanFrancisco, ©2006)

3 *Consider* him who endured such *hostility* against himself *from sinners, so that you* may not grow weary or lose heart.

-Hebrews 12:3, NRSV (Italics mine)

Here we have the cross set forth as an example of how to endure hardships. Christ's death is said to have been something done by "sinners", not the Father, and his patient endurance of their hostility serves as an example to us of how to lovingly endure persecution ourselves. Just as Christ endured the shame associated with crucifixion, choosing love and forgiveness over hatred and violence, so we ought to do the same.

Consider these words, from 1 Peter:

18 Slaves, accept the authority of your masters with all deference, not only those who are kind and gentle but also those who are harsh. 19 For it is a credit to you if, being aware of God, you endure pain while suffering unjustly. 20 If you endure when you are beaten for doing wrong, what credit is that? But if you endure when you do right and suffer for it, you have God's approval. 21 For to this you have been called, because Christ also suffered for you, leaving you an example, so that you should follow in his steps.

-1 Peter 2:18-21, NRSV

While this was clearly written in a different era of human history, in which a toleration for atrocities like slavery were a bit higher than ours today; and while this verse both can and has been used to justify great evil in the name of God, there is still a redeemable lesson present. We can lay aside the archaic belief that Christ's suffering gives a harsh slave master ownership over a man's soul, while not totally missing what was, perhaps, the deeper truth the author felt, but had no proper metaphor for. Here's his bottom line:

23 When he was abused, *he did not return abuse*; when he suffered, *he did not threaten*; but he entrusted himself to the one who judges justly.

-1 Peter 2:23, NRSV (Italics mine)

What we can take away from this passage is that the early church saw in Jesus' death an invitation into a life of enemy-love and forgiveness. Just as Jesus did not respond to violence with violence, so should we always take the high road of peace and non-retaliation. And while, yes, the example of Christ's suffering at the hands of those in power *can* be misunderstood, and used as justification for oppression, those who would use it to that end reveal how grossly they've misunderstood the suffering of Jesus, who dies, not as an example of how to commit great acts of evil, but of how to respond in a God-like fashion to great acts of evil. Here again, Christ's work is an example that we follow, not a payment made to God.

John sums this exemplary view of the cross up quite beautifully:

> 16 *We know love by this, that he laid down his life for us—and we ought to lay down our lives for one another.* 17 How does God's love abide in anyone who has the world's goods and sees a brother or sister in need and yet refuses help?
>
> -1 John 3:16-17, NRSV (Italics mine)

John does not present Christ's death as a blood payment to an offended, Moloch-like "god," but as the ultimate example of love. It is in the free giving of his life into the hands of those who would do him harm, and his refusal to avenge himself or seek out retribution when they do, that God reveals to us what love actually looks like. Love is a free giving of ourselves for the benefit of another, regardless of the personal cost. John then uses this example to spur on the church to take care of the poor and needy, not to rest assured that the wrath of God has been appeased.

Finally, in 2 Corinthians 5, Paul sees Christ's death as a representation of the death of an old creation, or an old way of framing and understanding the world. Having seen this, Paul also begins to see the whole of humanity in a new light:

> 14 For the love of Christ urges us on, because we are convinced that *one has died for all; therefore all have died.* 15 And *he died for all, so that those who live might live no longer for themselves*, but for him who died and was raised for them. 16 *From now on, therefore, we regard no one from a human point of view*, even though we once knew Christ from a human point of view, we know him no longer in that way.
>
> -2 Corinthians 5:14-16, NRSV (Italics mine)

Again, Paul sees in the cross a motivation for living in a brand new way -a way that rejects former categories of Jew and Gentile, male and female, slave and free, and instead sees humanity as a redeemed, liberated whole. Christ's death, here, is set forth as an example of how God has, in Jesus, put to death a system in which it is lawful to divide humanity into categories and judge them accordingly. For Paul, all of humanity is fully represented in Jesus, and all distinctions between them die at the cross.

I think by now you're seeing my point. The cross points us to living in a way that is contradictory to how the world is presently structured. It does not tell you that your sins have all been thrown onto a scapegoat, and so now you're free to go your own way, but that because Christ, who is God, responded to the evilest of acts with the purest of love, we can and should live lives that emulate such a love.

Lest I scare away any of my Grace-leaning friends for fear that I'm preaching "works," I assure you that I believe this emulation to be something only accomplished by the Spirit, and is not a mere human effort. But we are, in fact, enabled to complete what is lacking in regards to Christ's afflictions by giving ourselves just as Christ gave himself. The cross does not tell us that Christ took credit for what we had done wrong, was judged accordingly, and so now we can sit back taking credit for all the good he had done. It tells us that Christ has revealed to us the divine mystery of love, and now, empowered by the Spirit, calls us to follow his example.

Hitchens says of this immoral idea that Christ took responsibility so that we wouldn't have to:

> We cannot, like fear-ridden peasants of antiquity, hope to load all our crimes onto a goat and then drive the hapless animal into the desert. Our everyday idiom is quite sound in regarding "scapegoating" with contempt. And religion is scapegoating writ large. I can pay your debt, my love, if you have been imprudent, and if I were a hero like Sidney Carton in *A tale of Two Cities* I could even serve your term in prison or take your place on the scaffold. Greater love hath no man. But I cannot absolve you of your responsibilities. It would be immoral of me to offer, and immoral of you to accept. [90]

I *must* reject the PSA model of atonement for precisely the same reasons as Hitchens lays out. Again, to quote Wink, the revolt of atheism against such a "god" is an act of pure religion, and as MacDonald suggested, it would be better to abandon the concept of "god" altogether, rather than worship one like this. In Hitchens' words, though coming from a wholly atheistic perspective, I hear the wisdom of the God of Jesus, the preaching of apostles, and the thunderings of a prophet. God does not absolve us of responsibility through a sacrificial exchange, but rather reveals to us what true, God-like love looks like. We are called to leave behind the Moloch-like beings who call for blood in exchange for blessing, flesh in exchange for forgiveness, and follow instead the one who says that even the greatest of our crimes is met with mercy. The

---

[90] Christopher Hitchens, God is Not Great (New York: Twelve, 2007.)

example of Christ is one we are called to follow, and the responsibility he takes up is a responsibility we are moved to mirror. Regardless of how thorough and complete of a "work" Christ's death was, it still leaves something lacking, and that *something* is what we are called to complete in our Spirit-empowered emulation of the Crucified One. To accept an absolution of responsibility through a sacrificial exchange would be to accept something highly immoral, and it would mean the one offering such absolution was immoral as well.

REDEFINING SACRIFICE

Ultimately, I think our problem comes down to the concept of sacrifice, and our inability understand the death of Christ outside of preexisting sacrificial paradigms. We have, as I've already stated, fed the death of Christ into a pagan narrative about sacrifice, and have arrived at many of our present atonement theories precisely because of this error. We have imagined sacrifice as all ancient cultures have, in the sense that they are blood payments to deities that we make in order to secure peace, blessings, or forgiveness, and, since the New Testament writers use the word *sacrifice* regarding Jesus' death, have assumed that it worked the very same way. But what if the cross, far from confirming pagan suspicions about sacrifice, directly contradicts them, and seeks to redefine sacrifice as something else entirely?

In Hebrews chapter 10, the writer tells us plainly that God has never desired burnt offerings or sacrifices, including those specifically required by the Mosaic Law. The writer then speaks of Jesus' coming into this world in order to carry out the will of his Father, which the aforementioned sacrifices were incapable of carrying out. This, however, is spoken against the backdrop of God's rejection of the practice of sacrifice as humanity has traditionally understood it. Whatever it is Jesus came to do, though, it's still called *sacrifice*, but it isn't sacrifice as we have imagined it:

> 4 For it is impossible for the blood of bulls and goats to take away sins. 5 Consequently, when Christ came into the world, he said, "*Sacrifices and offerings you have not desired, but a body you have prepared for me; 6 in burnt offerings and sin offerings you have taken no pleasure. 7 Then I said, 'See, God, I have come to do your will, O God' (in the scroll of the book it is written of me)."* 8 When he said above, "*You have neither desired nor taken pleasure in sacrifices and offerings and burnt offerings and sin offerings*" (these are offered according to the law), 9 then he added, "See, *I have come to do*

your will." He abolishes the first in order to establish the second. 10 And it is *by God's will that we have been sanctified through the offering of the body of Jesus Christ once for all.*

-Hebrews 10:4-10, NRSV (Italics mine)

The writer, in a brilliant move, detaches the will of God from ritualistic concepts of sacrifice, stating that what Jesus accomplished in the body, while representing the will of God, was not aligned with Mosaic commands regarding sacrifice. Therefore, to read Jesus into the narrative of Leviticus, for example, is to sort of miss the point. Yes, the writer indicates that sacrifices were mere shadows of Christ's suffering, but in stating that God never desired these "shadows," and in detaching them from the will of God, he is also suggesting that Christ is not seeking to accomplish the things they were thought to accomplish.

In verse 9, after very clearly telling us that Jesus did not come to be a sacrifice as the Law demanded, or, I think we could add, according to the way sacrifice was framed in pagan myth, he tells us that God, in Jesus, "abolishes the first in order to establish the second." The "first" in question seems to be the former way of understanding sacrifice, whereas the "second" is the new and revolutionary understanding that Jesus introduces us to. This seems to clearly be what the author is doing, as in verse 10, after having told us in no uncertain terms that Christ is not in the business of offering ritualistic sacrifices, nor God in the business of accepting them, Christ's death is spoken of in sacrificial language: "the *offering* of the body of Jesus Christ once for all."

It seems the author is trying to show that in Jesus' death, God is initiating a shift in the way we understand sacrifice. It cleanses us, but we are also told clearly that it is not a sacrifice of the Mosaic, ritualistic order. So what is it cleansing us from? Is it cleansing us from sin through the offering of blood? Through the original sin of Adam, as taught by Augustine? If you go back to chapter 9, the writer is already speaking of Christ in sacrificial terms, while also laying out what it is this "sacrifice" redeems us from:

> 13 For if the blood of goats and bulls, with the sprinkling of the ashes of a heifer, sanctifies those who have been defiled so that their flesh is purified, 14 *how much more will the blood of Christ, who through the eternal Spirit offered himself without blemish to God, purify our conscience from dead works to worship the living God!* 15 For this reason he is the mediator of a new covenant, so that those who are called may receive the promised eternal inheritance, because *a death has occurred that redeems them from the transgressions under the first covenant.*

-Hebrews 9:13-15, NRSV (Italics mine)

The writer, writing to a Jewish-Christian audience, uses their own language to explain how they can understand Christ's death as freeing them from their former way of life. If the sacrifices offered under the Law were able to accomplish ritual cleansing for those involved, how much more will Christ's death purify the *conscience* of the worshipper? It is not that there needed to be a removal of literal sin from the person, or that God's wrath needed to be satisfied, but that the conscience of the one approaching God was still haunted by "dead works," or sins committed under the Law. By God's account, these sins were as good as dead and of no account, but the presence of the Law continually breathed life into them, causing them to appear as issues when they weren't. These weren't a problem on God's end, but on the end of those seeking to approach him. The death of Christ, then, can be understood by the Jewish Christian as being the thing that annuls the covenant that caused their consciences to be haunted in the first place. The death of Jesus, and his non-retaliatory response to being murdered, proves that all of our sins are as good as dead in his sight, but the Law keeps them alive and kicking in our minds. The Law had become the problem, not God. The death of Jesus, then, is an act in which the Jew can understand the system keeping their sins alive and their consciences haunted, as having been dealt with, that they might approach God with a clean and pure conscience!

This is the "will of God" which, in chapter 10, the writer claims Christ accomplished! We are cleansed, not because God accepted Christ as satisfaction for our sins, but because the system that insisted our transgressions still lived was annulled! It was a merciful act for our benefit, not God's!

This turns the concept of sacrifice on its head, as it has always been understood as something offered to the gods. In Christ, though, we have an offering made to God in a symbolic sense, but it was for the benefit of humanity. How could Christ offer a sacrifice to God that was for our benefit? The sacrifice in question was his carrying out of his Father's will, or his obedience, which was ultimately for us. The writer seems to be reinterpreting sacrifice as an act of obedience toward God that leads to the betterment of humanity.

In Hebrews 13, after this lengthy deconstruction of the process and principles of sacrifice, sacrificial language reappears. When it reappears, though, it has changed forms significantly, and no longer looks like a gift of blood to the "gods," but as the gift of hospitality to humans:

> 16 Do not neglect to *do good* and to *share* what you have, for *such sacrifices are pleasing to God.*

-Hebrews 13:16, NRSV (Italics mine)

The God of Jesus Christ is a God who rejects, and wants nothing to do with, bloody sacrifices aimed at appeasing his wrath. He rejects all such sacrifices, and instead, in the person of his Son, lives out and embodies his will, and then presents it to us as the true meaning of sacrifice. Doing good, sharing what you have, showing hospitality, loving one another, and all of those other Christian virtues that tend to get swept under the rug once we begin discussing the finer points of our atonement theories, are all that God has ever been after. The "offering," or "sacrifice," is our loving obedience in filling up what lacks in regards to Christ's afflictions. There's no wrath to be appeased or angry "gods" to be placated, only a Father who loves and serves humanity, and tells us that we look most like him when we are doing the same.

Our problem is that we have let go of God's redefinition of sacrifice in Jesus, and have allowed pagan concepts to reenter our narrative. As Wink notes, early Christians were "not able to sustain the intensity of this revelation," and thus reinterpreted it in light of the sacrificial doctrines and practices of old. The God of Jesus does not require violence in order to have a relationship with humanity or forgive their sins. Such ideas are nonsensical, and lead only to a vampiric form of faith that distorts the image of God, removes our responsibilities to the world, and kinks the hose of hospitality. What God has always desired was that we would be the recipients of his love, and therefore complete what it lacks in the world by emulating it and giving it away. This is the goal of the cross, and the true definition of the will of God and sacrifice. God did not need to have his frown turned upside down or his wrath removed through an offering of blood. What he needed was to show us what love looks like, so that we could be transformed by it, and in turn serve the world with it.

Ladies and gentlemen, regardless of how gracious and compassionate he is spoken of as being, I have no desire to live under the same roof as the wrath-drunk, abusive "god" of PSA; the "god" who must beat and murder our elder brother in order to treat us like children he loves. Even the acceptance of salvation on these terms seems to be an affront to justice, and an insult to the God Jesus has shown us. I cannot, in good conscience, stand within a world plagued by bloodshed, wars, domestic abuse, and violence of all sorts, and proclaim as the answer, a deity who could not resolve his problems without resorting to violence himself.

As a moral individual, who takes Jesus seriously, and sees the cross as a call to love, not as a blood debt paid to an offended god, I must reject this deity, in all of its various forms. I cannot, with my integrity intact, call myself a Jesus-follower while reading him into a narrative that contradicts the power of his message, and ultimately his death. I cannot look into the face of the non-violent, enemy-loving Jesus, who said that to see him was to see the Father, and claim that this very same Father demanded a type of sacrifice that the life and message of his "exact representation" exposed as hollow and meaningless. To look upon the cross and to understand its implications, and to then feed it back into pagan myth, is just not a move I'm willing to make.

I join with Hitchens the atheist, and MacDonald and Wink the theologians, in my atheism concerning this "god," an atheism that "he" has worked very hard to earn.

I stand unswervingly with Jesus, the enemy-lover, forgiver of sins, and revealer of the Father in his theism, and though that may make me an atheist to some, it's a pure religion I'll happily practice.

7 | GIVING THE ABSENT GOD EXISTENCE

"There is no God and we are his prophets."
-Cormac McCarthy

"The poor are the presence of the absent God..."
-Franz Hinkelammert

"God does not exist. God insists."
-John D. Caputo

There are places where God does not exist, but these are precisely the places where he is present, and calling to be brought into existence.

What could that possibly mean? We'll get there, don't' worry.

In Cormac McCarthy's bleak, apocalyptic novel, The Road, the two main characters, a father and a son, encounter an old man named Ely, who makes several statements that are equal parts profound and confusing. One of his statements, in particular, has always stuck out to me, haunted me even, and robbed my mind of many moments of rest. When the subject of God comes up in their conversation, the old man states matter of factly, "There is no God and we are his prophets."[91]

This statement bothered me for quite some time. What could it mean? What could the old man, and the author, be trying to say here? It could just be what the philosopher Daniel Dennet has dubbed a *deepity*[92], that is, a nonsensical statement that sounds profound, but is actually meaningless, like so many of the spiritual sounding, inspirational quotes we see bandied about on social media and hear in sermons. I think there's more to it than that, though.

"There is no God and we are his prophets."[93]

My guess would be that, in the context of the book's dark setting, in which men murder and cannibalize one another with the same degree of casualness we nod and smile at one another, the old man is saying that a desperate and suffering humanity has become a collective of prophets, uttering the oracles of a non-existent God. All one needs to do is look upon the blood, and bones, and brutality, and hear in them the thunderous prophetic declaration, "There is no God!" Atheist Dan Barker has said similarly, "All you have to do is walk into any children's hospital - and you know there is no god."

As I said in this book's opening line, I tried to be an atheist. As a pastor who was struggling with, among other things, questions concerning the goodness of God, I came to a place where the sight of so much meaningless suffering, with no apparent intervention by God, led me to conclude that he either didn't care, or that he didn't exist. As Sam Harris has famously said, "Either God can do nothing to stop catastrophes...or he doesn't care to, or he doesn't exist. God is either impotent, evil, or imaginary. Take your pick, and choose wisely."[94] Even more pointedly, Epicurus, the great pre-Christian, Greek philosopher, once said:

> Is God willing to prevent evil, but not able? Then he is
> not omnipotent.

---

[91] Cormac McCarthy, *The Road* (New York : Alfred A. Knopf, 2006.)

[92] Daniel Dennet, *Intuition Pumps and Others Tools For Thinking* (New York : W.W. Norton & Company, 2013.)

[93] This line is possibly a take on a famous remark made by Wolgang Pauli, concerning his friend, and scientist, Paul Dirac: "Well, our friend Dirac, too, has a religion, and its guiding principle is 'God does not exist and Dirac is His prophet.'"

[94] This quote is taken from a debate between Sam Harris and William Lane Craig, which can be seen here in its entirety: https://www.youtube.com/watch?v=yqaHXKLRKzg

Is he able, but not willing? Then he is malevolent.

Is he both able and willing? Then whence cometh evil?

Is he neither able nor willing? Then why call him God?

These thoughts began to pile up like a log jam in my soul. More and more, my traditional approach to God and his activity in the world, seemed to be stalling out. If God existed, but didn't care, why should I care for the manner in which he existed? Why was it that I had to watch the most devout, faithful, and prayerful of mothers, bury a child whom they had fully believed would be healed by a God of love? Why did it seem like the best people always had the worst cards dealt to them? Why, in a matter of a few months, did I have to see two different families torn apart by, thanks to cancer, the deaths of two of the godliest individuals you could have ever hoped to meet, both of whose healing I, and a multitude of others, prayed, fasted, and believed for earnestly? Why was it that I was constantly hearing testimonies of someone losing their car keys, and then finding them after prayer, and a week later hearing the news of a teenager, with a bright future ahead of them, dying in a car accident? If God can help you find your keys, why can't he keep them hidden them from those whose finding them would result in the loss of a life?

The pile up continued, and I had no answers. And as a pastor, as "*the guy,*" if you know what I mean, I was expected to have the answers. Every answer I'd give, though, was forced, and made me feel ill. I had none, and I knew it. In fact, slowly but surely, the questions that begged answers were becoming prophetic proclamations to me that there was no God. These horrific events were merely this non-existent being's mouthpieces, uttering with biblical urgency what I feared, deep down, was true.

As I said in earlier chapters, my attempts at atheism eventually failed me when I realized I was simply projecting onto atheism what I once projected onto God or "god." I was seeking refuge in it from pain, and using it as a distraction from reality. Eventually, even if only in desperation, I began to reexamine my Christianity, hoping to find in it *something* that spoke to these issues. As time passed, and I was able to think through this more completely, I started to realize that I wasn't so much convinced that God did not exist, as I was that God did not exist in the way I once thought he did. Now, was this a cop-out on my part? Was this just me returning to a belief system that I was comfortable with, since I was...comfortable with it? Perhaps. Who knows? What I can say, though, is that, in the Jesus story, I did, in fact, find a voice that spoke to the log jam in my soul. And while it did not answer all of my questions (not even close), it spoke to me. And that was enough.

Now let me explain what I'm getting at here.

In the last chapter we talked about the cross, and the "traditional" PSA approach to understanding atonement. For so many, that is the only version they've ever heard, and, for some, it has come to be the very definition of the Gospel. Because of this, we typically don't think any more deeply on the cross than this doctrine will allow. After all, if it's about satisfying the wrath of God against us hell-deserving sinners, why try to peer deeper? I mean, that's enough to warrant our devotion for an eternity, if it's true. Thankfully, though, I do not think it is true, but accepting that it wasn't proved to be quite difficult. I mean, what do you do when the central figure of your religion is an execution victim, if he is not serving as some kind of human sacrifice, or wrath-short-circuiting lightning rod? Well, that's what I want to talk about.

For me, the cross is to be understood as the place where God does not exist, but is present, and calling to be brought into existence. It is the voice of the prophet, whose suffering proclaims the inexistence of God, but, stranger still, identifies precisely where it is that he's present, and then commissions us to turn his presence into his existence. Now, I know, that all sounds confusing and purposely obtuse, and it is, but hopefully I'll be able to explain what I mean by all this.

Franz Hinkelammert, describing *liberation theology*, a branch of theology concerned mostly with things pertaining to social justice, and, as its name suggests, the liberation of people and people groups, writes:

> The existence of God, its Trinitarian character, redemption, etc., upon being professed as acts of faith, independent from their historical and concrete insertion, become nothing more than empty abstractions that compose a dogmatic whole without content. Liberation theology's problem is not to deny these beliefs, but to question their significance. Therefore, its question is not "Does God exist?' but "Where is God present?" and "How does God act?".[95]

Now, I don't intend to launch into an explanation of liberation theology here, and so I won't. But in order to get at the heart of what Hinkelammert is saying here, I will allow him to give us the most basic and pedestrian of explanations. In his words, it isn't about whether or not God exists. In fact, such questions are of little consequence in the real world. The real questions needing to be asked, says Hinkelammert, are "Where is God present?" and "How does God act?".

---

[95] David B Batstone, *Liberation Theologies, Postmodernity and the Americas* (London ; New York : Routledge, 1997)

So, *"where?"* and *"how?"* then?

He goes on to explain that liberation theology's answer lies in something called "the preferential option for the poor," a term intending to suggest that God is one to always side, or stand with the poor-and poor here speaks of more than *just* literal poverty, but of oppression of any sort. God is one who stands with those who are trampled upon, marginalized, excluded and otherized, and so, in liberation theology, God is *present* and standing with those who suffer in such ways.

He goes on to suggest that, when there is mutual acknowledgement between humans, a recognition that we are "needed beings," in some sense, God is present:

> The absence of this mutual recognition between human beings is present in the poor then...God is present wherever this acknowledgment occurs. The fact that this has not happened demonstrates a human relationship bereft of God. The existence of the poor testifies to the existence of a Godless society, whether one explicitly believes in God or not. This absence of God is present wherever someone is crying out.[96]

And here's the part I really want you to catch:

> The poor are the presence of the absent God.[97]

For Hinkelammert, the absence of God, or God's inexistence, *occurs* as an event whenever there is not mutual acknowledgement between humans that the other matters. When this acknowledgement is not present, be it in the form of literal poverty, social injustice, racism, war, etc., it is a prophetic declaration of God's absence. The poor, or the suffering, are literally the presence of a God who is absent. The old man from *The Road* was right in a sense, in that there is no God in the suffering of humans, and their suffering prophesies this absence. When I am not acknowledging your value, nor you mine, and our relationship fractures and things turn ugly, it is a relationship in which the qualities of God are absent, and therefore, it can be rightly said that the presence of such a relationship is a presence testifying to God's absence.

Wherever there are humans "crying out," their cries are equal parts expressions of injustice, and prophecies concerning God's inexistence. However, there is a third element to these cries as well, and that's that they are indicators of where God is present. God's attributes might not be in existence in situations of this sort, but the *preferential option for the*

---

[96] Ibid.
[97] Ibid.

poor declares that God is present with, and standing among, the suffering. Wherever, then, there is a cry of suffering, you will find God both absent and present. He is absent in the sense that the quality that defines him, *love*, is not on display, but is present in that he always opts to stand with those who suffer.

For Hinkelammert, one need not even explicitly believe in God in order to grasp what he's saying. Even if it is understood strictly as metaphor, the principle is still clear as day. In his own words: "God's absence is a place that can be pointed to." In other words, the *absence of God* is an event, as it were, even as philosophers like John Caputo speak of the presence of God as an event. God, to Caputo, is not necessarily a literal force one can come in contact with, but a call that is responded to, that then *happens* in the real world. This can look like the feeding of the poor, or the liberation of those unjustly oppressed. But whatever it looks like, God *happened.* In the same way, Hinkelammert speaks of God's absence as such an event in reverse. When there is no justice, compassion, or mutual acknowledgement among humans that the other matters, the absence of God occurs. When there *is* a mutual acknowledgment, however, and this acknowledgement leads us to love, serve, and give to one another, the cry is silenced, and absence is replaced by presence. God is present, not in some nebulous sense, or as some phantom in the air, but tangibly, in our actions as we acknowledge one another's necessity.

The cries of human suffering, then, as we've already said, do three things:

1) They reveal a situation in which God is absent
2) They reveal that God is present where he's absent
3) They commission us to actualize God's presence, or bring him into existence, by acknowledging the necessity, and value of the one suffering

THE GODLESS CRY

Throughout the Hebrew Scriptures, we hear this cry. For example, in Genesis 4, the cry of the unjustly murdered Abel reaches the ears of God, and we find him standing with Abel, the victim of a Godless relationship. The same word used to describe Abel's cry of suffering is used again, later on in Genesis, in chapter 18, to describe "outcry against Sodom and Gomorrah" that had reached God's ears. We typically understand this to mean that God heard tell of all the "bad things" going on within their city walls, and typically assume all those "bad things" equaled homosexual behavior. That's not what the text itself says, however. The actual suggestion is that Sodom was not protecting its guests, but victimizing and taking advantage of them. Hayes has written:

> ...the idea that the fundamental sin of Sodom was its homosexual nature is not at all clear in the Hebrew Bible...The Sodomites are guilty of gang rape, and the gender of the victims is hardly relevant. The Sodomites, like the generation of the flood, stand condemned by the "outcry" against them, a Hebrew term generally associated with the appeal of victims of violence, bloodshed, and oppressive injustice. The Sodomites' violation of the unwritten desert law of hospitality to strangers, their violent desire to abuse the strangers they should have been sheltering, is evidently merely one instance of their violent brutality.[98]

The way that God discovers that the outcry, or the cry of Sodom's victims, matches up with reality was through its treatment of the two angels sent to investigate. This is obviously meant to be contrasted with the way that Abraham welcomes and cares for these same angels in Genesis 18. If you recall, three men appear to Abraham, one of whom is said to be God, himself, and the others the angels who are sent to Sodom to investigate. Before going that way, however, Abraham hosts them, feeding and providing them with a place to rest:

> 2 He looked up and saw three men standing near him. When he saw them, he ran from the tent entrance to meet them, and bowed down to the ground. 3 He said, "My lord, if I find favor with you, do not pass by your servant. 4 *Let a little water be brought, and wash your feet, and rest yourselves under the tree. 5 Let me bring a little bread, that you may refresh yourselves*, and after that you may pass on—since you have come to your servant." So they said, "Do as you have said."... 20 Then the Lord said, "How great is the outcry against Sodom and Gomorrah and how very grave their sin! 21 I must go down and see whether they have done altogether according to the outcry that has come to me; and if not, I will know." 22 So the men turned from there, and went toward Sodom, while Abraham remained standing before the Lord.

> -Genesis 18:2-5; 20-22 NRSV (Italics mine)

---

[98] Christine Elizabeth Hayes, Introduction to the Bible (New Haven : Yale University Press, [2012])

Again, just as in the case of Abel's blood, we have an outcry making its way to God, who stands in solidarity with those crying out. In Exodus 2:23, this cry reappears, as the Israelites find themselves enslaved by the Egyptians, and cry to God for deliverance:

> 23 After a long time the king of Egypt died. The Israelites groaned under their slavery, and cried out. Out of the slavery their cry for help rose up to God.

> -Exodus 2:23, NRSV

And then again, in Isaiah 5:7, we read of this outcry:

> 7 For the vineyard of the Lord of hosts is the house of Israel, and the people of Judah are his pleasant planting; *he expected justice, but saw bloodshed; righteousness, but heard a cry!*

> -Isaiah 5:7, NRSV (Italics mine)

Commenting on this passage, Nahum Sarna writes that, "An outcry is the negation of justice and righteousness..."[99] Wherever there is a cry, as Hinkelammert wrote, "the absence of God is present." And yet, in all of these instances, this cry that prophesies God's absence, also prophesies his presence. He is never far from those who suffer, but stands with them, advocating for them.

Another example of this in scripture is Israel's exile, after Jerusalem is destroyed by the Babylonians in 586 BCE, and many of its citizens are carried off as slaves. The Psalmist sings of this exile in Psalms 137, and of how their captors demanded they sing for them the songs of their homeland. He laments, however, that they couldn't, and so refused, since:

> 4 How could we sing the LORD's song in a foreign land?

> -Psalms 137:4, NRSV

In many cultures of the day, and apparently within certain schools of Jewish thought as well, if a city were destroyed, and its inhabitants carried off as slaves, the gods they worshipped would stay behind, and eventually abandon the city. Naturally, then, the exiles would take on the customs, including the religion and the gods, of the land to which they were carried. In the Psalmist's words we find evidence of a similar belief. In their mind, Yahweh did not travel with them to Babylon, but stayed behind, and so they could not sing the songs of Yahweh in a foreign

---

[99] Nahum Sarna, Understanding Genesis (New York, Jewish Theological Seminary of America [1966])

land, being that he did not inhabit that land. The cry of the exile, then, was, similarly, a godless cry, a lament of abandonment and hopelessness. There was no God, and they were his prophets.

The prophet Ezekiel, however, has a striking vision in Ezekiel 10 & 11, in which he sees the Glory of God depart from the Temple in Jerusalem, and make its way east, toward the exiles, until Ezekiel is carried by the Spirit back among them, where we are to assume the Spirit itself took up residence as well. The imagery is powerful, and suggests a change in the way that God was understood. While they felt as though they were in exile minus God, the truth was that he had moved east with them, living among them in exile as well. Again, the cry that indicted God on charges of inexistence, was at the same time a cry that indicated he was present.

The very idea that the Christ-follower can somehow attain to a level of superior spirituality, in which sorrow no longer touches their lives, or the lives of anyone they touch, is directly contradicted by all of these stories and more. The New Testament too is filled with tales of suffering of the most meaningless sort, touching the lives of the most faithful sort. There are no promises of a present world in which these things will be banished, and never touch the lives of the "righteous." It was we who decided that the Gospel could make us impervious to pain and suffering, but nowhere is such a promise ever made to us. It is due in part to this false hope that suffering has come to prophesy God's *literal* non-existence to us. Sure, as Hinkelammert and the prophets suggest, a lack of justice *is*, in a very real sense, a lack of God, but it does not necessarily testify that there is no God. Rather, it testifies to the fact that there is a lack of Godly virtue being demonstrated in the situation. It is also a declaration that there is no "god," in the sense where "god" is imagined as an idealized version of ourselves, and therefore a type of savior figure. The "god" who is free from suffering, and promises that we can escape it as well, so long as we say the right magic words, recite the right creeds, and believe just the right way, exists only in our imaginations, and it is only here that it ever will exist.

The very fact that God chooses to embrace, and swallow into his being, human suffering and the experience of godlessness, proves that a place free of suffering is as mythical as the Asgard of Norse mythology. If it were to exist anywhere, certainly it would exist in God, but when we see God himself suffering as we do, we are met with the cold, hard reality that no such place exists. As we've said in past chapters, when faced with suffering, regardless of the size or shape of it, we will seek solace in "god" figures. Sometimes those figures are merely human idols, who represent to us what we wish we were. We might idolize a television dad, and aspire to be just like him, like the one played by Bill Cosby on the Cosby show. When it was shown, however, that Mr. Cosby actually looked nothing like the Phil Huxtable he portrayed on television, it could prove to be somewhat traumatic. Why? Because the revelation of Cosby's lack-of-Huxtable-ness, communicates to us that the one place such paternal perfection would exist, if it existed at all, is a place in which it clearly does not exist. This sort of derails our hopes of ever becoming a Huxtable-like patriarch, since not even "Huxtable" himself actually was.

It works the same way with Jesus. We like to imagine that somewhere in the cosmos exists a place where the sort of suffering we undergo does not exist, and, naturally, for a theist, that place is God. What we see in the crucifixion, however, is that even God himself suffers. Meaning that the one place wherein protection from suffering would exist, if it existed at all, is a place that does not exist. If God suffers, even to the point of experiencing the pain of godlessness, then there is no salvation, at least in the way we tend to think of salvation, from suffering.

G.K. Chesterton, in *Orthodoxy*, has written:

> That a good man may have his back to the wall is no more than we knew already, but that God could have His back to the wall is a boast for all insurgents forever. Christianity is the only religion on earth that has felt that omnipotence made God incomplete...In this indeed I approach a matter more dark and awful than it is easy to discuss; and I apologize in advance if any of my phrases fall wrong or seem irreverent touching a matter which the greatest saints and thinkers have justly feared to approach. But in the terrific tale of the Passion there is a distinct emotional suggestion that the author of all things (in some unthinkable way) went not only through agony, but through doubt. It is written, "Thou shalt not tempt the Lord thy God." No; but the Lord thy God may tempt Himself; and it seems as if this was what happened in Gethsemane. In a garden Satan tempted man: and in a garden God tempted God...When the world shook and the sun was wiped out of heaven, it was not at the crucifixion, but at the cry from the cross: the cry which confessed that God was forsaken of God... but let the atheists themselves choose a god. They will find only one divinity who ever uttered their isolation; only one religion in which God seemed for an instant to be an atheist.[100]

For Chesterton, Jesus' absorption of, or solidarity with, human suffering, for a moment, transforms God into an atheist. He literally takes up the cry

[100] G.K. Chesterton, The Collected Works of G.K. Chesterton (San Francisco: Ignatius Press, ©1986-<©2012>)

of Abel, Sodom's victims, the enslaved Israelites, and the exiles; the cry of the godless:

> 34 At three o'clock Jesus cried out with a loud voice, "Eloi, Eloi, lema sabachthani?" which means, *"My God, my God, why have you forsaken me?"* 35 When some of the bystanders heard it, they said, "Listen, he is calling for Elijah." 36 And someone ran, filled a sponge with sour wine, put it on a stick, and gave it to him to drink, saying, "Wait, let us see whether Elijah will come to take him down." 37 Then *Jesus gave a loud cry* and breathed his last. 38 *And the curtain of the temple was torn in two, from top to bottom.*

-Mark 12:34-38, NRSV (Italics mine)

In this moment of intense suffering, Jesus chooses to express his agony by quoting the first verse of Psalms 22 (My God, my god, why have you forsaken me?), even though we know from Jesus' own words elsewhere in the Gospels that he was not *literally* forsaken, or abandoned by his Father (John 8:28-29). In my first book, I devote an entire chapter to debunking the popular idea commonly associated with the PSA theory that the Father had to literally forsake Jesus in order for atonement to be made. That is just simply not the case, though, and not in any way what Jesus seems to be implying here. The very same prophetic Psalm from which he quotes culminates with the Psalmist proclaiming that he had not, in fact, been abandoned or forsaken:

> 24 ...*he did not hide his face from me*, but heard when I cried to him.

-Psalms 22:24, NRSV (Italics mine)

Why, I wonder then, if Jesus had available to him a more theologically accurate line from the same Psalm, did he choose to quote a line that did not reflect upon the reality of the situation? Why choose to declare himself forsaken, when he could have just as easily and justifiably declared himself beloved, and in the Father's embrace? Why leave subsequent generations open to wrongly seeing in his words a God who *literally* forsook him in his wrath and anger against sin? I think, here, Jesus is joining the exiles in proclaiming, in a sense, that he could not, or would not, sing the songs of Yahweh while in a "foreign land," or a godless situation. It is here that Jesus shows us a path of salvation from suffering, not by literally rescuing us from it, but by showing us that God, in his omnipotence and omniscience, knows what it is to feel impotent, and knows what it is to know he does not exist. God offers us salvation in the form of solidarity, showing us that the only real way out is to embrace where we are, and realize that God, in some sense, though we feel his absence, is very much present.

In one sense, I think Jesus is dispelling the myth of the sort of "god" Dietrich Bonhoeffer called a deus ex machina, a reference to a character who, in ancient theatrical presentations, would be brought into a scene via a "machine," or a sort of mechanical device, in order to solve unsolvable problems in a seemingly supernatural manner. He writes:

> Religious people speak of God at a point where human knowledge is at an end (or sometimes when they're too lazy to think further), or when human strength fails. Actually it's a deus ex machina that they're always bringing on the scene, either to appear to solve insoluble problems or to provide strength when human powers fail, thus always exploiting human weakness or human limitations.[101]

So, maybe suffering is not so much a prophetic proclamation that there is no God, as much as it is that there is no "god?" Maybe there is no beanstalk onto which we can climb and escape the sometimes bleak world that prophesies this inexistence, and perhaps, instead, we must simply make peace with the God who is. And maybe that God is not a deus ex machina who can be invoked whenever we don't like the circumstances we find ourselves in, even when those circumstances are downright unjust and evil. Maybe God's solidarity with human suffering and his absorption of the Godless cry is meant to show us that there is no actual, literal salvation from suffering. If it exists in God, then it exists, and will certainly come to exist in our own lives at some point. However, though we feel abandoned by God in these moments, it is simply the non-existence of a "god" we were never promised existed in the first place that we are feeling, but the God who is, is a God who suffers with us, not a God who causes us to suffer apart from him.

See, I don't claim to have figured out the answer to the problem of evil, or to why suffering is a reality. No, I think those are questions we'll be asking until our tongues no longer move, and our brains no longer function. Suffering just is, and I don't think that saying "we live in a fallen world," is in any way a proper or helpful reply. We live in a chaotic, magmatic, sometimes order-less universe, and things happen, events occur, and people do things, that are mind-blowingly terrible, and no deeper meaning behind them might exist. In a universe such as this, of course we want a deus ex machina. Of course we want a super hero who gets lowered in to rectify our circumstances every time things get a

---

[101] Dietrich Bonhoeffer; Eberhard Bethge, *Letters and Papers From Prison* (New York : Macmillan, 1972, ©1971.)

little hairy. That "god," though, despite our wishes and desires, just doesn't seem to be the God we have.

The God we have is the God who has chosen to identify himself in the person of Jesus. And more specifically, he is the God who has chosen to reveal himself in the cross. And what we have in the cross is a God who joins himself to the Godless cry. The cross is, in a sense, Yahweh identifying and standing with Abel, Sodom's victims, and the enslaved Israelites. It is God refusing to sing the songs of God when he's absent, but also moving east toward the exiles, and acknowledging the absence present in their suffering, but also proving himself present in suffering. The cross is the place where all of this, at least for the one who takes it seriously, is made terribly and beautifully plain.

I can't help here but be reminded of a story shared by Elie Wiesel, in his book *Night*, which documents his horrendous time spent in Auschwitz, as well as his struggle to hold onto his faith in God. He tells a story of watching a young boy die on the gallows, but because of his weight, it took him something like an agonizing half an hour to die. As all of this was going on, he hears a man ask aloud: "Where is God now?" then writes: "And I heard a voice within me answer him: 'Where is He? Here He is-He is hanging here on this gallows.'"[102]

The point is to say that, for Wiesel, God was in a slow process of dying already, and this event was something of the sealing of the deal. A God who can allow such suffering must be a God who simply does not exist. The young man's excruciating death was, in a sense, God's as well.

When we look at this event through the lens of the God revealed in the cross, however, we see that it might not be so much that God is dying on the gallows with the boy, in the sense that his inexistence is being exposed, but that God, literally, dies with the dying, suffers with the suffering, and cries with the Godless. The God of Jesus, while absent in the sense that there was nothing God-like about the event, was also present in that he is a God who *always* stands with those who are persecuted, trampled upon, victimized, and ravaged by a Godless system.

While Jesus' cry does identify him with such system's victims, it, at the same time, exposes the true and Godless nature of the systems themselves. It was, after all, the religious system of the day, in bed with empire and corrupt government that was responsible for his death, but it was a system that believed it had God on its side. God was with them and against him, and so whatever they did to him was justifiable in their minds. Notice what occurs, though, in the actual narrative itself. Jesus

---

[102] Elie Wiesel, Marion Wiesel, *Night* (New York, NY : Hill and Wang, a division of Farrar, Straus and Giroux, 2006)

declares himself forsaken, and breathes his last after emitting a loud cry. What was that cry? If we sort of smoosh the Gospel narratives together, which isn't always a good idea, mind you, but if we do it in this instance, we get this:

> 46 Then Jesus, crying with a loud voice, said, "*Father, into your hands I commend my spirit.*" Having said this, he breathed his last...

-Luke 23:46, NRSV (Emphasis mine)

Where Mark just simply has Jesus crying a "loud cry," Luke elaborates, and has that loud cry be Jesus placing his spirit into the loving hands of his Father. In Mark's Gospel, it is after the cry that the Temple curtain is ripped in two, from top to bottom. This we often liken unto God telling the human race that it's now safe to come back over to his place, since, in Jesus' death, he's found a cure for his debilitating wrath-aholism. What is more likely, though, is that the bankrupt nature of the religious institution was being laid bare before the eyes of the people. There had been no ark, no *glory*, present behind the veil for centuries, and the tearing of the veil revealed its absence. At the same time, however, Jesus declared where it was the Father was actually present, and it was with him, tending to the care of his spirit.

What I want you to see here is a beautiful picture of both God's presence and absence in the death of Jesus. Jesus was forsaken of God, in the sense that, those charged with justly manifesting God's character in the world had done just the opposite. There was no glory behind the veil, and there was just as much on display in the unjust murder of the innocent Jesus. His crying out from this justice-deprived, righteousness-impoverished place, is quite literally the "presence of the absent God." Jesus had become devalued and dehumanized by a system to such a degree that his torture and death were considered justifiable acts. The Godless nature of the relationship between Jesus, and all victims of such systems, is testified to, both in his cry of forsakenness, and in the vacant holy of holies.

At the same time, though, Jesus' affirms that the Father was actually with him, at the very moment it is revealed he is not within the system. In a symbolic sense, God abandons the structure and stands with this victim of unjust suffering, even as he left the Temple in Ezekiel's vision, in order to move east and stand with the exiles. There is no God in this situation, as Jesus' cry prophesies, and yet God is present, as he always is with the Godless. What is missing from this situation, though, is one who will fill in the gaps, as it were, recognize who it is God is standing with, and then choose to stand with them as well. Perhaps, in a sense, we can find that in the centurion's declaration of "Truly, this man was God's son!" (Matt 27:54) and "Certainly this man was innocent!" (Lk 23:47). Perhaps, though compulsory, it is present in Simon of Cyrene's carrying of his cross, the thief's declaration of his innocence, or even in the actions of whomever gave him the wine on a sponge in John 19:28-29. The system, however, did not recognize God as with him, and so crucified him unjustly. The powers that be, refused to recognize the value of his humanity, and therefore deprived him of life, justice, and in a sense, the living reality of God that manifests in healthy human relationships.

I opened this chapter with this line: *There are places where God does not exist, but those are precisely the places where he is present, calling for us to give him existence.* So far we've looked at what I mean by there being places where God does not exist, as well as what I mean when I say that these are precisely the places where he is present. How, though, is it that we give God existence in such situations?

The philosopher, John Caputo, has written, "God does not exist. God insists." Now, what in God's name does that even mean? Caputo explains:

> Without God we can do nothing, but then again without us God can do nothing. Without us, nothing gets done in the name of God, since the name of God is the name of a call for something to be done by us. So we each need each other, God and the world...the name of God is the name of a deed. God's need for us is God's need for deeds to actualize the divine call...Otherwise the name of God is sounding brass and a tinkling cymbal. It comes down to deeds, or rather it spirals up to and breaks out into deeds...[103]

Essentially, what Caputo is saying is that God does not exist or subsist in the world as something physical or tangible that you can wrap your fingers around, nor as the deus ex machina criticized by Bonhoeffer. God's name, he argues, is the name of a call for something to be done. Unless that call is heard and responded to by us, nothing gets done. God insists on finding existence by continually sounding his call of love in our ears, but it is only in our response that God gains tangible existence in the world.

In 1 John, we read similarly:

> 11 Beloved, since God loved us so much, we also ought to love one another. 12 *No one has ever seen God; if we love one another, God lives in us, and his love is perfected in us.*

---

[103] John D Caputo, *Hoping Against Hope: Confessions of a Postmodern Pilgrim* (Minneapolis : Fortress Press, [2015])

-1 John 4:11-12, NRSV (Italics mine)

God's love for humanity, he tells us, is something that predates any human response to it, but is ever calling for a human response. No one has ever seen God, says the writer, but when we respond to the love with predates us, God comes to exist in our fellowship with one another. The insistent becomes existent when acted upon by us. We do not create it, we simply bring into existence what already is.

This is, I think, what James has in mind when he writes of faith without works being dead:

> 14 What good is it, my brothers and sisters, if you say you have faith but do not have works? Can faith save you? 15 *If a brother or sister is naked and lacks daily food, 16 and one of you says to them, "Go in peace; keep warm and eat your fill," and yet you do not supply their bodily needs, what is the good of that?* 17 So *faith by itself, if it has no works, is dead.*

-James 2:14-17, NRSV (Italics mine)

When our only response to the insistent call is to give mental assent to it, it is useless as far as the world is concerned. Even if that mental assent is in the form of "faith," it is useless unless acted upon. No one has ever *believed* food into a hungry person's stomach, clothes onto the body of the naked, or shelter over the heads of the homeless. No, God only comes to exist in such situations when we act upon his insistence, and give it existence through action.

Hinkelammert writes:

> God's absence is a place that can be pointed to. One can protest god's abandonment and God's absence, one can reclaim the assumption of responsibility for this absence, and one can call for the acknowledgement of God, which can also mean a call for this absence to be transformed into presence. The presence of God is no longer an internal emotion, but rather is transformed into praxis (orthopraxis). Its criteria lie in actual reality. God is present if there is no poverty. God's presence is a doing, a praxis.[104]

The presence of the poor or oppressed person, the one crying out represented in James's brother or sister who is "naked and lacking in

---

[104] David B Batstone, Liberation Theologies, Postmodernity and the Americas (London ; New York : Routledge, 1997)

daily food," is the presence of a God who is absent. God's absence is an occurrence that can be pointed to in real time, but so is his presence. When we act upon the insistent call of love coming to us from the cross, which calls us to transform this absence into presence, God comes to exist. The presence of God *happens* when we see those with whom God is standing, and actualize his stance through action.

Elsewhere, Caputo has written:

> When I speak of the insistence of God, I mean that God does not exist or subsist but that God insists, while it is the world that exists...The name of God is the name of an insistent call or solicitation that is visited upon the world, and whether God comes to exist depends upon whether we resist or assist this insistence...God is an insistent claim or provocation, while the business of existence is up to us...[105]

Atheist Sam Harris has said similarly, "To not believe in God is to know it falls to us to make the world a better place." Now, obviously, Caputo and Harris are coming from two different places; one being a theist of sorts, and the other an avowed atheist, but both are essentially saying the same thing. Realizing, or coming to believe that there either is no God at all, or that there is no God existing in certain situations, calls us, and no one else, to make the world a better place. There is no deus ex machina who will do it, nor is there some caped, superhero deity who will crash through the wall and save the day. There is, however, an insistent call and provocation to love and give ourselves for the benefit and betterment of others, and it is when we, in Caputo's words, "assist this insistence" that God gains existence in this world.

For the Christian, this call rings out to us from the cross. It is in the Godless cry of God himself that we realize all such situations are ones in which God does not properly exist, but where he is nonetheless present, calling for us to give him existence.

In Colossians 1, the apostle Paul writes:

> 24 I am now rejoicing in my sufferings for your sake, *and in my flesh I am completing what is lacking in Christ's afflictions for the sake of his body*, that is, the church. 25 *I became its servant* according to God's commission that was given to me for you, to make the word of God fully known,

---

[105] John D. Caputo, *The Insistence of God: A Theology of Perhaps* (Bloomington : Indiana University Press, 2013.)

-Colossians 1:24-25, NRSV (Italics mine)

We've already covered this in the last chapter, but it is strikingly relevant in our present discussion, and so I'll risk repeating myself in bringing it up again. To one who holds to a sacrificial understanding of the cross, as we also deconstructed in the last chapter, a statement like this would seem like borderline blasphemy. How can Paul, a mere human, suffer in a way that puts him on par with Jesus? And how could he even for a second insinuate that there was something missing, or lacking, in Christ's afflictions? I mean, wasn't it "finished" at the cross? How could Paul possibly complete something that Christ already completed?

Paul is essentially making a statement here about the very thing Caputo writes of. The cross is the place from which God's solidarity with the Godless rings out, but the implications of what God communicates to the world through that event are still absent from all such similar events. God, in Jesus, shows us what Godlessness looks likes, and that it is always the place where we will find him, but it is still up to us to bring his presence into existence in these situations. It is when we give ourselves for another, as Paul did for the church, that that which was set forth and revealed in Jesus is transformed from the insistent to the existent.

What else could Jesus have had in mind but this in Matthew 16:24, when he tells us that all disciples must take up their crosses and follow him? If the cross represents a literal blood sacrifice offered to an offended deity, does this mean we are all to be micro-sacrifices to this "god" as well? And how would that square with the idea that Jesus was the ultimate, once-for-all, never-to-be-repeated sacrifice? Clearly, Jesus had in mind something more in line with what Paul communicated. Taking up our crosses and following Jesus is how we bring the insistent love of God, and his solidarity with the suffering and the Godless into existence. This may even be why, in Galatains 6:17, the same Paul could refer to the physical wounds he incurred in his service of the church as "the marks of Jesus." In following the others-centered example of Jesus, what is only insisting in the cross, came to literally exist in Paul's actions. The wounds Christ incurred to show his solidarity with the Godless leave the realm of potential, insistent things, and become tangible, existent realities when a one like Paul sees where it is God is standing, and completes what is lacking by "moving east" and standing there as well.

The traditional sacrificial view of the cross, or the PSA theory, cannot offer us this insight. In that view, the cross is doing something for God. It is satisfying his wrath, and getting him off of humanity's back. Once we allow that God to be done away with, however, we can rediscover something beautiful and exemplary that has come to be buried beneath forensic, transactional, and sacrificial language. The cross is where God shows his solidarity with the suffering, and it is in us hearing and responding to that insistent call coming from the cross that what it communicates and calls for comes to exist.

So, again, there are places where God does not exist, but those are precisely the places where he is present, calling us to give him existence.

The way of Jesus is the way of the cross. And the way of the cross requires that we come to terms with the God who himself becomes an atheist, and disavows all notions of a "god" who is literally absent from human suffering. This disavowal says to us that God is actually present wherever he is absent. At the same time, though, he also disavows the deus ex machina, who acts independently of you and I. Jesus suffers the death of the Godless, to show us that wherever there is such suffering, God is absent, but present, calling for existence. And it is only when we respond to the insistent cry of love ringing out from the cross that God comes to exist in reality.

"There is no God and we are his prophets." a suffering world calls to us.

"There is no 'god,' and in that place of godlessness I stand and bear witness," the cross replies, "but it need not stay this way. The Godless need not stay as such, and God need not continue in inexistence."

Suffering indeed prophesies of a God who does not exist. At the same time, though, it prophesies of a God who stands with those suffering from his inexistence. Unless, though, we hear this prophetic call, and "fill up in our own flesh what is lacking," that will be the end of the story. When we hear more than a nihilistic declaration of God's inexistence, though, and instead hear and respond to a commission to "assist the insistence," the game changes, and God gains existence.

A "god" who requires suffering in order to forgive humans who suffer is not worth calling God. A God, however, who joins himself with the Godless, is the only hope for the suffering.

May we come to grips with the true words of atheists like Sam Harris, needless sufferers like Elie Wiesel, theologians like Hinkelammert, and Jesus himself, who tell us that suffering is proof enough that we find ourselves in a place bereft of God. But may we, instead of collapsing into a bitter acceptance of this inexistence, see it transformed into existence.

"There is no God and we are his prophets."

But there can be a God, if only we'd heed and assist the insistence.

8 | DEAD MICE AND GOD'S AILIBI

[THE IMMORALITY OF HELL]

"…the last thing that the accursed sinner should and will hear when he takes his first step into hell, is all of creation standing to its feet and applauding God, because he has rid the earth of him.
-Paul Washer

"No statement, theological or otherwise, should be made that would not be credible in the presence of burning children."
-Irving Greenberg

"So God created the cultural isolation of the Hindus. He engineered the circumstance of their deaths, in ignorance of revelation. And then he created the penalty for this ignorance, which is an eternity of conscious torment in fire…if there is a less moral, moral framework…I haven't heard of it."
-Sam Harris

I killed a mouse recently.

Actually, in my tenure as husband, and defender of the realm against pests of all varieties, I've killed more than just one.

But this one was different.

I live in a semi-rural neighborhood, and on occasion have had a mouse or two make its way indoors. Last year, more than just one was able to breach the walls of my castle, and I realized that I had a decent-sized problem on my hands, and so declared war.

I purchased every sort of mouse trap I could find, from glue traps, to poison, to the traditional snap traps. It was war, after all, and no method was off the table. In the evenings, before going to bed, I would commission my two feline sentries to do whatever needed to be done, and would sleep well knowing that they were standing guard in my absence.

One evening, I was startled by a shrill scream, as my wife had walked in on one of our cats, as commanded, doing "whatever needed to be done." It had caught a mouse, but instead of simply ending its life in a quick and humane fashion, opted to have a little fun with it first. The mouse did not seem to be sharing in my cat's enjoyment of the moment, though, and was making its lack of enjoyment clear through a series of distressed squeaks and squeals.

Upon closer examination, I realized that the poor creature was in pretty rough shape, and knew I only had three options: 1) let my cat slowly torture it to death, 2) rescue it and throw it outside to die of its injuries, or 3) quickly and humanely put it out of its misery.

Despite the war I'd been waging, I didn't want to see (or hear) anything suffer in this way, and so I went for option number three. I did the deed quickly, and in a way that I hope caused as little pain to the tiny prisoner of war as possible. Yes, I killed it, but despite the fact that I killed it in the most merciful way possible, I still felt like a monster. When it looked up at me with its little mouse eyes, so as to say, "make it a quick death, sir" my heart was crushed, and the sight continued to haunt me for several days after the event.

Now, as I've already said, this wasn't my first rodeo. I've killed other mice in my lifetime. In fact, I like to think I'm somewhat notorious within the mouse community, but this one was different. This was the first mouse that I had *directly* killed. All of the others had died in traps that I'd set, or at the paws of one of my feline goons, but this death required my direct participation.

So, why did this disturb me so deeply? Why did it *seem* so different to me than all of the other times I'd killed mice indirectly? I mean, slowly dying on a glue trap is surely a much worse way to go than the quick, and humane death I delivered. I slept just fine knowing that traps with the potential to inflict quite a bit of pain were set at various points in and around my home, but the thought that I humanely, but directly, brought harm to a mouse, disturbed me far more than any of those things.

THE TROLLEY PROBLEM

The difference, I think, can be seen in an illustration often used by moral philosophers, called "the trolley problem." It goes something like this: You are walking along two sets of railroad tracks, when you spot a train speeding directly toward a group of five men, all of whom are completely unaware of the danger. There is no time for the train to stop, and, for whatever reason, no time for them to get off the tracks. Their fates seem sealed. That is, until you see a lever that you could pull which would reroute the train down another set of tracks. The only problem is that there is a man standing on those tracks as well, who is also completely unaware of the approaching train, and who also happens to not have enough time to make it off the tracks. No matter what choice you make, somebody is going to die.

So, do you allow the train to continue on its present path, killing five people? Or do you pull the lever, and send it instead toward a single individual? While it would not be an easy thing to do either way, most who are asked this question agree that they would pull the lever, and sacrifice one life for the sake of five.

In the next scenario, you are to imagine yourself walking along a footbridge, with train tracks running directly beneath you. You again see a train speeding toward a group of five unsuspecting individuals, only this time there is no hope of diverting it onto another set of tracks. The only way to save these five men would be to put a very large object into the path of the oncoming train in order to slow it down or stop it altogether. As providence would have it, there happens to be an extremely large man walking near you; a man *just* large enough to bring the train to a halt. At this point, you have to make a decision: Do you push the man into the path of the train in order to *save* five lives? Or do you allow the train to continue on its present course, which will tragically *end* five lives?

This is where it gets interesting, because while the vast majority of those presented with these hypothetical situations will opt for flipping the switch and sacrificing one for the sake of five in the first scenario, almost no one is willing to sacrifice one for the sake of five in the instance where direct contact with the "sacrifice" would be necessary. In other words, in the scenario where the only thing required is the flipping of a switch, most people see it as a moral action to sacrifice one for the sake of five. However, in a very similar scenario, only where the flipping of a switch is exchanged for the pushing of a man from a footbridge, almost everyone agrees it would be an immoral action.

Why is this? Why is one scenario so similar, and yet so different from the other? The difference seems to lie in the fact that one does not require you to bring direct harm to another. It requires only the indirect action of flipping a switch, and nothing more. The other, however, demands that you physically push a man to his death. Both instances require that you make a decision that costs one man his life for the sake of five others, but one requires *direct* action and the other, only an *indirect* action.

SEPARATION FROM GOD?

Now, I want to ask you a question: have you ever been told that hell is a place of eternal separation from God? I have too. But why are we taught this? Is it because there is a list of proof texts a mile long that can be used to support it?

As far as I can tell, there's really only one passage that could be used as evidence for this idea, and it is 2 Thessalonians 1:9, which reads:

> 9 They will be punished with everlasting destruction and *shut out from the presence of the Lord and from the glory of his might*
>
> -2 Thessalonians 1:9, NIV (Italics mine)

Now, if you're already predisposed to think of hell as a place of eternal separation from God, it would be very easy to read that understanding into a passage like this. It certainly seems to be suggesting that unbelievers will spend their eternity separated from the "presence of the Lord and from the glory of his might." The text does not actually say "unbelievers," as in anyone who has never accepted the Gospel message, though, but simply "they." So, who are "they," in context? We will need to back up several verses in order to find the answer:

> 4 Therefore, among God's churches we boast about your perseverance and faith in *all the persecutions and trials you are enduring.* 5 All this is evidence that God's judgment is right, and as a result you will be counted

worthy of the kingdom of God, for which *you are suffering.* 6 God is just: *He will pay back trouble to those who trouble you* 7 *and give relief to you who are troubled, and to us as well. This will happen when the Lord Jesus is revealed from heaven* in blazing fire with his powerful angels. 8 He will punish those who do not know God and do not obey the gospel of our Lord Jesus. 9 *They* will be punished with everlasting destruction and shut out from the presence of the Lord and from the glory of his might.

-2 Thessalonians 1:4-9, NIV (Italics mine)

The identity of the "they" of verse 9 is found in verse 8, which tells us that it is those who "do not know God and do not obey the gospel of our Lord Jesus." While this sounds as though it's describing those we might call "unbelievers," the author has a more specific category of people in mind. In verse 4 we are told that those reading or hearing the words of this epistle were enduring intense persecution and trials, and in verse 5 are told that they are suffering for the sake of the message they preach and believe. Then, in verse 6, the author tells us specifically who it is he has in mind when he speaks of "those who do not know God" or "obey the Gospel." It is those who are troubling the Thessalonian believers and causing them to suffer. They are the "they" of verse 9, meaning that this is not a general statement about the fate of every human being whose life ends before they hear the Gospel or believe in Jesus.

Also, it is said in verse 7 that the judgment of verse 9 will bring relief to the persecuted Thessalonians, as well as to other segments of the church who were suffering similar things at the same time in history. How is it that a final fiery judgment at the end of time would bring relief to those who were being troubled and persecuted in the first century? It wouldn't, which means that the event the writer had in mind dealt, not with a fate that people would meet after death or at a still-future-to-us resurrection. He had in mind a judgment that he saw as being imminent in his day. Jesus, so the thought was, would in some way appear, judge the individuals harming and persecuting the church, and usher in a period of peace.

When looked at in its fuller context, it's clear that this is not a declaration about an unbeliever's postmortem fate, but about specific people who were troubling the recipients of the epistle, and others living in the same time period. The troublemakers responsible for the suffering were, so the writer claimed, to be repaid with trouble, which would in turn bring relief to the troubled. Now, if this were some postmortem, eschatological fate, the first century sufferers would be long dead before any relief could be brought to them, and while some might claim that the "relief" would come in the form of heavenly rest, any honest reader knows that that is not what's being discussed.

What then are the events being discussed, if not a literal hell? That is not something that I will attempt to answer in this book, but it is important to note that very few scholars consider 2 Thessalonians to be among the genuine Pauline epistles, meaning that we are not required to try to fit this event into Paul's eschatology, which seems to be much more inclusive and lacking in the sort of language used here. While I will not attempt to answer the "what" of the event the writer had in mind, it does seem to be something more in line with what many Jews living in the Second Temple period were expecting. This looked more like an earthly judgment of some kind, followed by a time of peace and Jubilee, and less like a postmortem hell.

More pertinent to our present discussion though, is the NIV's rendering of verse 9, which makes it sound as though the punishment in question is something to occur while those suffering it are "shut out from" the presence of God. The words "shut out" do not actually appear in the Greek text, and other translations have the "everlasting destruction" as coming "*from* His presence," meaning that that the destruction is not a separation *from* God. This is beyond an important point as, if this translation is correct, and the text is better rendered as "from his presence" rather than "away from his presence," it would leave us with absolutely no excuse for using the passage to justify the belief that hell equals eternal separation from God.

Just consider the problems this creates for many who hold to the belief in a hell that equals separation from the divine. Many insist that the Hebrew word *Sheol*, when used in the Old Testament, should be translated as *hell*. In fact, many of the depictions of hell we are used to hearing come from Old Testament passages in which the King James Bible has translated *Sheol* as *hell*. The problem with this way of interpreting *Sheol* arises when we look at passages like Psalms 139:9, for instance::

> 8 If I ascend to heaven, you are there; *if I make my bed in Sheol, you are there*

> -Psalms 139:8, NRSV (Italics mine)

Here, the concept that *Sheol* and hell are the same places, and that it's a fiery chasm devoid of God's presence, is turned on its head, as *Sheol* is spoken of by the Psalmist as a place where God is still present. How one can insist *Sheol* be rendered as *hell*, while also claiming hell to be a place of separation from God is beyond me, in light of passages like this.

Or consider the fact that most ardent hell-believers will insist that certain judgment passages in the highly metaphorical, apocalyptic book of the

Revelation are meant to be understood as being about hell. When you examine just one of the favorite "gotcha" passages often used to justify their belief, again, the notion of hell being as a place of separation from God finds itself refuted:

> 9 Then another angel, a third, followed them, crying with a loud voice, "Those who worship the beast and its image, and receive a mark on their foreheads or on their hands, 10 they will also drink the wine of God's wrath, poured unmixed into the cup of his anger, and *they will be tormented with fire and sulfur in the presence of the holy angels and in the presence of the Lamb*. 11 And the smoke of their torment goes up forever and ever. There is no rest day or night for those who worship the beast and its image and for anyone who receives the mark of its name." -Revelation 14:9-11, NRSV (Italics mine)

I've heard the above passage used rather effectively to do everything from terrify teenagers in youth groups to abstain from premarital sex, to warn of the dangers of technology (the mark of the beast). Now, I'm not going to take time speculating on what this does or does not mean, but what it cannot be used to do is prop up the idea of a hell that is a place of separation from God. Verse 10 could not be any clearer that whatever the torment is that the author has in mind, it occurs *in* the presence of both God and the holy angels, not away from it.

So, if there are not a mountain of proof texts lying around that can be used to prop up this idea of hell as a place of eternal separation from God, why do so many cling to it? I believe the reason to be, as the mouse and trolley problems demonstrate, that those with normal functioning brains have an extreme disdain for the thought of causing direct harm to other living creatures. Indirect harm is one thing, but direct harm is something that an empathetic brain simply will not allow us to get behind. Pulling levers and setting traps is acceptable, but pushing men from bridges and killing even rodents with our hands makes us feel queasy and uncomfortable. When it comes to a God we've been told is love personified, and who is perfectly merciful in all that he does, we simply cannot fathom his participation in activities which we know, deep down, are fundamentally evil and immoral. We can cope with a God who creates a place of punishment that exists apart from himself; a trap into which those who live disobedient lifestyles fall if they are not careful, if you will. But we cannot fathom a God who actively participates in, and eternally prolongs, the suffering of others.

Since we do not wish to worship such a God, we construct doctrines, as well as eschatological scenarios, from which he is absent. We sleep better at night knowing that the "bad guys" are getting what they deserve, but that God is not directly involved.

Being that hell is supposed to represent God's wrath, however, can it really be that he plays no active part in what occurs within its gates? How could an attribute of God which would seem to demand emotion, find expression in a place from which he is absent? If God is not present in hell, how can it actually be equated with his wrath? Both Greek words rendered *wrath* in the New Testament denote strong emotion, and a place that would require strong emotion to function, and a place like hell, that would require strong emotion in order to function, would certainly require the presence of an emotive being. So, in order for hell to truly be a manifestation of God's wrath, he would have to be personally involved in meting it out in some way.

Now, not only must God play an active part in the torments of hell, he must actually be the source of all of it. Hell, after all, whatever it actually is, could not have spontaneously generated out of thin air when we are dealing in a worldview where God is creator. This means that whatever you believe about hell must also be, on some level, what you believe about God. You simply cannot separate the two. If hell *really* is what many Christians would like for us to believe it is, then it isn't just "hell" that is horrifying, but God himself, for he created it, and anything created has to somehow reflect on the character of the creator.

Some might argue that there are a great many evils in the world that do not originate in God, and so call my point moot. Some might say that since we live in a fallen world, it cannot be rightly argued that simply since something evil exists that it must be a reflection on God. I would, in large part, agree with that statement, but hell is never touted as being a product of "the fall" in modern Christianity, only as a place of punishment for things fallen. Hell, though, if it is to represent God's perfect justice and righteous anger towards sin, must be untouched by corruption, and therefore a perfect picture of his nature. So, again, whatever one believes about hell, they also believe about God. There is simply no way around this.

Honest believers in this doctrine have no problem owning up to it, and do not see the things we've been looking at so far as problems, but rather as things to be celebrated. One very popular Calvinistic preacher has gone as far as saying:

> It is not an exaggeration to say that the last thing that the accursed sinner should and will hear when he takes his first step into hell, is all of creation standing to its feet and applauding God, because he has rid the earth of him.[106]

---

[106] Paul Washer, *The Gospel's Power and Message* (Grand Rapids, Michigan: Reformation Heritage Books, [2012] ©2011)

While this isn't mainstream Christian thought, it is what the mainstream actually does believe at the end of the day, they just aren't as abrasive or vocal about it. While such a claim might make your typical, hell-believing Christian uncomfortable, hell, if it's truly to be understood as an uncorrupted creation of God, must be something deserving of applause. How could it be anything else, at the end of the day? If it represents perfect justice and righteousness, how dare we, mere humans, do anything *but* applaud it? Would not a refusal to applaud God for doing what he supposedly does to the wicked be an act of defiance and rebellion?

If you're like most decent human beings, the thought of applauding the sight of billions of souls in torment makes you recoil in disgust, but if you cannot say that hell is good, and if you cannot applaud the things said to be happening within it, are you *really* convinced that *God* is good? I would submit that if you believe in the eternal conscious torment model of hell, but cannot bring yourself to confess that it is good, or to applaud what you believe is occurring there, then you do not fully believe in the goodness of your God.

Think about it. When you raise your hands on Sunday mornings, and sing words like, "How Great is Our God," or, "You are Beautiful in All of Your Ways," is it hell that you picture? Do you imagine God actively participating in the torture of billions of departed souls? Do you imagine children screaming, begging God for mercy, when these lyrics escape your lips?

Quite to the contrary, it is typically the outwardly and obviously beautiful things that you think upon. You have in mind the love he showed you in freely giving you forgiveness, the grace he extended in helping you turn your life around, etc. You may picture majestic mountains, and fiery sunrises, but I would be willing to wager that it is not the souls of the damned whose tortured screams move you to declare God's ways to be beautiful. And yet, if you believe in that model of hell, it is precisely such actions that you *are*, even if you do not have them in mind, praising. You cannot, after all, believe in this type of hell and confess God to be good, without also confessing hell to be good. If this hell exists, it is undeniably an extension of God, and therefore a reflection on him.

Let us try a little thought exercise, shall we? I want you to close your eyes, and begin, in your own way, to thank God for his goodness. Thank him for your health, your children's health, money in the bank, food on the table, and all of the other things that we are very quick to acknowledge as being reflections of his goodness. Now, I want you to change gears. I want you to imagine the gruesome hell that your theology demands you believe in, and I don't want you to water anything down. Imagine it just as it is preached to you.

See the disembodied souls, some of them just old enough to be considered to have passed the "age of accountability" (that's right around 12 or 13 in most preacher's opinions), being tortured and screaming for relief. Feel the hopelessness which fills their hearts as they replay, on loop, for all of eternity, each and every missed opportunity they had to believe the gospel. And consider the fact that it is "God" who somehow has granted them the ability to do this. Feel the despair overtaking their entire beings like a cancer, and watch as they writhe and tremble beneath the weight of the most extreme emotional and physical pain imaginable.

Feel the heat, the hatred and the hopelessness present in this hell. Feel the grief, the despair, the anger, and the terror.

It's all rather hellish, isn't it?

Now, I want you to turn your eyes to your Heavenly Father once more, and begin thanking him for his goodness in carrying all of this out. Thank him for every tribesperson who now burns eternally, whose only crime was being born in isolation, unable to hear the name of Jesus before their deaths. Thank him for his goodness in torturing Grandmothers right next to rapists, pedophiles and serial killers.

Now, let's turn the volume up on our praise, shall we? Dance before the Lord like David as you imagine him tormenting the multitudes who once truly believed themselves to be saved, but who were not taught the Gospel 100% correctly, and thus were damned forever. Thank him for his greatness in inflicting horrific pain upon the soul of the young woman who all of her life was raped and molested by her father, and committed suicide as an atheist because God seemed deaf to her cries for deliverance. Thank him that, while in life she experienced abuse on a finite scale, she will now experience those things on an infinite scale.

Praise him for the elderly Jewish man who died cursing God in the ovens of Auschwitz because he could not understand why the God of Abraham would allow his people to suffer so, and so now burns permanently in the ovens of God's wrath! He died experiencing the worst that men could dish out, and will now forever suffer the worst that God can dish out.

Having trouble getting into worship with all of that in mind? If you didn't, let me encourage you to seek professional help, sooner rather than later. If you're like most of us, though, you found each of those scenarios to be utterly repugnant, and extremely difficult to even read. Allow me to remind you, though, that if you believe in a hell of that nature, those scenarios are things that you *should* be applauding! After all, they represent the goodness of God, and should be as easy to praise him for as the air in our lungs or the food in our cupboards. So why isn't it? Why

187 | JEFF TURNER

can't we think of such things while praising God for His goodness? Could it be that something deep within us knows better?

In our hearts we know that to attribute such things to God is to put him on the same level as a psychopath or a serial killer. He is capable of the unspeakable, and the only way for us to praise him for it would be to lie to ourselves, or sink in to a state of moral degeneracy that, in a world where hell exists, would likely land us there. In the worldview where hell is presented in the ways we've been discussing, we are forced to believe that behind Jesus' innocent and loving facade hides something dark and sinister. The same mind that we are told contains loving thoughts concerning us, also conceived and created a place that not only rivals Auschwitz, but compared to which it would seem like an oasis.

And this is where our problem arises. We simply cannot look at our Sunday school Jesus and imagine him being guilty of active participation in such things, and so we seek to theologize him out of the picture. Instead of questioning the entire notion of a place of eternal conscious torment, we simply find an alibi for God. *He's not there,* we claim, for hell is a place of eternal separation from him, and so cannot represent his active wrath. It's more of a mousetrap he sets, but not his active participation in the pain and suffering of others. This we seem to be able to live with, even though the sufferings said to occur in a hell from which God is absent are still horrendous. Really, this is just a convenient, though probably unconscious, way of getting God off the hook for the heinous acts his participation would demand he stand accused of.

But facts are facts, and as we have already discussed, there is no getting God off the hook here. There is no alibi we can construct to place him elsewhere. If this version of hell exists, God is not only there, but actively participating in all that occurs within its gates.

FOR THE DEVIL AND HIS ANGELS?

The last resort of many is to claim that hell is actually a prison originally created for the devil and his angels, and so was never intended for human beings. It is only when we align ourselves with the devil (which apparently, in the case of isolated tribes, includes having never heard of him or his arch nemesis) that we become deserving of the same fate as he. In this last ditch effort to salvage hell and exonerate God, it is often claimed that he does not actually send anyone to hell, but that they send themselves there. Have you heard that one before? That people *choose* to go to hell when they decide to "live for the devil", and that God is simply incapable of doing anything to alter their fate?

Not only is this an absurd claim, it is also a butchering of scripture. Matthew 25:41 is the proof text used to prop it up, but it is lifted from the *parable* of the sheep and the goats, which, as its name suggests, is a parable, and not intended to teach us literal truths about eschatology or the afterlife. To interpret it as though it is meant to do these things is to do violence to the writer's intent, and to totally miss the meaning behind the parable. It is simply not OK to isolate a single verse of scripture from its larger context, and then build an entire theological or eschatological view from it. That is just not how the bible works.

But let's say for a moment, just for the sake of argument, that that is how the bible works, and that the claim is true. Hell remains the terrible place we've been told of, it's just that it wasn't created for us. It was created for celestial criminals and outlaws, guilty of high treason against the God of heaven. The torturous scenarios remain the same, and it still amounts to an eternity's worth of agony, it's just that it was created for the devil and his fallen angelic thugs, not humans. What would that change? I mean, God would still have dreamt up a place that exists solely for the purpose of torture, with no remedial or redemptive purpose to speak of. His sole intent in creating this hell, even when it was intended only for the devil and demons, would have been to inflict pain and agony with no greater purpose in mind.

The fact that this hell is outfitted with the means of causing *eternal* pain would suggest that the devil for whom it was created is capable of feeling pain eternally, again, meaning that the purpose of hell, regardless of who goes there, has always been the same. It has always been about inflicting pain, simply for pain's sake. Even if it was originally designed for a rebellious cherub and his goons, God would still have created it knowing that he would have to play an active role in the endless suffering of beings capable of feeling and emotion. Sure, maybe they deserved punishment, but endless pain and misery, with no end in sight? After a quadrillion years, even the torture of a Hitler-type would seem a bit redundant.

And speaking of Hitler, since he always comes up in discussions of this nature, what if it was one day discovered that the methods and means of torture used in Nazi concentration camps were originally created by the same regime to punish the "bad guys?" What if the Nazis, prior to becoming the genocidal regime we all love to hate, had created camps like Auschwitz in order to punish sick and demented men *like* Hitler? What if their intended inhabitants were murderers, pedophiles and other moral degenerates, and that they were only used by the Third Reich on innocents after they themselves fell into moral degeneracy? While we might be able to empathize with their creators, we'd still have to wrestle with the morality of the things being done to the types of people most of us would be happy to see rot in prison. Prison time is one thing, but gassing them alive, or burning them in massive ovens? That's a little over the top, regardless of the level of one's criminality. If the Nazis, at a more moral point in their history, had developed methods of hurting human beings that boggle the mind and sicken the stomach, would it really reflect any better on them if they'd originally intended to use them against the evil instead of the innocent? One's morality, after all, is not determined only by how they treat their friends, but their enemies as well.

You see, constructing doctrines saying that God did not intend hell for man but for the devil, still does very little to help his reputation. He was still the mastermind behind the most horrendous place of pain that has ever existed, and he created it in such a way that those who go there will never be released from their misery, but forced to endure it forever. Even if it was created for some diabolical force, it does not change the fact that it would have to be a creation of God, and therefore a reflection of his nature. Can you really feel safe in the arms of one from whose heart emerged such horrors?

The fact is that *if* the now-popular version of hell is real, God is to blame for its existence, as well as for what goes on within its confines. This is not something that any honest soul should simply acquiesce to believe, without at least a bit of wrestling. This hell, as most truthful Christians would confess, *is* representative of the wrath of God against a sinful humanity, and gentle Jesus meek and mild is therefore *directly* responsible for the unspeakable pain billions and billions of people are presently suffering.

Look again at the Jesus you imagine when you pray or sing love-centered worship songs. Can you picture him laying his hands on a twelve year old child, and squeezing their arm until the skin breaks? Can you imagine him walking up to a thirteen year old girl, who just years before was dressing up in princess gowns, and loudly singing lines from her favorite Disney movies, and striking her in the mouth with enough force to knock her teeth out? Can you imagine him imprisoning children in a dungeon of his own making, depriving them of food and sunlight, in addition to torturing them day after day?

If you're like most Christians, the answer is no. You could never imagine Jesus being so cruel and heartless. Yet, if you're a hell-believer, you are required to believe that, at any given moment, he is doing far, far worse than this. The Jesus of that belief system is actively burning billions of souls, making sure that they are unable to grow accustomed to the pain and agony, lest it be normalized. The cruelties of this "Jesus" are new every morning, and never lose their torturous sting. And remember, it isn't just the Hitlers or Stalins who are on the receiving end of it, but the thirteen year old former princesses, who were just old enough to have passed that mythical line we call the "age of accountability," but who, sadly, either neglected, or never had the opportunity, to pray a "sinner's prayer" in their lifetimes. If you insist on hanging on to the eternal conscious torment model of hell, you are forced to believe that the one you adore and have pledged your life to is presently causing millions of little children's nerve endings to scream for relief, and has no intention of stopping, despite the outrage we might feel at the thought of it.

HELL AT THE GATES OF AUSCHWITZ

The Jewish theologian, Irving Greenberg, commenting on the horrors of the holocaust, and how they ought to shape and inform our theology, has written: "No statement, theological or otherwise, should be made that would not be credible in the presence of burning children."[107] Now, Greenberg did not say this in the context of hell, but it most certainly can still apply here. Another theologian, Roger Olson, has written: ""If a theology is worth believing, we should be able to preach it standing in front of the gates of Auschwitz."[108] Taken together, a hybrid quote of both Greenberg and Olson could read, "Any theology that is of any inherent worth, should be able to be taught within a stone's throw of children burning and suffering due to human cruelty." Could you, however, stand at the gates of Auschwitz and preach eternal conscious torment? Could you feel the heat of its ovens, as they vaporized innocent children, and proclaim that God is presently doing the same, and much worse, to billions upon billions of people? Including some of the very ones being sent up the chimneys as ash?

There's nothing right or OK with a belief system like this. If you have to push past your gag reflex in order to call your "god" perfect and loving, you're simply worshipping the wrong God. And if his actions cannot be emulated without landing you in prison, on the wrong end of an angry mob's pitchforks and torches, or on trial in Nuremberg, atheism would be the most moral path you could take.

I need to be honest with you here, if God is capable of such things, not only do I not wish to worship him, but think that worshipping him would be to participate in the grossest form of immorality possible. Any being who can act this way, even if he *is* a "god," deserves the rebellion and resistance of those he created, not their adoration and obeisance. The most immoral thing one could do is to fully believe in a "god" like this and then continue to worship him as if it's perfectly normal to do so. Any family who could live in a penthouse atop Auschwitz, enjoying steak

---

[107] Irving Greenberg, *Cloud of Smoke, Pillar of Fire*, in *Auschwitz: Beginning of a New Era?* (New York: KTAV, 1977)

[108] Roger E Olson, *Against Calvinism* (Grand Rapids, Michigan : Zondervan, 2011)

dinners, fine wine and music, while Jews were being gassed and burned alive just stories below them, would be seen as sick and morally degenerate human beings, who, despite their social status, deserved disrespect and ridicule. Simply because they were German citizens, and their government sanctioned the activities of their living quarters' lower levels, would not mean that it was morally acceptable for them to turn a blind eye and pretend that all was well. When everything inside of you perceives an act as evil, and your perception is not the result of an askew moral compass or psychosis, then no amount of authority in the world should be able to convince you that such things are OK, let alone "holy." Furthermore, rejoicing at the harm you are avoiding by worshipping such a dictator is repugnant, and the quality of life you give to your family in light of your immoral, blind-eye-turning ways, is not admirable, but despicable.

Yet, year after year, we continue to teach and preach that God does things that would make even the Nazis blush, and no moral outcry arises from those calling themselves "the church." We are happy to accept his sovereign decree that all who believe differently than we will burn forever, and we happily accept the prospect of living in a heavenly penthouse built atop hell, so long as its flames are kept from touching us. We've been taught to push down and suppress our own sense of outrage at the things God is reportedly doing since, you know, his ways are higher than ours and all that, but the sane among our number know in their heart of hearts that hell is not a moral idea. If we believed it was a just, moral, and good decision on God's part, why does the thought of it turn our stomachs? Why does the thought of a loved one ending up there make us weep?

Because we know better.

DO AS I SAY, NOT AS I DO

Whenever one makes such complaints known, however, they are quickly told that we, as fallen humans, simply cannot trust our own sense of right and wrong, as it is so diluted and polluted when it comes to understanding God's holiness that things which seem repugnant to us may actually be perfectly in line with his goodness and love. He is allowed to repay "evil with evil," and practice an "eye for an eye" brand of justice. And while, sure, he calls us to abstain from such things, it's only because vengeance is his, and not ours.

The problem with this idea, though, is that Jesus seems to believe something completely different:

> 38 *"You have heard that it was said, 'Eye for eye, and tooth for tooth.'* 39 *But I tell you*, do not resist an evil person. If anyone slaps you on the right cheek, turn to them the other cheek also.
>
> -Matthew 5:38, NIV (Italics mine)

Or how about this one:

> 43 *"You have heard that it was said*, 'Love your neighbor and *hate your enemy.'* 44 *But I tell you, love your enemies* and pray for those who persecute you,
>
> -Matthew 5:43, NIV (Italics mine)

While these exhortations most definitely seem to stand opposed to the retributive doctrine of eternal conscious torment, many simply assume that God is permitted to behave in ways that we're commanded not to. They will find ways to proof-text their beliefs into sound doctrine with a verse about vengeance belonging to the Lord, and firmly assert that for us to act as God does would be to trespass on his turf. *We* must forgive our enemies, they inadvertently claim, but *God* is permitted to hold onto his grudges forever. *We* must never respond to the evil actions of another in kind, they say on accident, but God is allowed to do so eternally. Why? Because vengeance is his, not ours.

But is this really what Jesus advocates for? Maybe we should let him speak:

> 44 But I tell you, love your enemies and pray for those who persecute you, 45 that you may be children of your Father in heaven. He causes his sun to rise on the evil and the good, and sends rain on the righteous and the unrighteous. 46 If you love those who love you, what reward will you get? Are not even the tax collectors doing that? 47 And if you greet only your own people, what are you doing more than others? Do not even pagans do that? 48 Be perfect, therefore, as your heavenly Father is perfect.
>
> -Matthew 5:44-47, NIV

The point Jesus makes is that when we live an enemy-forgiving, grudge-releasing, non-retributive lifestyle, we look like children of our Father. We are reflecting the Father's perfection, which is seen in His willingness to forgive, turn the other cheek, and do good to those who despise him. In Luke's account of this passage, the Father's perfection becomes his mercy, making Jesus' point even clearer.

Jesus does not call us to walk this way despite the Father's nature, but in Spirit-influenced mimicry of it. If he calls us to forgive our enemies, it's because his Father does the same. If he calls us to do good to those who do us evil, it's because that's what His Father does. If he calls us to live a life of mercy, it's because his Father is defined by mercy. Yet, according to popular views of hell, the Father is also an eternal grudge-holder, a doer of evil to his enemies, and merciful only until your heart stops beating. Can you imagine how robbed of beauty the Sermon on the Mount would be if it were built upon the foundation of the god of hellfire and brimstone, instead of the loving Abba of Jesus? There would be much we would be called to do, but it would all be despite the fact that the "god" we were being called to follow was permitted to do the opposite. Those timeless and beautiful words would need to come with a note attached reading: *You have heard it said, do as I do. But I say unto you, do as I say, not as I do.*

While we're at it, we'd might as well bring up the fact that Paul says that vengeance, as far as he is concerned, looks like doing good to those who do us wrong:

> 17 *Do not repay anyone evil for evil, but take thought for what is noble in the sight of all.* 18 If it is possible, so far as it depends on you, live peaceably with all. 19 Beloved, *never avenge yourselves, but leave room for the wrath of God; for it is written, "Vengeance is mine, I will repay, says the Lord."* 20 No, *"if your enemies are hungry, feed them; if they are thirsty, give them something to drink; for by doing this you will heap burning coals on their heads."* 21 *Do not be overcome by evil, but overcome evil with good.*
> -Romans 12:17-19, NRSV (Italics mine)

This text is often taken to mean that when we love our enemies, we create the conditions in which God can do his work of judgment, or, that we do good only because we know in the back of our minds we know that they'll eventually get what they've got coming. That is not the tone of Paul's words at all, however. He seems to be suggesting, not that we do good with the intention of causing pain, or that we do good knowing that God will later cause our enemies pain, but that the way we combat evil, or "heap burnings coals" upon its head, is by loving those ensnared by it. God does not respond to evil in kind, but with kindness, and when we do the same, we overcome it just as he did. After all, the vengeance of God from Calvary looked like "Father, forgive them, for they know not what they do" not, "Father, slay them all, for they know precisely what they do."

No, to act vengefully and retributively is to betray the nature of the God we're called to follow. To forgive, and to love, and to show mercy to those who show us none of the above, is to live as God lives.

To follow the "god" we insist into being when we follow the eternal conscious torment model of hell, though, one would have to set aside and negate the most basic and foundational of Jesus' teachings, which would, by Christian standards, put them in the category of a non-believer. To follow his path would be to walk one that went against everything the Christian is called to believe and live out, and could not in any way, shape, or form, be called "the way."

I think, though, that there is an even more subtle form of immorality we can fall into when we follow such a "god" and believe in a place like hell. It isn't nearly as overt, and it's something you'd likely not even notice if you were only looking on the surface, but it is there, to be sure.

Let me illustrate. A few months back I was listening to an interview conducted by a group of Christians with a former pastor who had chosen to live a year of his life as though God did not exist. The man was in something of a faith crisis, and wanted to honestly determine for himself whether or not his faith made a difference in his life. At the time of this writing, the former pastor is an atheist, though of the very meek, and non-combative sort.

In the interview, the former pastor was asked something akin to, "So why choose to live a 'year without God?' Why not live a 'year as a child abuser,' or a 'year as a rapist,' or a 'year as a dictator?'" The former pastor was noticeably bothered by this question, as any thinking person would have been, and simply answered with something like, "Because I'm none of those things. I'm a moral person who is just not sure if he believes in God anymore." This answer did not satisfy the interviewer, however, who went on to insist that, for him, to live without God would be to resort to such behaviors. For him, a belief in God and normal human emotion went hand in hand, and to lack the former would inevitably lead one to lack the latter.

As I pondered why this man's sense of morality was so shallow, I could only think that it had something to do with his belief in eternal judgment. In his mind, the only thing keeping him from living in ways that most would think immoral, was the threat of punishment in the afterlife. Now, certainly this man was capable of thinking in a more sophisticated manner about morals and morality, but maybe he simply never had? I mean, after all, when the threat of eternal punishment looms, why think beyond that? What more motivation do you need?

Sadly, this is how many Christians approach the subject of morality, and were it proven to them tomorrow that there were no hell, they would find themselves scrambling for reasons to live moral lives. The sad truth is that when one's belief system includes a belief in endless agony for the unbeliever after death, there is no reason to think past that when it comes to morality. Thus, while so many Christians seem to live squeaky clean lives, it's usually a fear-based response to an unsound belief. Beneath the surface, regardless of how whitewashed things appear, I'm tempted to think that their moral scruples lie grossly underdeveloped.

The point I'm trying to make here is that following the "god" of hellfire can do nothing more for us than lead us toward a life of immorality. There is no "way" in this belief system. No one to emulate or follow. There is no higher path of living and existing in the world that leads to peace, defuses violence, and moves us forward as a species. There is, sadly though, the opposite, in copious amounts.

If we set aside the teachings of Jesus, and instead follow the actions of hell's "god," we would not be fit to live in a civil society. We simply could not take the ethics and morality inherent within that view and translate them into real world actions. The God of this view is one before whom we can bow and tremble, but he is not one we can follow, and so most of us don't, even though we like to loudly proclaim that we do. To deny him altogether would be to risk his wrath, and so we openly confess his deity, but we do not live in ways that reflect that belief. Yet, if looking like "god" is what makes one moral, and one's "god" is the fuel sustaining hell's torturous flames, would it not be immoral to walk morally? Would not our lack of emulation of this "god" render us unholy? Logically, the answer to that question has to be *yes*, but if we opted to live like this "god," we would go against everything Jesus ever taught, and end up in prison rather quickly.

It seems no matter which way you turn, the belief in hell is problematic in light of Jesus, and immorality seems to be lurking around every corner.

The more subtle form of immorality we discussed, where we live certain ways only out of fear, but never develop the deep love, empathy and compassion for human beings present in the life of Jesus, is just as problematic as its less subtle sibling. It might not be as pronounced, nor actually present in our actions, but immorality remains lodged in our hearts, as it has yet to be forced out by a greater example of goodness. This immorality is subtle, under the surface, and might not actually ever be revealed, but if one suddenly lost their belief in a deity or hell, they would also find themselves without a moral compass, or, at the very least, with a malfunctioning one.

Again, following the "god" of hell seems to lead to only one place, and that's to immorality.

As my final illustration for this we will look to the next life.

If you ask a believer how they plan on experiencing heaven as a place of joy when they know that, somewhere in the universe, there exists a place of endless suffering that some of their own loved ones may be occupying, you'll likely be met with a response like, "Well, the bible says that God will wipe away every tear from our eyes and banish all sadness. So, somehow, God is going to keep us from feeling the pain of having a loved one in hell so that we can enjoy the reward of heaven forever." I suppose if one believes in hell, and also believes that heaven will be a place of eternal bliss, there's really no other way around the problem. You would have to imagine that your deity would keep you from knowing that other human beings, and specifically your loved ones, were suffering if you were going to experience peace in heaven.

I want to point out to you, though, the immense problems with this view. You see, in order for God to be able to take away your knowledge of the suffering of others, he would have to somehow alter your brain (or however that works in the great hereafter) so that it was only capable of processing pleasure. As a result, you would lose your ability to feel pain, or to empathize with the pain of others since, who needs such things in a place like heaven, right? The only problem is that morality is largely determined by our ability to empathize with the pain of others, and to be moved when others suffer. To lose that is to lose something foundational to being human, and to essentially become a sort of robot who is less alive as a heavenly creature than it was as a mere human.

When one considers the fact that Jesus' Father's perfection is said to be his mercy toward others, his enemies included, how could it be possible that our most God-like state would be one in which we have become indifferent to the suffering of others? How could we truly be experiencing perfection when we lack the ability to feel, or to desire to extend mercy to another? This would be neither a perfect place nor a perfect state, in light of Jesus' own definition of God. If billions of souls were suffering and writhing in agony, but we had been reprogrammed to lack empathy and feel only bliss, we would be in the most ungodly state imaginable. In order for this to truly be perfection, God himself, the definition of perfection, would need to be indifferent to the suffering of those in hell, which would make him anything but a figure I would want to spend my eternity with.

Equally problematic would be the fact that we, as humans, are social creatures. Our relationships, in many ways, define us, and without them we truly cease to be the people we think ourselves to be. We are, in actuality, the sum total of our relationships with others, and there really would be no you, no me, no any of us, if we were all to be suddenly divorced from one another. My relationship to my wife defines me, as does my relationship to my children, my parents, my neighbors, and so on. If, then, I had to have those relationships permanently severed from my memory in order for my experience of heaven to be an enjoyable one, I would actually cease to be me, since I am the sum total of relationships that I may, or may not, be permitted to have any recollection of.

Matt Dillahunty, an atheist speaker and activist, has said along these same lines:

> My mother is a fundamentalist, committed Christian who loves me dearly…and thinks I'm working for satan and sending people to hell. She also believes that she's gonna go to heaven, and she's absolutely wrong. Even if she's right about there being a God and a heaven, she's not going. Because she believes there's no sorrow in heaven, and there's no way that my mother could be in heaven with me in hell, and not be sorry. Which means whatever ends up in heaven is not my mother; it's some doppelganger of my mother that has been stripped of all of the things that make her her. [109]

If we have to have our most important relationships wiped from our memory in order for heaven to be heavenly, truly, it will not be us who is in heaven, but some clone that looks like us, but that is not, in any way, actually us. In that sense, then, I can comfortably say that if we must lose those deep connections with other humans in order to go to heaven, nobody goes to heaven, since those connections are what makes us human.

This seems to be something of what Paul had in mind when he spoke of the eternal endurance of love, in 1 Corinthians 13. At the revelation of perfection, Paul argues, only that which is born of love will endure, since love is the only truly enduring thing. Love, after all, is God, and God is love, and so while everything else will perish, love will endure forever. If, though, our relationships must cease to be in order for us to experience heaven, love will have ceased to endure, and since God is love, God will have ceased to exist, leaving you in a Godless universe.

The other option would be that, upon death, we would experience a profound change in our sense of right and wrong, and what seemed horrible to us on earth would suddenly seem like something worth breakdancing about. As we covered earlier, many Christians, both past and present, have stated that in heaven the believer will feel the urge to praise "god" for his torture of the damned. You'll recall Jonathan Edwards' insistence that a father, upon seeing his child in hell, will have his "bliss increased rather than diminished by the sight of it".

---

[109] https://www.youtube.com/watch?v=dnkW5A124Eg

The so-called *golden mouthed* preacher, Tertullian once said:

> At that greatest of all spectacles, that last and eternal judgment how shall I admire, how laugh, how rejoice, how exult, when I behold so many proud monarchs groaning in the lowest abyss of darkness; so many magistrates liquefying in fiercer flames than they ever kindled against the Christians; so many sage philosophers blushing in red-hot fires with their deluded pupils; so many tragedians more tuneful in the expression of their own sufferings; so many dancers tripping more nimbly from anguish than ever before from applause.[110]

And then there's this comforting though from St. Augustine:

> They who shall enter into [the] joy [of the Lord] shall know what is going on outside in the outer darkness...The saints'...knowledge, which shall be great, shall keep them acquainted...with the eternal sufferings of the lost.[111]

These saints of old seemed to all agree that, in heaven, the Christian will not find themselves bothered by the suffering of those in hell, nor will they find themselves lobotomized, and therefore unable to contemplate it. On the contrary, they will now see something beautiful and wondrous in something that once turned their stomachs and made them weep. Morality will have been redefined for them, and they will, it seems, have been gifted with a sort of supernatural schadenfreude[112], enabling them to take delight in things that, in life, they would have considered revolting. Even the basest, and most primal of human instincts seem to be taken from us in this version of heaven. According to Edwards, even the sight of one's own children in agony will cause them to praise "god"! Even an animal knows that a child in distress is not a cause for celebration, but intervention, but that instinct will be taken from us in the sweet by and by.

Nietzsche, in *On the Genealogy of Morals*, writes in his inimitable scathing way:

> In my view, Dante was grossly in error when, with an ingenuity inspiring terror, he set that inscription over the

---

[110] Tertullian; Emanuele Castorina, *De Spectaculis* (Firenze, "La Nuova Italia" editrice [1961])

[111] Augustine, Saint Bishop of Hippo.; E B Pusey; Marcus Dods; J J Shaw, The Confessions ; The City of God ; On Christian Doctrine (Chicago: Encyclopaedia Britannica, [1955, ©1952])

[112] The taking of pleasure in the pain or misfortune of others.

gateway into his hell: "Eternal love also created me." Over the gateway into the Christian paradise and its "eternal blessedness" it would, in any event, be more fitting to let the inscription stand "Eternal hate also created me"—provided it's all right to set a truth over the gateway to a lie! For what is the bliss of that paradise? Perhaps we might have guessed that already, but it is better for it to be expressly described for us by an authority we cannot underestimate in such matters, Thomas Aquinas, the great teacher and saint: "In the kingdom of heaven" he says as gently as a lamb, "the blessed will see the punishment of the damned, so that they will derive all the more pleasure from their heavenly bliss."[113]

I refer back to my illustration of a family who was able to live comfortably in a penthouse atop Auschwitz. It wouldn't matter how indoctrinated by the state they had been, or how many threats had been hurled at them by the powers that be, to live normally in such a manner would be an indictment against their character and morals. And I submit that if a heaven exists in which we become indifferent to the sufferings of others, either by force or by having morality redefined for us, it would be an indictment against the character and the morals of the "god" who would call such a hell "heaven." There would be nothing perfect, beautiful or holy about it, and like any other dictatorship, it would be worthy and deserving of revolt and insurrection. Any being who called such a place perfect, regardless of the power he or she wields, would not be one that any moral individual should bow to in worship. This being, were it to exist, would deserve the upraised fist of revolution, not uplifted hands of human praise.

Again, the doctrine of hell seems to only be able to lead us to a place of immorality, whether in this life or the next. If followed through and taken seriously, it forces us to abandon the very principles Christ called God-like, and to behave in a vile and criminal manner. Even in death this fate would be inescapable, as even heaven would become a type of hell, and we some sort of lobotomized shells of our former selves, if a hell of this variety exists.

I know that at this point I've likely lost quite a few readers, and some who remain might be on the verge of tearing this book in half. My comparisons and illustrations have likely angered quite a few, and that is something I'm aware of, even as I write. I really want you to think, though, about what it is you could possibly be angry about? Why do my comparisons of the "god" of hell to men like Hitler anger you so? I mean,

---

[113] Friedrich Nietzsche, *On the Genealogy of Morals* (New York, 1969.)

I really *do* understand, as I've been in the same place myself. But if we're really honest with ourselves, why would it anger us for someone to say that a "god" who tortures people endlessly, with no redemption in sight, is an immoral being who is undeserving of worship?

For a very contemporary example, I want you to think again of ISIS, or the Islamic State, who have masterminded terror attacks of all sorts, and committed horrid acts of murder, torture and rape on everyone from elderly men and women, to innocent children. Humanity's collective loathing for this group is palpable, and most would be behind bombing them to "hell" at a moment's notice. One incident that really gripped the attention of the world was their burning of a man alive in a cage. When news of this incident broke, an outcry was heard across the world through news outlets, social media, and water cooler conversations. They literally locked a man in a cage, doused him in gasoline, and set him on fire. All the man could do was futilely attempt an escape while he slowly burned to death.

It really doesn't get much more disgusting than that.

However, the man whose horrific death made headlines, was himself a Muslim, just of a sort ISIL did not think radical enough. This means that, by "Christian" standards, the moment this man's soul exited his charred body, he immediately went to hell. In other words, "god" locked him in a cage and set him on fire. The only difference is that ISIL's actions look quite tame and compassionate when compared to those of "god," for at least the man in the cage could hope for the sweet relief of death to end his suffering. To the hell-believer, however, "god" is *still* tormenting this man at this very moment, and will continue to do so forever. In fact, ISIL could only dream of being able to inflict the sort of misery the "god" of hell is presently causing this man to suffer.

My question, then, is how can we possibly justify being outraged at the actions of the Islamic State, while claiming that "god" is good and justified in doing what he did, and is presently still doing, to their victim? Why does the outrage we feel toward ISIL not transfer over to the "god" who does far worse than ISIL ever could?

It's precisely conundrums such as these that force us to come up with beliefs like those in which hell is a place of eternal separation from God.

We *know* the action itself to be immoral, and also know that to attribute a worse action to God would be to turn him into a devil. Our only recourse, even if it's unconscious, is to craft an alibi for God that places him elsewhere. Hell is just a trap the man fell into. It's just a switch that was flipped. But God himself was not involved. We know that any being who would do such things is repulsive and evil, but we feel we must find a way of saving its reputation and worshipping it, lest we end up in the very place we are trying to save it from being complicit in. This separation of "god" from direct involvement in the torments of hell, however, really does nothing to save or salvage his reputation, but simply makes him the cruelest of beings, who has ensured a vast majority of humans will suffer forever, but they will do so while he remains aloof and at a distance.

My comparisons of this "god" to unpleasant figures, I think, unearths the equally unpleasant truth that any "god" who exists alongside hell is no God at all, but a monster. We know this, but we try to keep this hidden, even form ourselves. We do so by insisting he remains separate from hell somehow, and try to never think too deeply on the subject, lest our fallacious reasoning be exposed, but such reasoning simply cannot remain unchallenged anymore. The days we live in, and the Jesus whom we claim to follow, demand that we reevaluate this most important of subjects. How, after all, can we claim outrage at the actions of groups like ISIL, while praising the goodness of a "god" who, mere moments after they struck the match, struck his own eternal match? The belief in a hell of this type *literally* short circuits our ability to speak against injustices and atrocities, and, ultimately, our ability to claim we follow Jesus.

Look, I know I didn't answer every scriptural question regarding hell in this chapter, but I did that purposely. Sure, there are still many passages one could turn to in order to find justification for a belief in it. What I want to ask you, though, is why do we unconsciously feel the need to separate God from it? And if we don't, and choose to claim that God is actively involved in the torments of hell, what kind of "god" are you serving, exactly?

If deep down you know better, don't you think maybe God does too?

If deep down you feel a burning desire to separate God from such an evil concept, maybe God burns to be separated from it as well?

If we really want to save the reputation of the God we call "good," perhaps we should separate him from hell, not by distancing him from it in space or in our theology, but by burning the traditional concept of it to the ground, thereby separating him and the rest of us from it entirely. Perhaps, instead of taking hell seriously and then trying to figure Jesus into, our out of, the equation, we should start by taking Jesus seriously, and seeing if traditional concepts of hell have any place in a world over which he is Lord.

Maybe, just maybe, being true theists in the order of Jesus, demands that we become atheists about "gods" whose very existences would turn even heaven into hell. And perhaps true "heaven," both in our character and in our experience, awaits only on the other side of such an atheism.

Perhaps.

9 | FORSAKING HEAVEN
[MEANINGFUL MEANINGLESSNESS]

"When my head rolls off, someone else's will turn, but while I'm alive, I'll make tiny changes to earth."
-Scott Hutchison of the band *Frightened Rabbit*

"…when all hope of a just reward is gone, then righteousness becomes an intrinsic value."
-Christine Hayes

"Lord, when..?"
-The "sheep," Matthew 25

Now this is going to sound a little confusing and purposely obtuse, and that's because it's a little confusing and purposely obtuse. But here goes:

Life is meaningless, and that is precisely why it is meaningful.

What do I mean?

We'll get there.

When you let go of the idea of hell as punishment, what are you left with? While many who've undertaken this deconstruction process have happily tossed that doctrine into the rubbish heap, many are still very comfortably keeping heaven around. Now, don't get me wrong, I believe whatever lies on the other side of our final breath looks like God, and since God is love, I think that's a good thing. I may not be able to tell you precisely what it's like, how it all unfolds, or how you will experience it, but I believe that to be absent from the body is to be present with the Lord, and so, whatever it is, I believe it's good. On all of the little details, however, I'm quite comfortable, along with the late Marcus Borg, testifying to my agnosticism. And by that I mean only that I don't know what lies beyond, mostly because I've never been there, and even the bible doesn't have nearly as much to say about it as we like to pretend it does. I just want to be clear, that in the language I use in this chapter concerning heaven, I'm not speaking literally as much as metaphorically. So don't panic, I'm not throwing heaven away. At least not totally.

I will say, though, that if we are going to get rid of hell as punishment, it seems logical that we must, likewise, rid ourselves of the concept of heaven as a reward. The key words in my argument are "as a reward," as I still have hope that what *is,* is not all that there is (not that it would be all that bad of a thing if it were). While the believer in a doctrine like eternal conscious torment has that odious view constantly at work in their minds, driving them to behave in certain ways, and not in others, the doctrine of heaven as a reward has a similar effect. And, I will say, until we can rid ourselves of this concept, we will not be operating, morally speaking, in the way that Jesus did. In fact, I would go as far as to say that while we may be performing moral acts, they are not coming from a moral place.

The teacher in Ecclesiastes, whom we often conflate with the biblical figure of King Solomon, writes in some rather drab and dreary terms concerning his outlook on life. In chapter 3 of his book, he tells of all the pleasures he has indulged in, all of the wealth he's amassed, and the influence he's attained. Basically, if it was to be done in the ancient world, he'd done it. He'd seen it all, owned it all, slept with it all, and then some. Every veil behind which we might imagine significance and purpose as lying, are veils he had not only peeked behind, but lived behind, and returned from with what, on the surface, sounds like a depressing message: *it's all meaningless.*

After concluding that pleasure is a dead end, he searches for significance and meaning in the amassing of political power, and speaks of becoming king and of all the glory accompanying such a lofty position. Much to our dismay, however, he returns from his fling with political power with the exact same message: *it's all meaningless.*

He then changes his strategy, deciding to instead seek out wisdom over wealth. Perhaps here he will find the peace, sense of significance, and lasting legacy he desires. But again, he comes back with the same message. Here it is in full:

> 15 Then I said to myself, "What happens to the fool will happen to me also; why then have I been so very wise?" And I said to myself that this also is vanity. 16 For there is no enduring remembrance of the wise or of fools, seeing that in the days to come all will have been long forgotten. *How can the wise die just like fools?* 17 So I hated life, because what is done under the sun was grievous to me; for *all is vanity and a chasing after wind*
>
> -Ecclesiastes 3:15-17, NRSV (Italics mine)

Having amassed pleasures, wealth, and now wisdom, the teacher realizes that even the loftier pursuits of life end in meaninglessness. He concludes that, when he dies, his brain and body will rot just the same as the one who has spent their days in foolish pursuits, and so what was the point in accumulating all of that knowledge and wisdom? I can surely relate. It seems such a great, terrible tragedy when a bright young person, with the whole world ahead of him, dies tragically and unceremoniously, while meth dealers and crack heads seem to cheat and avoid death with the skill of an immortal. But I digress.

The teacher continues, and things don't get any brighter or sunnier from there. All is vanity. Everything is meaningless. Nothing means anything, and anything you can think of means nothing.

When we get to chapter 9 of Ecclesiastes, the teacher has had some time to write and think through his thoughts on all things existential and miserable, and gives us these beautiful and ironically enduring words:

> 1 All this I laid to heart, examining it all, how the righteous and the wise and their deeds are in the hand of God; whether it is love or hate one does not know. Everything that confronts them 2 is vanity, since the same fate comes to all, to the righteous and the wicked, to the good and the evil, to the clean and the unclean, to those who sacrifice and those who do not sacrifice. As are the good, so are the sinners; those who swear are like those who shun an oath. 3 This is an evil in all that happens under the sun, that the same fate comes to everyone. Moreover, the hearts of all are full of evil; madness is in their hearts while they live, and after that they go to the dead. 4 But whoever is joined with all the living has hope, for a living dog is better than a dead

lion. 5 The living know that they will die, but the dead know nothing; they have no more reward, and even the memory of them is lost. 6 Their love and their hate and their envy have already perished; never again will they have any share in all that happens under the sun.

-Ecclesiastes 9:1-6, NRSV

Regardless of how one lives, says the teacher, regardless of their religion or irreligion, their theism or atheism, their scrupulous morals or complete lack thereof, everyone goes to the same place in the end: the ground. Everybody dies, and in death, there is no distinction between great and small, rich or poor, wise or foolish. When it's over, it's over, and so even the weakest and most pitied among the living are to be envied by the greatest among the dead, because when you're dead, you're *dead*.

His conclusion, while a bit on the fatalistic and nihilistic side, is also, in my opinion, one of the most beautiful calls to live in the whole of scripture. He writes:

7 Go, eat your bread with enjoyment, and drink your wine with a merry heart; for God has long ago approved what you do. 8 Let your garments always be white; do not let oil be lacking on your head. 9 Enjoy life with the wife whom you love, all the days of your vain life that are given you under the sun, because that is your portion in life and in your toil at which you toil under the sun. 10 *Whatever your hand finds to do, do with your might; for there is no work or thought or knowledge or wisdom in Sheol, to which you are going.*

-Ecclesiastes 9:7-10, NRSV (Italics mine)

There is no heaven or hell in the teacher's thinking. There is just Sheol, or the grave, and everyone who has ever lived or will ever live is either there, or headed there. There's no stopping it. We're all on the fast track to Sheol, and try as we might, there's nothing any of us can do to slow down. Once there, he says, there is no work to be done, no knowledge or wisdom to be had, no pleasures to be experienced. Nothing. It's all over.

So what is his conclusion? That we take up residence in the nearest corner, and commence sucking our thumb while rocking back and forth in the fetal position? No. For the teacher, all of his ruminations on the finitude and corresponding meaningless of existence, has not led him to opt out of life, but to jump into it with everything he has. Eat, drink, enjoy your relationships, he tells us, and above all, find something to do, and then do it with all of your might. Why? Because none of it lasts? What sense does it make to pour my all into something that will vanish like a puff of smoke? Why live and be passionate about it, if life is meaningless?

The reply comes from the teacher: "Because it's meaningless."

Now, something you have to bear in mind here, is that many of these writings come to us from a place in Jewish history when many were wrestling with the problem of suffering, and questioning how it was that God could have or would have allowed such evil to befall them. In 586 BCE, the Temple in Jerusalem was burned and destroyed by the invading Babylonian horde, and many of its citizens were taken to Babylon as slaves. For a people who believed it was promised to them that they would be something of a master race, from whose capital city God would rule the world, and to whom all other nations would stream and pay tribute, this would be a most perplexing place to find oneself in. Beyond perplexing, it would hurt like hell. You would feel abandoned, forsaken, rejected, and set aside. How could this have happened?

As is always the case, many voices arose to give an explanation. For some of the prophets, this great evil befell Israel because of their great evil. They had broken covenant with God, and rejected his prophets, hence their sufferings. This was in line with what is called the Deuteronomic worldview, which essentially says that good things happen to good people, and bad things happen to bad people. It's a rather all too simple approach to the problem of evil and suffering, and really only works until suffering comes knocking at your door, at which point one quickly begins to rethink their reasoning on why it is bad things happen. This same view can be seen in the Proverbs, many of which consist of overly simple ideas about the good being blessed, and the evil being cursed.

When God's "very own people" undergo suffering like this, there are bound to be questions and even protests. And that's precisely what we have. The book of Ecclesiastes is one such likely protest, as its blunt statements about the same fate awaiting both the good and the bad fly in the face of the Deuteronomic hermeneutic and worldview. When so many were looking for a purpose in their suffering, either as a punishment, or as serving some greater purpose, as in the case of Isaiah 53's suffering servant, the teacher in Ecclesiastes simply says that it means nothing. Zilch. Nada.

The book of Job was likely written, or at least adapted and canonized, for a similar purpose. In it, we have the main character, Job, a man whose righteousness is praised to the point of exaggeration, who finds himself the victim of the most hideous kind of suffering. He loses his family, his wealth, his status, and everything else that a man could value, and to top it all off, his "friends" decide to pay him a little visit. These "friends" insist that such things as those Job was suffering simply do not happen without there being a cause. Righteous people don't experience such calamities, in their thinking, and so Job must have been guilty of some terrible, terrible crime. It reminds me of the time my dad needed to have cataract surgery, and a preacher friend of his asked him with a deadly seriousness, "What have you been looking at on the internet?" insinuating, of course, that an internet porn problem was the reason for his ocular malady.

Job, like my dad, insisted on his innocence, however, and finally resolved to take his case before God with such determination that he was even willing to be struck down by his wrath if need be. He would have his day in court with this God who had allowed such injustices to touch his life, even if it kills him. When he finally does have his day in court, however, he's met with something of a surprise. Not only are his friends wrong, Job is as well. His friends are wrong for assuming Job to be on the receiving end of divine justice, but Job is equally wrong for assuming that his friends were operating on a sound principle. Even when Job comes to see that there is no such principle at work, and, as the teacher in Ecclesiastes states, both the righteous and the wicked experience life the same, he feels that there *should be* such a principle at work, and is here shown to be in the wrong. It isn't merely that Job's friends' accusations were false, but that the very idea of suffering only visiting the sinner, while blessings always come to the saint, is flawed to its core, and not representative of how the world actually works.

Job's friends, according to G.K. Chesterton, in his *Introduction to the Book of Job*, are the sorts who think there is a neat, clean, tidy answer for everything. The world is simple, and so when things go awry, as in the case of Job, the answer must be equally simple. You sinned, God punished you. Or your children sinned, and God punished them. Case closed. Chesterton writes of this sort of approach: "The mechanical optimist endeavors to justify the universe avowedly upon the ground that it is a rational and consecutive pattern. He points out that the fine thing about the world is that it can all be explained."[114] In other words, you have cataracts? You must have porn addiction. Case closed. Simple as that.

That's not, however, the way God sees it.

Chesterton continues:

> That is one point, if I may put it so, on which God, in return, is explicit to the point of violence. God says, in effect, that if there is one fine thing about the world, as

---

[114] G.K. Chesterton, The Collected Works of G.K. Chesterton (San Francisco: Ignatius Press, ©1986-<©2012>)

far as men are concerned, it is that it cannot be explained. He insists on the inexplicableness of everything. "Hath the rain a father? ... Out of whose womb came the ice? (38:28f). He goes farther, and insists on the positive and palpable unreason of things; "Hast thou sent the rain upon the desert where no man is, and upon the wilderness wherein there is no man?" *38:26. God will make man see things, if it is only against the black background of nonentity. God will make Job see a startling universe if He can only do it by making Job see an idiotic universe. *To startle man, God becomes for an instant a blasphemer; one might almost say that God becomes for an instant an atheist.* He unrolls before Job a long panorama of created things, the horse, the eagle, the raven, the wild ass, the peacock, the ostrich, the crocodile. He so describes each of them that it sounds like a monster walking in the sun. The whole is a sort of psalm of the sense of wonder. The maker of all things is astonished at the things he Himself has made.[115]

Neither Job nor the reader is intended to have seen that coming, I'm sure.

In God's response to Job, there is no karma-like principle at work, ensuring that everyone gets what they have coming to them. There is, on the contrary, only a chaotic universe, in which good and bad happen to all equally. Job's God, to Chesterton, becomes a blasphemer and an atheist for questioning the idea of there being any rhyme or reason to it all- a system of good for good, and bad for bad. If one seems to be the recipient of more bad than good, or more good than bad, it's either an illusion, or a coincidence, because Job's God is not pushing buttons, pulling strings, or ensuring that everyone gets their just deserts. There is, in the world of Job's God, no moral order, as it were, but just a massive universe in which stuff happens. The good, the bad, and the ugly come knocking on everyone's door equally. God is an atheist, in a sense, who rejects the concepts of a rewarding and punishing "god," in favor of one who is astounded by the insanity of his own world.

What's most interesting to me about the book of Job, though, is that, even prior to hearing God's reply, Job, beginning to suspect that life and God are unfair, uncaring, or maybe a mixture of the two, refuses to let go of that quality that made him the target of this spectacle in the first place. His righteousness, even though it was earning him no gold stars or brownie points, was something he simply would not forsake.

---

[115] Ibid.

Christine Hayes has said:

> ...even in the depths of his anguish, and even though he is now convinced that God does not enforce a moral law in the universe, Job clings to one value: righteousness is a virtue in and of itself, and even if it brings no reward, Job will not give up his righteousness. Faced with the shocking insight that good and evil are met with indifference by God, that righteousness brings no reward, and wickedness no punishment, Job, although bitter, refuses to succumb to a moral nihilism...In his darkest, most bitter hour, with all hope of reward gone, Job clings to the one thing he has: his own righteousness. *In fact, when all hope of a just reward is gone, then righteousness becomes an intrinsic value.* (Italics mine)[116]

Jewish scholar, Moshe Greenberg, writes similarly:

> The universe has turned its back on him [Job], we may add, he believes God has turned his back on him, *yet Job persists in his affirmation of his own worth and the transcendent worth of unrewarded good.* (Italics mine)[117]

And this ultimately seems to be the message of the book of Job. Righteousness, or doing right, in spite of the fact that, more often than not, it goes unrewarded, is still worth clinging to. It is its own reward, and even in the face of a universe that is, to quote Chesterton, "inexplicable," and "much stranger...than Job ever thought it was," one's uprightness ought not to be cast aside. Even in a world where God himself is an atheist, who disavows the existence of a moral order, morality is no less a virtue. As the glum teacher of Ecclesiastes has suggested, sure, everything is meaningless, and sure, everybody ends up the same way, but this should be the very thing that motivates us to find something to do, and to then do it with all of our might. It will one day be forgotten, there can be little doubt about that, but we should not sink into "moral nihilism," simply because we live in a universe that won't always publicly acknowledge us for our hard work and well-earned significance, or manifest our already-possessed significance by elevating us to lofty heights. *Unrewarded good* has transcendent value, and it is, in fact, only when we lay aside the hope of reward that "righteousness becomes an intrinsic value."

---

[116] This quote comes from a lecture given by Christine Hayes. The full lecture can be seen here: https://www.youtube.com/watch?v=RxENRH-vOXk
[117] Quoted by Christine Hayes in a live lecture. The full lecture can be seen here: https://www.youtube.com/watch?v=RxENRH-vOXk

In other words, life is meaningless, but that is precisely why it's meaningful.

If there was always a reward for doing good, living right, or for doing whatever it is one does with all of one's might, it would cease to have meaning. Why? Well, because our reason for doing it would be only for what comes to us as a result. It would be a self-centered morality, which reality isn't morality at all, since morality deals with us seeking the betterment of all, and not just ourselves.

SIGNIFICANCE THAT CRIPPLES

We all crave significance, don't we? Whether it's in the eyes of humans, God, or the "gods," we all want to feel like we matter and like we mean something, and ultimately, we all want to be rewarded for mattering. When it comes to God, some of us already feel significant, beloved, and as though we are the center of his universe, and desire for this to be manifested before the rest of the world in some way, be it through our being endued with miraculous abilities of the Charismatic order, or simply by having our lives come to reek of blessing and favor. Others of us, who maybe grew up with a harsher, less-loving portrait of God, feel that significance in God's sight is something we must earn, and pay for through sweaty devotion. Depending on the portrait of God one has in mind, the way we approach this idea of significance will vary.

For me, I grew up believing in a being who was profoundly disappointed in me. I did not have this projected onto me by parents or the church I grew up in, which didn't deal in this sort of depressing theology. I'm not sure where I picked it up, but from a very young age, I felt as though God were sorely displeased with me. His brow eternally furrowed, his arms forever crossed, and his mouth ever positioned in a frown, I took it upon myself to earn from him what I felt I was lacking in. So, the first thing I needed to do was to identify what it was about me that made him so disappointed. Sin, was the obvious answer, coupled with a lack of devotion, fervency in my faith, and intensity in my pursuit of him. So, I set about to right all of these wrongs, and become the polar opposite of the person I felt God was disappointed with.

I kid you not when I say that I prayed 8-12 hours a day, and not just for a week or so after returning home from church camp, but for years. I read the bible for hours on end, hoping God was watching and taking notes, consumed every book on living radically for God I could get my hands on, and evangelized every creature with cognitive abilities above those of worms. I began (and broke) more forty day fasts than most ever even dream of attempting, and eventually settled on every other day as an appropriate, and more realistic approach. I wanted to be *the* guy, if you catch my drift. I would read portions of scripture, like Genesis 6, in which we're told that God repented of ever creating humankind, but that Noah found favor in his eyes, and determined I was going to be the "but" in my generation. In the midst of a crooked, corrupt, spiritually bankrupt, and bent-in-all-kinds-of-wrong-directions era, I was going to be the "but Noah," and I pursued that position like a madman.

Eventually, however, after years of struggling under the weight of hyper-insignificance, I crashed, burned, and realized I simply could not do it anymore. I was killing myself, my family, and everyone within a thousand mile radius, and, if I was going to continue doing this Christianity thing, needed to find a better way. It was then, after much exhaustion, fatigue, and damage done to my relationships, in my very early 20's, that I began to discover a more gracious version of God. God was not the angry, disgruntled dictator, but a loving, caring Father. I wasn't loathed but loved! I wasn't abhorred but adored! I wasn't insignificant needing to earn significance, but the most significant creature in the universe, needing only to realize and manifest my already significant state!

Now, those first two statements are true. Certainly, I *am* loved and adored. That is at the very center of the Gospel message. It's in that third statement that things can start to get problematic. I did not need to earn significance with God, obviously, but I had simply gone from one extreme to the other, from the right end of the canoe to the left, and was in just as much danger of it capsizing here as I was over there. The thing about extremes is, though they feel very different from one another, they are actually the very same things. To react against a thing, and, in protest, run from it as far and as fast as you can, is still to be controlled by it. And the same pitfalls you encountered that made you flee it in the first place, are the same pitfalls you'll encounter in the fleeing.

When I took upon the posture of hyper-significance, this is precisely what I encountered. In my former life, preaching, teaching, prophecy, and everything in between, were all aimed at pointing out sin, areas of compromise, lukewarm-ness, and a lack of spiritual passion, but on the other side of the canoe, all of those things were flipped on their heads. Now, preaching, teaching, prophecy, and everything in between, were aimed at pointing out how nothing was wrong with you, and everything was right with you. On top of all of that, everyone and their brother was called to be a god-like, anointed superhuman, commissioned to take the Gospel to the nations, and on any given Monday should be raising the dead, and banishing any and all demonic forces back from whence they came.

It was exciting, and certainly more fun and uplifting than my former approach, but I soon began running into problems. You see, the constant emphasis on my hyper-significant state was having the same effect on my emotions that rapid weight gain has on the body. The "skin" of my expectations about life and what it should look like was being stretched to its limits by my ever expanding sense of significance: I'm a prophet, a healer, a deliverer, a revivalist, an apostle, a part of a chosen generation, a leader in an end time army, etc. This made being the things that I actually was, like a dad, a husband, a payer of bills and earner of paychecks, that much more difficult to accept, since these were mere human trivialities. I found that, the more I became puffed up and bloated by a sense of hyper-significance, the less I was able to be good at the things I actually was; things that, in truth, were the most important things in my life. Engaging in them, though, seemed below me, and sent my mind back to that place of feeling like the earthbound, unimportant and insignificant wretch that I had worked so hard to overcome.

In the years that have followed, I've watched many individuals struggle to pick up the pieces after the "weight" itself disappears, and they are left with nothing but the "stretched skin" of over-expanded expectations, and find being a regular human being to be a most difficult task.

The funny thing is, when I lived with a sense of hyper-insignificance, I felt it equally difficult to be a regular human, with regular, but extremely important, things to do. Just being a husband, father, employee, or what have you, served only to remind me that I *wasn't* the spiritual giant I longed to be, and was just as normal as everyone else. I would speak of these things in terms of being mere shadows of truer and more powerful realities, and so found justification for belittling those relationships while pursuing what I thought was a greater one.

You can see what I mean here about extremes. In both instances, I was equally kept from things that mattered by what seemed like two opposing ideas, both of which communicated to me the idea that the things that mattered didn't. When I felt hyper-insignificant, normal human tasks only reminded me of how normal and human I was, and when I felt hyper-significant, normal, human tasks seemed below me, like a "coming down from the mountain," if you will. The two thoughts seemed completely different from one another, and yet both had the same effect of plucking me from the real world, and, in turn, keeping me from doing any real good in it.

The problem, in both cases, was the desire for significance and reward. In the first, I was trying desperately to earn it, and in the second, I was trying desperately to rest and believe enough in order to manifest it. In one instance, I wanted to be rewarded, and in the other I thought I already had been, and so became frustrated when life didn't match up to what I thought it should be for a hyper-significant one like myself. All the while, though, things that needed to be done, people who needed to be loved, a wife who needed her husband present and in the room, and kids who needed their dad home, and not at prayer meetings or prophetic conferences, were neglected. As I searched for, and attempted to manifest significance, truly significant things suffered.

And here is why I say that the teacher of Ecclesiastes makes one of the most profoundly moral statements in scripture. There is no reward in his worldview. There is no hell, no heaven, no afterlife to speak of whatsoever, in fact. There is no karma, no moral order, no good stuff for the good guys and bad stuff for the bad guys. For the teacher, valleys are exalted and mountains made low. Everyone gets what everyone gets. The rain falls and the sun rises on just and unjust, righteous and unrighteous alike. And yet, none of this moves him to lay aside the responsibility of morality and uprightness. Instead, he says to find something to do, and to give it your all.

Job's is a similar story. In it, God, at least in the eyes of Job's friends, whose "god" was one of rewards and reprisals, is essentially an atheist. The "god" of Job's friends does not exist, and instead we have a universe that never repays you, and sometimes gives you the shaft when you deserve a crown. Sometimes you have to watch the wicked prosper while you beg, and the lazy thrive while you struggle to survive. It doesn't make any sense, in such a world, to live uprightly, but it is precisely what Job chooses to do, and it is precisely why he is the book's hero.

In both of these cases we have examples of characters who have laid hold of a form of morality, far superior to what we find in most religions, popular Christianity included. Heaven and hell hang over us constantly in religion, threatening us, and promising us, and while many of us have set aside the fear of hell, we still have, in one form or another, the idea of heaven motivating us. Now, to reiterate, I'm not being literal here when I speak of forsaking heaven. I, again, affirm that whatever awaits us postmortem, looks like God. But if we set aside hell as a punishment, and as an impetus for avoiding evil, we must also set aside heaven as a reward, and as an impetus for doing good.

Now, heaven for you might not be a literal castle in the clouds, located just behind yonder cumulonimbus formation, but simply the thought of arriving at some form of utopia in response to how you live, or how you believe. It might look like being rewarded with a great calling or anointing, or with a blessed and prosperous life. It could be any number of things, but I think you get the point. "Heaven," here, is simply a reward for doing what you think good, or for the good you already are. Both of these ideas, however, at least in my experience, and based on my observation of the experience of others, become unbearable burdens that keep us from doing actual good, while we desperately strain for the unreal. We want to accomplish things so lofty, that anything smelling of planet earth repulses us, or feel so significant and lofty that we are scrambling to, in a figurative sense, leave all that is earthly behind. While I'm not saying that nothing positive can ever come from it, the idea of reward, of "heaven," if you will, poisons us, cripples us, and crushes us beneath the weight of either hyper-insignificance, or hyper-significance. We are either trying to purchase our admission, or manifest our admission-worthiness, and in both cases we will walk right past the things that matter, while pursuing things that don't.

In Jesus' parable of the sheep and goats in Matthew 25, we see this illustrated in a most beautiful way. We have in it a picture of all nations being brought before the Messianic king, to be either punished or rewarded. Now, remember, this a parable, not a prophecy, or a literal, eschatological teaching on how things will pan out in the end. Jesus is simply taking stories and beliefs that were in common use in his day, and altering them just enough to leave his audience reeling, thinking, and scrambling to pick their jaws up off the floor. Now, the manner in which Jesus presents himself here is very important. He's a king, seated on a glorious throne, accompanied and attended to by angels. This is precisely the sort of glory that any reasonable, heaven-expecting, reward-anticipating person is expecting to be on the receiving end of for their good deeds.

When Jesus makes his division between sheep and goats, righteous and unrighteous, the curious thing is that the righteous literally have to have their righteousness spelled out for them. Jesus explains:

> 35 For I was hungry and you gave me something to eat,
> I was thirsty and you gave me something to drink, I was
> a stranger and you invited me in, 36 I needed clothes
> and you clothed me, I was sick and you looked after me,
> I was in prison and you came to visit me.'
>
> -Matthew 25:35-36, NIV

The righteous, however, are absolutely taken aback by Jesus' statements, and ask:

> 37 ...'Lord, when did we see you hungry and feed you,
> or thirsty and give you something to drink? 38 When did
> we see you a stranger and invite you in, or needing
> clothes and clothe you? 39 When did we see you sick or
> in prison and go to visit you?
>
> -Matthew 25:37-39, NIV (Italics mine)

To which Jesus replies:

> 40 ...'whatever you did for one of the least of these
> brothers and sisters of mine, you did for me.'
>
> -Matthew 25:40, NIV

I want you to feel the gravity of what is happening here. These individuals, who are about to be rewarded with "the kingdom prepared for you since the creation of the world" (verse 34), have no idea why they are being thus rewarded. Jesus tells them, essentially, that whenever they saw him in need, they took care of him. They still don't get it. "Lord, when? Lord, when?" they ask, to which Jesus finally replies, "Anytime you took care of those thought not to matter, you took care of me. Whenever you did that for which you thought there would be no reward, you did what mattered."

These individuals had no idea what they had done, meaning that they weren't going around, helping the poor with ulterior motives. They weren't feeding the hungry, all the while thinking, "You know, what I do for the least I do for Jesus. So I sure earned me some points today!" No, Jesus has to explain that principle to them, meaning it was not functioning in their belief system when they did the things that they did. What they did, they did without any expectation of reward, or without any thought being given to the fact that someone was watching or keeping score. When we do something for the "least," we, by necessity, do so without the expectation of being rewarded or paid back, since it is not within their abilities *to* pay us back.

The moral of the story here is not that we ought to do good because doing so ensures we'll reach Scrooge McDuck status in the afterlife, but that real righteousness is that which we do without any expectation of reward. It's the stuff we do with all of our might, even after concluding that it's meaninglessness that means something. It's the refusal to slip into moral nihilism, and the determination to walk uprightly, even though we live in a universe where God is an atheist, and denies the existence of a moral order, or a greater purpose behind our works, that constitutes righteousness from God's perspective. These individuals did not have a Messianic king figure in mind when they did their works. No, they were doing for those who could do nothing in return, and had no expectation of either earthly or heavenly reward. And that, from God's perspective constituted righteousness.

John Caputo writes:

> My idea is not to beat religion senseless but to claim that religion is constantly getting in its own way by its built-in tendency to shrink down the unconditional gift...into an economic exchange. It allows itself to be led into the temptation to turn works of mercy into coins in the realm of the economic system of the kingdom of God. In this world virtue goes unrequited; but in the next one we will be rich as hell-or rather heaven. When these works of mercy have that religion up their sleeve, by which I mean the economy of salvation, that is not the gift. The relief

> packages are distributed as part of a package deal put together by the proselytizers who make it clear that these are not just works of mercy. These works are also the work of celestially minded mercenaries, works with mercenary value... That reduces the gratuity of their grace to a delayed gratification. [118]

When works of mercy become the "work of celestially minded mercenaries," gracious guns for hire, who do what they do only in the hopes of receiving a reward, they cease to, in fact, be works of mercy at all. They are things done wholly and solely for oneself, or, at the very least, things done mostly for oneself. We are, when we act with "heaven," in all of its various forms in mind, acting on pure survival instincts, ensuring that we live on, and do so sumptuously, either in this world or the next. That is not the modus operandi of the righteous sheep, Job, or the teacher. Beyond that, however, it is also not that of Jesus.

Stop and think for a moment who it is, as a Christian, you follow. I'll help, in case you're stuck: it's Jesus. Who is Jesus, exactly? According to Paul, he is, "the one who knew no sin," but who was, "made to be sin." (2 Cor 5:21). Now, what that means, quite literally, is that Jesus, in knowing no sin, was absolutely innocent of any and every charge ever made against him. Despite this, he was "made to be sin," that is, treated as though he were guilty of sin, and punished in like manner. This treatment does not come from the hands of God, even though many translations add the word "God" to Paul's statement, making it read something like, "God made the one who knew no sin to be sin for us." From hence comes all sorts of notions of Jesus as a literal human sacrifice offered to God, and such, but the real thrust of Paul's words is that we, the human race, rewarded Jesus' innocence with the punishment reserved for criminals and sinners.

Theologian Michael Hardin has rendered the verse thusly: "The one who was innocent was deemed guilty by humanity..."[119]

That, ladies and gentlemen, is meaningless.

In fact, I'll go as far as to say (and risk losing my head in the process) that the death of Jesus was meaningless. What do I mean? Well, think about it. What inherent meaning is there in a young man, in the prime of his life, and at the height of his career, being unjustly executed by the state? There's no meaning there, in fact, Paul states in 1 Corinthians 2:8

---

[118] John D. Caputo, *Hoping Against Hope: Confessions of a Postmodern Pilgrim* (Minneapolis : Fortress Press, [2015])

[119] Michael Hardin, *The Jesus Driven Life: Reconnecting Humanity With Jesus* (Lancaster, PA : JDL Press, ©2010.)

that, "had the rulers of this age understood the wisdom of God, they would not have crucified the Lord of Glory." The death of Jesus was not an inherently wise or beautiful thing, but an injustice. A travesty. A meaningless, senseless lynching of an innocent man.

And yet, this injustice came upon a man who "knew no sin." That was his reward. That was his heaven. The same, unceremonious death that the two thieves on either side of him underwent, the one who knew no sin underwent as well. Barabbas, a brigand, murderer, and insurrectionist, on the other hand, gets off scot-free, and goes on to do God knows what with a life many would say he didn't deserve to keep. Where's the justice? Where's the reward? Where's the heaven for that? Now, I know, I know, I've preached those sermons, so I know the host of others' texts that could be brought about the "joy set before him" and whatnot, but for the sake of the point I'm making, set those aside for a moment, and just track with me. If anyone, anywhere, and at any time, ever deserved to be rewarded for his significance, or was significant enough to have it manifested publicly for all to see, it was Jesus. And yet, here he is, asphyxiating on a Roman cross, like any common criminal, while other common criminals breathe easily.

Are we to assume Jesus did not know it would end like this? Of course not, as the Gospels tell us otherwise at numerous points. Yet, did he sink into moral nihilism? Did he curl up in the corner, rocking back and forth in the fetal position, whilst sucking his thumb? No. He found something to do, and did it with all of his might. He, being God, embraced a universe in which the "god" of moral orders, karma, and eye for an eye, just doesn't exist. In Chesterton's words, he became an atheist, embraced the meaninglessness, and in that found meaning.

Beyond just the way that he lived, look at what this unjust murder of an innocent man became! In 2 Corinthians 5:21, Paul not only declares Jesus' innocence and unjust execution, but also the effect of the injustice: we become the righteousness of God! In other words, we are revealed to be in right standing with God. How can that be? How can humanity's unjust treatment of the ultimate innocent reveal us to be right with God? Well, it is certainly not the act itself that reveals this, but, rather, God's response to the act. We are told in verse 19 that, "God was in Christ, reconciling the world to himself, not counting men's sins against them." This means that God, even after experiencing the absolute worst that humanity is capable of, responded to it, not in kind, but with kindness. Not with lightning bolts, but with love. Not malevolence, but mercy. This most meaningless act was seized upon by the Godhead to show humanity the sheer depth, width, height, and breadth of their love for us.

Here's Hardin's translation of the rest of verse 21: "...inasmuch as we made a wrong judgment about the innocent Jesus, God is right to make a 'wrong' judgement about us and declare us, who are guilty, to be in right relationship with God."[120]

The cross was a meaningless, wrong judgment on our part, but the Godhead mined meaning from out of it.

Were the death of Jesus inherently meaningful, and were God the one pulling the strings and flipping the switches in order to ensure that it all happened according to plan, it would be absolutely stripped of meaning. What it shows is that humanity's worst is met with God's best, but were God the mastermind of the whole thing, there would be no crime to declare us innocent of, and no sin to forgive. Were it a meaningful event, in itself, it would be meaningless, but it is precisely its meaninglessness that makes it fertile enough soil for meaning to be harvested from.

My friends, the only meaningful way to live is in light of life's meaninglessness. Righteousness, as God sees it, only springs forth from soil that expects nothing in return for what it is, and is content to watch its uprightness dry into dust and be carried away by the wind. In the song *Heads Roll Off,* by the band, *Frightened Rabbit*, Scott Hutchison, himself an atheist sings:

> You can burn me, 'cos we'll all be the same
>
> ...dirt in someone's eyes cried down the drain
>
> ...but while I'm alive I'll make tiny changes to earth.[121]

That all might sound gloomy, moody, and needlessly depressing, but it contains some deep, deep truths; truths that the teacher discovered, truths that Job and Job's God knew, and truths that Jesus embodied. When we embrace the reality that everything is fleeting, meaningless even, and that our lives may never earn us a pat on the back, a packed church filled with signs and wonders, or a vault filled with heavenly accolades, and yet still determine to "make tiny changes to earth," we choose what matters. When I let go of "heaven," in that sense, suddenly, the small things become the big things, and the big things become the small things. Sitting with my son and playing Mario Kart, talking My Little Ponies with my daughters, taking my wife out for dinner, and doing all of those things my former self thought small, become the most significant things in the cosmos. Doing little things, for people that, from the perspective of one who thinks themselves hyper-significant, are just as small; people who can't pay you back, reward you, make you famous, or your life any more cushy, are the things that actually have meaning.

[120] Michael Hardin, The Jesus Driven Life: Reconnecting Humanity With Jesus (Lancaster, PA : JDL Press, ©2010.)
[121] Hutchison, Scott (Heads Roll Off.)

Were there some deeper meaning to doing them, meaning would be drained from them. In Hayes' words, "when all hope of a just reward is gone, then righteousness becomes an intrinsic value." Righteousness is its own reward in a universe free of award-giving "gods," and it is only in such a universe that we are free to truly become upright, and Jesus-like people. As Caputo writes, "...works of mercy *are* the kingdom of God; the Kingdom of God is not a reward..."

My friends, if we are going to choose to become atheists as it concerns the "god" of hellfire, it is only logical that we join Job's God, and Jesus' Father, in disavowing the god of "heaven," as well. Life is meaningless, and that is precisely why it's meaningful. "Heaven" does not always await the one who follows "the way," and that is precisely why following it means something. Working with "all of our might," only in light of what we'll gain in return, is a bankrupt, backwards, and, ultimately, disillusioning path. But the way of Jesus is a way without karma, rewards, or reprisals; a way without "heaven," a way of meaninglessness, and it is on this path that we come to actually experience fulfillment and meaning.

In 1 Corinthians 1, Paul speaks of the Jews' expectations of a Messiah of power, and the Greeks understanding that a Messianic figure would be one of great wisdom. In Jesus, however, both groups are presented with something that seems wholly antithetical to what they desired. A crucified Jew, taken out in the prime of his life, at the height of his career and influence, certainly does not look like power. And surrendering to an unjust verdict, when it was in your power to protest it and then some, certainly does not look wise. And yet, for Paul, this same event that was seen as both foolish and weak to some, represented wisdom and power.

As we move on in the letter of 1 Corinthians, and come to chapter 13, often called the "love chapter," we find Paul critiquing the Corinthian church's obsession with spiritual gifts and manifestations that are of a more outwardly powerful order. Perhaps, like the Jews who demanded signs, and the Greeks who desired wisdom, the Corinthians too had certain ideas about what the truly significant looked like. For them, it was prophecy, speaking in other tongues, and other such exotic gifts. Paul, while not discouraging their pursuit of, or desire for such things, still sees that in their pursuit of the outwardly and obviously supernatural, they're missing the bigger picture:

> 1 If I speak in the tongues *of mortals and of angels*, *but do not have love, I am a noisy gong or a clanging cymbal.* 2 And if I have *prophetic powers, and understand all mysteries and all knowledge*, and if I have *all faith, so as to remove mountains, but do not have love, I am nothing.* 3 If I give away all my possessions,

and if I hand over my body so that I may boast, but do not have love, I gain nothing.

-1 Corinthians 13:1-3, NRSV (Italics mine)

Here Paul appeals to his audience's love for the obviously supernatural, by exaggerating gifts of the Spirit in which the Corinthian church was operating. You've all spoken in tongues, Paul says, but let's say I take it a step further, and speak in angelic languages that no human could possibly know? You've all prophesied, but what if I arrive at a place in my gifting where I can fathom *all* mysteries, and *all* knowledge? Obviously, he's again being hyperbolic since, in verse 9, he states that at present we only know and prophesy in part.

His point is obvious. Even if he is demonstrating the *obviously*, and *undeniably* supernatural, if love is not at the center of these things, they are literally meaningless. In verses 8-12, he writes:

> 8 *Love never ends. But as for prophecies, they will come to an end; as for tongues, they will cease; as for knowledge, it will come to an end.* 9 For we know only in part, and we prophesy only in part; 10 but *when the complete comes, the partial will come to an end.* 11 When I was a child, I spoke like a child, I thought like a child, I reasoned like a child; when I became an adult, I put an end to childish ways. 12 For now we see in a mirror, dimly, but then we will see face to face. Now I know only in part; then I will know fully, even as I have been fully known.

-1 Corinthians 13:8-12, NRSV (Italics mine)

When the "end" comes, whatever that is and whatever it looks like, and perfection itself is fully unveiled, everything that is incomplete and imperfect will vanish. When this occurs, Paul assures his audience that all of the things they value, tongues, prophecy, and all things obviously supernatural, will be but dust. Gone forever. Never to return. In other words, these things which they place eternal value upon, are by no means eternal. They are as temporal, fleeting, momentary and meaningless as the sod beneath their feet, even when they appear in exaggerated, and undeniably supernatural ways. *Love*, however, never ends. And when perfection is revealed, love will not vanish, since it is beyond a human invention or emotion, and is, in fact, the very essence of God, that upholds the cosmos.

If, however, the temporal, the fleeting, and the meaningless, have love at their center, they, though they remain ultimately meaningless, become eternal in quality, and therefore meaningful. In Chapter 14, Paul goes on to explain what he means when he speaks of great gifts divorced from love, and it is the use of gifts simply for the sake of using gifts, as opposed to using them for another's betterment. Even the most trivial of things, when done with the knowledge that it won't last, but with the intent of bettering another's existence, becomes of the same substance as that which will never cease. The unenduring, un-eternal, temporal, and meaningless becomes the most enduring, eternal, and meaningful of things.

Here's what I'm trying to get at in this chapter: it is truly only in the face of meaninglessness that anything becomes inherently meaningful. For the teacher, something becomes worth doing with all of our might only when we conclude that it will not last. If it lasted, and if we were to receive some cosmic pat on the back for doing it, it would not mean what it means when we do it despite its meaninglessness. For Job, righteousness became a valuable thing, precisely because it seems to go completely unrewarded. In Jesus, the cross comes to communicate the most meaningful message to humanity, only because it was undeserved, unjust, and unfair. It was met with kindness, mercy, forgiveness, and a revelation that humanity's worst will only ever be met with love on the part of the divine, but were it somehow eternally just, or a sacrifice demanded by God, it would be reduced to nothingness as far as forgiveness is concerned. Finally, in Paul we see that it is when we choose love, even though faced with the fact that the act itself will fizzle out and one day be remembered no more, that moments take on an eternal quality, and join the company of the unending and enduring.

As Chesterton said so beautifully, it is when God becomes, in a sense, an atheist, that we are forced to face the facts that a world in which scales are always evenly balanced, and fairness will always win the day, is not the world that we live in. It is a willingness to cling to righteousness, to love with no reward, and to do with all of our might something that won't ultimately survive, that represents the most Jesus-like mode of existence.

I refer back here to the interview I spoke of at the end of the last chapter, in which several Christians interviewed a former pastor who had decided to do an experiment in which he lived a year of his life as though there were no God, in order to determine whether or not such a belief made any actual difference in his life. He was obviously already in a questioning phase, and had, at least in part, begun to lose his faith a bit, but his quest was sincere. Towards the end of what was an enjoyable interview, as I've already stated, one of the interviewers asked, in a tone which betrayed that which he'd taken throughout the bulk of the interview, something akin to, "Why not just try on pure evil for a year instead of just being an atheist?"

The shock in the interviewee's voice was palpable, and the revulsion I felt at hearing the question must have been as well.

He answered, in a somewhat baffled way, that he was disturbed by the question, and that having doubts about God's existence had nothing to do with whether or not he was a violent or immoral person. One of the hosts then went on to say that, for him, were he to ever find himself without his faith, he knows that he would very quickly sink into moral degeneracy.

I ask again, what on earth would possess a person to say that? That if they found themselves without a specific type of faith, they would sink into moral degeneracy? Why would that be the case? Well, again, if you consider the position of most theistic religions, we live the way that we live, and believe what we believe, in the hopes of one day being rewarded for it. Or, the reverse, we live and believe certain ways in order to avoid being punished. If that is the case, though, my friends, is what you have actually morality? If losing your faith would cause you to sink into moral nihilism and degeneracy, and lose all motivation for doing good in the world, was what you had prior to the "sinking" a real, true, heartfelt morality, or just fear and instinctual, me-first survivalism?

This is why I think the whole idea of "heaven," in the figurative sense I'm using it here, is so problematic. If you live in an upright manner, only to avoid punishment, or to be rewarded in some significant way, there's no reason to think that anything significant or substantial has occurred within you on a heart-level. If your faith in God, or some "god," motivates you only through promises, what will happen to you when those promises fail to manifest? It is likely, at that point, you would conclude that all you had done was meaningless and worthless, and begin to live in the way the aforementioned interviewer suggested he would. I mean, sure, I'd rather have you not killing and robbing out of fear than still doing it while you wait to discover a better reason not to, but ultimately, even in an extreme case like that, one who avoids harming others, only to avoid harm being done to them, is not living a moral life, but a fearful, self-centered life. I simply can't abide the idea that the Gospel operates this way, calling us to "holiness," only so that we can save our own skin.

In this regard, I have to say that many atheists I know, and whose works I've studied, are far more moral individuals than many Christians I know. I don't say this because one group's works outweighs the others, but because one group has a very clear and stated motivation for doing what they do, and the other has only the doing itself as motivation. The atheist, and even the Christian who embraces the way of atheistic theism, does not have a kingdom promised to them as a reward for what they do, but a kingdom that consists of what they do, that is its own reward. In Caputo's words, "works of mercy are the Kingdom of God."

Christopher Hitchens, who I've quoted several times throughout this book, was arguably one of the greatest thinkers and most polished orators of the 21st century, and also one of its most notorious atheists. He obviously did not espouse a belief in either a hell or a heaven, which he mockingly referred to as, "some theme park; one nice and one nasty," and yet, somehow, found plenty of motivation for living and being alive. Though he, as much and maybe more than most, understood the ultimate meaninglessness of his own work, after being diagnosed with cancer in 2010-a cancer that would ultimately kill him-he, like Job, like the teacher, and dare I say it, even like Jesus, refused to allow the meaningless to remain as such. His wife, in the afterword to his final collection of writings, *Mortality*, writes:

> During this time of what he [Hitchens] called "living dyingly," he insisted ferociously on living, and his constitution, physical and philosophical, did all it could to stay alive.[122]

What would motivate an atheist, one with no fear of punishment, or hope for reward, to continue living, even while dying, instead of simply sinking into a dark hole, and allowing the meaninglessness to eat him alive along with the cancer? Once asked by an audience member what it was that gave meaning to his life, despite his disbelief in a transcendent, supernatural being, Hitchens responded:

> You want to know what makes my life meaningful? Generally speaking, it's been struggling myself to be free...and trying to help others to be free as well. That's given a lot of meaning to my life, and does still. Solidarity.[123]

While I'm sure I won't win any popularity contests saying so, but I believe that a man who, even when faced with certain death and utter meaninglessness, would choose to continue living at a pace, and with a passion that most healthy persons never reach, all because he burned to free himself and others from things, thoughts, and ideas he thought destructive, is a man who has surpassed the one who strives to obey God or the "gods" out of fear of punishment, or hope for reward. A man who, even when given an unpardonable death sentence, and has no fear of hell or faith in heaven, continues living for others to his very last breath, is a man who has learned what it is to love, and love endures all things.

---

[122] Christopher Hitchens, *Morality* (New York : Twelve, 2012.)
[123] This quote comes from a debate between Christopher Hitchens and William Lane Craig. The full debate can be found here:
https://www.youtube.com/watch?v=0tYm41hb48o

I know it's a bit beyond taboo to say so, but I think Hitchens was an example of someone who stumbled onto the "way," though completely by accident, and it was precisely the lack of a "god" like that of Job's friends in his belief system that likely landed him there. Sometimes atheism is closer to the "way" of Jesus than are so many of the systems that claim that title for themselves. Zizek claims that Christianity is the truest form of atheism, and I agree with him, but sometimes even an incomplete atheism that has yet to experience the dissolution of all "gods" in the person of Jesus, is still closer to Christianity than what often passes as it today. A man like Hitchens, in my opinion, embodied that reality.

The Jesus way is the way of the teacher and of Job; of the sheep who must ask "Lord, when?" and Paul, who tells us that even the perishable becomes imperishable when it acts selflessly, and out of love for another. The Jesus way is the way of the atheistic God. It's the way of the meaninglessly crucified One, who mines meaning from this darkest of moments by choosing love in the midst of it. Dare I say it? The way of Jesus is even the way of a Christopher Hitchens, who lived life with the freedom of others in mind, even while anticipating nothing more than nothing on the other side of his final breath. And who knows? Maybe Hitch, as he was affectionately referred to, will one day find himself among the "sheep" asking, "Lord, when? Lord, when?" only to hear, "Whatever you did with for the benefit of others, with no expectation of reward, you did for me. Whatever you did with all of your might, though you knew it to be ultimately meaningless and fleeting, you did for me."

May we all live lives so meaningless that we too must ask, "Lord, when?" and on that day may we be good enough Christians to be counted among atheists like Hitch, and good enough atheists to be among the Christ-like.

ACKNOWLEDGMENTS

This book absolutely would not be a reality were it not for the patience and loving support of my family.

Diana, you're my greatest treasure. Thank you for loving me and standing by my side. I love you.

To my kids, thanks for putting up with daddy writing for hours and hours on end. I love you more than you'll ever know.

To my parents, thank you for your loving support. You mean the world to me.

To the endless list of authors, theologians, scholars, philosophers, etc., who have influenced me on my journey-thank you! I wouldn't be where I am today were it not for what you've sown into my life. Michael Hardin, Brad Jersak, Peter Rollins, John D. Caputo, Slavoj Zizek, Leron Shults, Walter Wink, Thomas Altizer, Rene Girard, Marcus Borg, and literally a host of others who I'm only opting not to name so as to save space-I owe all of you a debt of gratitude that I'm afraid I'll never be able to pay. Though some on this list are no longer among the living, I am alive today because of their studiousness, devotion to scholarship, and willingness to dig in and endure the blows that many of us could never endure. Thank you. From the bottom of my heart, thank you.

To Caleb Miller, your friendship, devotion to your craft, and pretty much everything else about you inspires me. Thank you for being my friend.

To Beverly Dobrich, thank you for helping to correct my many grammatical errors. Your job was not an easy one. Thank you.

And finally, to my friends in the atheist and secular communities, you were there for me when religion was not. I don't know what my mental or emotional state would be today, had I not been allowed to sit at your feet and learn from you. Thank you for being the unwitting prophets that you are. The church needs you, and I appreciate you.

ABOUT THE AUTHOR

Jeff Turner is an author and speaker who travels throughout the United States teaching in churches and conferences on the love of God, and the necessity of deconstructing harmful god-concepts. He is a former pastor, with 15 years of ministry experience. Jeff presently resides in Port Huron, Michigan, with his wife, Diana, and their three children, Hannah, Samuel, and Abigail.

For more information, visit Jeff's website, at jeff-turner.org.

Made in the USA
Monee, IL
28 January 2021